The WHALE

SEAFARING AMERICA
Richard J. King, Williams College at Mystic Seaport, Editor

Seafaring America is a series of original and classic works of fiction, nonfiction, poetry, and drama bearing on the history of America's engagement with our oceans and coastlines. Spanning diverse eras, populations, and geographical settings, the series strives to introduce, revive, and aggregate a wide range of exemplary and seminal stories about our American maritime heritage, including the accounts of First Peoples, explorers, slaves, immigrants, fishermen, whalers, captains, common sailors, members of the navy and coast guard, marine biologists, and the crews of vessels ranging from lifeboats, riverboats, and tugboats to recreational yachts. As a sailor's library, Seafaring America introduces new stories of maritime interest, reprints books that have fallen out of circulation and deserve reappraisal, and publishes selections from well-known works that reward reconsideration because of the lessons they offer about our relationship with the ocean. For a complete list of books available in this series, see www.upne.com.

The Whale and His Captors; or, The Whaleman's Adventures
Henry T. Cheever, edited by Robert D. Madison

The Palatine Wreck: The Legend of the New England Ghost Ship
Jill Farinelli

In Pursuit of Giants: One Man's Global Search for the Last of the Great Fish
Matt Rigney

The Sea Is a Continual Miracle: Sea Poems and Other Writings by Walt Whitman
Walt Whitman, edited by Jeffrey Yang

Surviving the Essex: The Afterlife of America's Most Storied Shipwreck
David O. Dowling

THE
WHALE
AND HIS CAPTORS;
OR, THE WHALEMAN'S
ADVENTURES

HENRY T. CHEEVER
Edited and with an Introduction by
ROBERT D. MADISON
Afterword by MARK BOUSQUET

UNIVERSITY PRESS OF NEW ENGLAND

Hanover and London

University Press of New England
www.upne.com
© 2018 University Press of New England
All rights reserved
Manufactured in the United States of America
Designed by Richard Hendel
Typeset in Miller and Egiziano by Passumpsic Publishing

Afterword adapted from Mark Bousquet, "The Cruel Harpoon
and the Honorable Lamp: The Awakening of an Environmental
Consciousness in Henry Theodore Cheever's *The Whale and His Captors,*"
Interdisciplinary Studies in Literature and the Environment 19:2
(September 2012): 253–273, and used by permission of
the author and Oxford University Press.

For permission to reproduce any of the material in this book,
contact Permissions, University Press of New England, One Court Street,
Suite 250, Lebanon NH 03766; or visit www.upne.com.

Seafaring America is supported and produced in part by the
Maritime Studies Program of Williams College and Mystic Seaport.
Williams-Mystic empowers global, creative citizens while inspiring an enduring
relationship with the ocean. We create an open-minded, interdisciplinary
academic community, with experiential learning at Mystic Seaport,
along the coasts of America, and at sea.

Library of Congress Cataloging-in-Publication Data
NAMES: Cheever, Henry T. (Henry Theodore), 1814–1897, author. |
Madison, R. D., editor.
TITLE: The whale and his captors ; or, The whaleman's adventures /
Henry T. Cheever ; edited and with an introduction by Robert D. Madison;
afterword by Mark Bousquet.
OTHER TITLES: Whaleman's adventures
DESCRIPTION: Hanover : University Press of New England, [2018] |
Series: Seafaring America | Originally published: New York : Harper &
brothers, 1850. | Includes bibliographical references.
IDENTIFIERS: LCCN 2017049023 (print) | LCCN 2017053746 (ebook) |
ISBN 9781512602661 (epub, mobi, & pdf) | ISBN 9781512602647
(cloth : alk. paper) | ISBN 9781512602654 (pbk. : alk. paper)
SUBJECTS: LCSH: Whales. | Whaling.
CLASSIFICATION: LCC QL737.C4 (ebook) | LCC QL737.C4 C4 2018 (print) |
DDC 599.5—dc23
LC record available at https://lccn.loc.gov/2017049023.

5 4 3 2 1

FRONTISPIECE
Henry Theodore Cheever. Courtesy of the American Antiquarian Society.

Oh, the rare old Whale, mid storm and gale,
In his ocean home will be
A Giant in might, where might is right,
And King of the boundless Sea.

CONTENTS

ILLUSTRATIONS

Unless otherwise noted, the illustrations throughout
this edition are placed approximately as in Cheever's original.
The titles below are from Cheever's "List of Engravings," although
they do not always agree with the captions on the illustrations
themselves. The engravings followed by an asterisk (*) are by W.
Roberts; only one, the next to last, is signed by an artist, F. Purcell.
The variety of formats suggests the engravings in *The Whale and
His Captors* were gleaned, at least in part, from earlier works.

SERIES EDITOR'S PREFACE
Seafaring America

The Inupiat of far northern Alaska have for centuries said that the bowhead whale lives two human lifetimes. In *Moby-Dick*, the primary entrepôt of all American literature of the sea, Ishmael yarns about a stone lance in an old whale: "It might have been darted by some Nor'-West Indian long before America was discovered." By studying amino acids in the eyes of legally killed bowhead whales and dating the old lances of stone, ivory, and steel found buried in the blubber, twenty-first-century researchers have confirmed that some individuals of this species might indeed live over two hundred years. A bowhead swimming around the thinning ice of the Arctic in 2015, when the Cuban-American poet Richard Blanco wrote "we all belong to the sea between us," likely also swam in 1859 when Emily Dickinson penciled the lines, "Exultation is the going / Of an inland soul to sea"— and then put them in her drawer.

Since the first human settlement of our coasts, the voices expressing the American relationship with the sea have been diverse in gender, race, ethnicity, geography, and experience. And the study of maritime literature and history continues to converge and circulate with marine science and contemporary policy.

Seafaring America seeks to inspire and explore ocean study in this twenty-first century. The Taino chief Hatuey, James Fenimore Cooper, Harriet Beecher Stowe, Frederick Douglass, Walt Whitman, Winslow Homer, Alexander Agassiz, Joshua Slocum, Kate Chopin, Samuel Eliot Morison, Langston Hughes, Marianne Moore, Rachel Carson, Ursula K. Le Guin, Henry T. Cheever, and generations of other American mariners, artists, writers, scientists, and historians have all known that the ocean is the dominant ecological, meteorological, political, and metaphorical force on earth.

"The sea is History," wrote Derek Walcott in 1979, mourning the horrors of the Middle Passage and the drowned African American cultural memory. By the 1970s the sea was history in a new way. Americans began to perceive the global ocean as vulnerable to our destructive reach. The realization rolled in with the discovery of the dead zone off the Mississippi River delta, industrial overfishing off New England, and the massive oil spill that spoiled the same Santa Barbara sands on which Richard Henry Dana Jr. first landed his bare Boston Brahmin feet in 1835 after a passage of 150 days. Yet even today, the rising seas, floods, shipwrecks, and immutable tempests along the Great Lakes, the Gulf of Mexico, and America's Atlantic, Pacific, and Arctic coasts continue to remind us of an immortal and indifferent sea—a savage ocean that crashes and seeps over the transience of *Homo sapiens.*

Seafaring America is a series of new and classic works of fiction, nonfiction, history, poetry, and drama that engages with the country's enduring relationship with the oceans and coastlines. Seafaring America strives to introduce, revive, and aggregate a wide range of exemplary and seminal stories and verse about the American maritime heritage: to trace the footprints on the beach, the stone lances in the blubber, and the pearls in the drawer.

Richard J. King,
Williams College-Mystic Seaport

Series Editor's Preface

ACKNOWLEDGMENTS

This book would not have come about without the indefatigable imagination of Rich King (Williams-Mystic Maritime Studies) and chowder at Mystic Seaport's Galley. We owe a debt of gratitude to everyone at University Press of New England, especially acquisitions editor Stephen P. Hull, project editor Rachel Shields, and copy editor Lee Motteler. Hershel Parker cited the Cheever-albatross connection in the third Norton critical *Moby-Dick* even before we had a page number. Marie E. Lamoureux (American Antiquarian Society) yet again piloted us through the magnificent collections at Worcester.

In an increasingly materialistic world of literary criticism, long ago Stuart M. Frank (Kendall Institute, New Bedford Whaling Museum) insisted on the importance of American religious thought to maritime culture. We hope the present volume follows worthily in his wake.

INTRODUCTION
Henry Cheever and Stories of Whaling

When Henry Theodore Cheever took a holiday from inspecting the Protestant missions in the Hawaiian Islands, he chose a venue that might seem odd to us today: he accompanied a wooden whaleship in its wanderings in the South Pacific. But the choice was not such an odd one after all.

It is no accident that James Fenimore Cooper (1789–1851), teller of sea tales, began and ended his career with books that featured whaling scenes. In *The Pilot: A Tale of the Sea* (1824), Cooper deliberately attempted to show "the truth of the matter" where Sir Walter Scott had clumsily had his Orkney islanders put to death a right whale by means of pitchforks. An isolated scene in an island story, the passage from Scott's *The Pirate* (1822) cannot legitimately stand at the head of whaling fiction, but Scott's depiction casts a long shadow (Richard Henry Dana Jr., 1815–1882, may have read it while taking a break from stowing cowhides on the California beach in the 1830s). Cooper—who had never hunted whales but had been part owner of the whaleship *Union* in 1819, and who had traveled the length of Lake Ontario as a young naval officer—resented the misplaced praise Scott's book received and set out systematically to show how exciting sea scenes should be presented in fiction.

Only three episodes of *The Pilot*, a fictionalized treatment of an early cruise of John Paul Jones along the coast of England, demonstrate the unique potential of the sea story. Most of the book is conventional enough: a double love plot within a British military novel of manners. But Cooper interlarded his narrative with striking scenes of a whale chase, a bloody combat between two light vessels, and a relentless onshore gale. These three categories of literary tension—man against man, man against the sea, and man against the creature of the sea—account for nearly all that is exciting in a sea story. If there is a major category of tension that Cooper left out of *The Pilot*, it is probably the sublime moment of discovery—not unique to the sea but surely a staple of sea stories with Cooper himself from 1835 on. In that year, Cooper published his playful allegory of *The Monikins*, set in a Symzonian Antarctic and his last book before a turn to bitter social criticism that blighted most later novels.

The literature of discovery, as opposed to swashbuckling tales, replaced (or at least supplemented) danger with wonder in the sea fiction of Cooper's later years. It was, after all, an older genre, although it is surprising how tedious many voyages of discovery are. Dana parodied them in an oft-quoted passage from *Two Years Before the Mast* (1840):

> *Monday, Nov. 10th.* During a part of this day we were hove to, but the rest of the time were driving on, under close-reefed sails, with a heavy sea, a strong gale, and frequent squalls of hail and snow.
> *Tuesday, Nov. 11th.* The same.
> *Wednesday.* The same.
> *Thursday.* The same.[1]

Cooper interrupted his final sea story, *The Sea Lions* (1849), with another intrusive account of a whale chase. But by the time he wrote this second Antarctic allegory, the nature of both fictional and "true" accounts of life under sail had been subjected to another requirement: not only did the narrative voice need to be authentic; that voice itself needed to be an unhandselled utterance of the forecastle.

Although this Wordsworthian proposition did occasionally result in a celebration of maritime primitivism ("savagism," Cheever would later call it), Dana—the author who irrevocably established the voice of the common sailor as a criterion for authenticity—was, like Wordsworth (1770–1850) before him, not exactly an illiterate bumpkin or even a literate rustic in the tradition of Robert Burns (1759–1796). Instead, each was a product of his country's most elite institutions of higher learning. Even Herman Melville (1819–1891) was no whaleman speaking to whalemen ("Was ever any thing of this sort said before by a sailor?"[2]) but a writer clearly endued with a more lively sensibility and emphatically a more comprehensive soul than one would likely find before the mast. The great shift in literature of the sea that came with Dana's book is a direct result of the Emersonian (Ralph Waldo Emerson, 1803–1882, published in *Nature* in 1836) Wordsworthianism that would send Henry Thoreau (1817–1862) to the pond, Francis Parkman (1823–1893) to the plains, and Dana to the sea. In none of these cases do we get the voice of the Canadian woodchopper, the buffalo hunter, or the handsome sailor. Instead we get a Harvard student, or someone very close to the tradition ("A whale-ship was my Yale College and my Harvard"[3]).

Dana was a student at Harvard when he contracted an ophthalmic condition that made it painful to read. Some of Dana's biographers trace the condition to measles; others hint that it was more psychological. Perhaps a disproportionate number of self-rusticated students who went to sea wrote books. It is, of course, a rather circular observation that those who did would end up telling the story of a bright young man not entirely at ease with his shipmates, but there seems also always to be another sensitive young man in the fo'c'sle, educated, fond of reading and so forth, to share the narrator's predicament. In Dana's case, at one time there were only three or four men before the mast, and for two of these scholar-gypsies to be in the same watch seems somewhat miraculous. But perhaps certain ship owners made a practice of innocently shipping their colleagues' sick sons as green hands in a degrading trade.

Although Dana claimed to have kept a journal of his voyage to California, it isn't clear when he actually decided he was a young author. Back in his milieu of literary (and legal) Boston, however, he prepared his manuscript and through the agency of his family and friends was offered $250 for his book by Harper and Brothers, a New York company later known for tightfistedness—although the Danas reportedly turned down an offer based on sales. The sum accepted was no mean amount for a new author with a sea story, and the bitterness expressed toward the Harpers later in life must also express Dana's complicated frustration when his book did, in fact, turn out to be a best seller.[4]

Was Dana a whaling author? The fascination with whales—as with albatrosses—seems to have extended to those whose pursuits were not particularly cetacean. On the voyage out, Dana had been enchanted by the nighttime breathing of whales:

The calm of the morning reminds me of a scene which I forgot to describe at the time of its occurrence, but which I remember from its being the first time that I had heard the near breathing of whales. It was on the night that we passed between the Falkland Islands and Staten Land. We had the watch from twelve to four, and coming upon deck, found the little brig lying perfectly still, surrounded by a thick fog, and the sea as smooth as though oil had been poured upon it; yet now and then a long, low swell rolling over its surface, slightly lifting the vessel, but without breaking the glassy smoothness of the water. We were surrounded far and near by shoals of sluggish whales and grampuses, which the fog prevented our seeing, rising slowly to the surface, or perhaps lying out at length, heaving out those peculiar lazy, deep, and long-drawn breathings which give such an impression of supineness and strength. Some of the watch were asleep, and the others were perfectly still, so that there was nothing to break the illusion, and I stood leaning over the bulwarks, listening to the slow breathings of the mighty creatures —now one breaking the water just alongside, whose black body I almost fancied that I could see through the fog; and again another, which I could just hear in the distance—until the low and regular swell seemed like the heaving of ocean's mighty bosom to the sound of its heavy and long-drawn respirations. (29)

The Pilot aside, American whaling literature might be said to truly begin with that paragraph. Dana was more prosaic in describing the whale migrations of the California coast:

This being the spring season, San Pedro, as well as all the other open ports upon the coast, was filled with whales, that had come in to make their annual visit upon soundings. For the first few days that we were here and at Santa Barbara, we watched them with great interest—calling out "there she blows!" every time we saw the spout of one, breaking the surface of the water; but they soon became so common that we took little notice of them. They often "broke" very near us; and one thick, foggy night, during a dead calm, while I was standing anchor-watch, one of them rose so near, that he struck our cable, and made all surge again. He did not seem to like the encounter much himself, for he sheered off, and spouted at a good distance. We once came very near running one down in the gig, and should probably have been knocked to pieces and blown sky-high. We had been on board the little Spanish brig, and were returning, stretching out well at our oars, the little boat going like a swallow; our backs were forward, (as is always the case in pulling,) and the captain, who was steering, was not looking ahead, when, all at once, we heard the spout of a whale directly ahead. "Back water! back water, for your lives!" shouted the captain; and we backed our blades in the water and brought the boat to in a smother of foam. Turning our heads, we saw a great, rough, hump-backed whale, slowly crossing our fore foot, within three or four yards of the boat's stem. Had we not backed water just as we did, we should inevitably gone smash upon him, striking him with our stem just about midships. He took no notice of us, but passed slowly on, and dived a few yards beyond us, throwing his tail high in the air. He was so near that we had a perfect view of him, and as may be supposed, had no desire to see him nearer. He was a disgusting creature; with a skin rough, hairy, and of an iron-grey color. This kind differs much from the sperm, in color and skin, and is said to be fiercer. We saw a few sperm whales; but most of the whales that come upon the coast are fin-backs, hump-backs, and right-whales, which are more difficult to take, and are said not to give oil enough to pay for the trouble. For this reason, whale-ships do not come upon the coast after them. Our captain, together with Captain Nye of the Loriotte, who had been in a whale-ship, thought of making an attempt upon one of them with two boat's crews, but as we had only two harpoons and no proper lines, they gave it up. (131–132)

Despite the mystique of the whale itself, Dana had no use for the profession of whaling, "which a thorough sailor despises, and will always steer clear of, if he can" (176). Dana described the whaler *Wilmington and Liverpool Packet* as having a "certain slovenly look," with her decks "rough and oily" and "her rigging slack." "Her crew," Dana continues, "were not in much better order . . . the men looked more like fishermen and farmers than they did like sailors" (201). And yet that whaler was carrying nineteen hundred barrels of oil: not bad for farmers, and, after all, they were a sort of fishermen.

Dana's encounter with the albatross was archetypal:

This day we saw the last of the albatrosses, which had been our companions a great part of the time off the Cape. I had been interested in the bird from descriptions which I had read of it, and was not at all disappointed. We caught one or two with a baited hook which we floated astern upon a shingle. Their long, flapping wings, long legs, and large, staring eyes, give them a very peculiar appearance. They look well on the wing; but one of the finest sights that I have ever seen, was an albatross asleep upon the water, during a calm, off Cape Horn, when a heavy sea was running. There being no breeze, the surface of the water was unbroken, but a long, heavy swell was rolling, and we saw the fellow, all white, directly ahead of us, asleep upon the waves, with his head under his wing; now rising on the top of a huge billow, and then falling slowly until he was lost in the hollow between. He was undisturbed for some time, until the noise of our bows, gradually approaching roused him, when, lifting his head, he stared upon us for a moment, and then spread his wide wings and took his flight. (34)

The success of Dana's book made the Brothers Harper—and not Cooper's publishers at the time, Lea and Blanchard—the de facto publisher of choice for sea stories. Cooper himself came out with a "before-the-mast" book: the retold autobiography of an alcoholic shipmate from Cooper's youth named Ned Myers. Cooper cut Ned's book short in order, in part, to employ his narrative voice in *Afloat and Ashore* (1844), a monster novel even by Cooper standards that employs a first-person narrator but changes the narrator's social status from that of Ned to Cooper's own. None of the imitations of Dana, in fact or fiction, came close to matching Dana's success in sales or in synthesizing a common-sailor viewpoint with the stylistic clarity and precision of the Boston Brahmin. While Dana's vision of the common sailor was appropriately Wordsworthian, his language was not the extreme homeliness of some of the *Lyrical Ballads* (1798). What really distinguished Dana's book and gave it its lasting reputation is the modern quality of the prose: *Two Years Before the Mast* may be the best *told* sea story before the modernism of Joseph Conrad (1857–

1924). Conrad himself had said of Cooper that "He wrote before the great American language was born."[5] He would not have needed to offer that excuse for Dana.

In 1846, the same year they published their Family Library edition of the *Journal of Researches* by Charles Darwin (1809–1882), the Brothers Harper also published *Etchings of a Whaling Cruise* by J. Ross Browne (1821–1875), a work that followed the Dana model in its main narrative but included a substantial appendix on the economics of whaling. No doubt that appendix contributed significantly to the "useful knowledge" aspect of Browne's book and made it more attractive to the Harpers. The book, in fact, was so well done and comprehensive that when Melville reviewed it for the *Literary World* (March 6, 1847), he might well have felt that the subject of whaling had about been exhausted, at least in the mode of either Darwin or Browne. Although never receiving the acclaim of Dana's book, *Etchings* sold well enough that Harpers kept Browne on for several more books of travel, mostly about the American West (Parkman's *California and Oregon Trail*, published in book form by Harpers' competitor G. P. Putnam in 1849 and reviewed by Melville, would do for the Great American Desert what Dana had done with the voyage by sea). Although not stylistically in the same league as Dana, Browne's claim to being the voice of a common sailor was much more nearly true. He was no blueblood but an Irish immigrant. And his book may have tempted the Harpers to salivate when the prospect of other whaling books emerged.[6]

Harpers would shortly establish an uneasy relationship with Melville, publishing *Omoo* (1847) and reprinting an expurgated version of *Typee*. Despite its obvious fictional genre, they also published *Mardi* (1849). Each of these three books began with whaling but swiftly turned to more promising material. When the Harpers published his next two books, *Redburn* (1849) and *White-Jacket* (1850), it might have appeared to both the publishers and Melville that he had evolved from the man who had lived among cannibals to a straightforward author of sea stories, pretty much in the tradition of Cooper's first-person fictions but with more focus and a more metaphysical turn of mind.

This was the setting for *The Whale and His Captors*.

Henry Theodore Cheever (1814–1897) first went to sea after graduation at about the same age as Dana and Melville, but he was somewhat older when he made the whaling voyage recounted in *The Whale and His Captors*. By far the best account of Cheever's sea years is Randall Cluff's *Leviathan* article, "'Thou Man of the Evangelist': Henry Cheever's Review of *Typee*" (2001).[7] On the basis of Cheever family correspondence at the American Antiquarian Society and Cheever's later published writings, Cluff determined that Cheever, a boy from Maine, attended Bowdoin College (not Harvard or Yale, but good enough for Nathaniel Hawthorne, 1804–1864); that he went to sea in October 1842 hoping to cure a vocal impediment that would otherwise interfere with a career as a preacher; that the vessel was the *Wales*, Captain Landon, on a scientific cruise; and that he arrived in Honolulu in early May 1843, where he occupied himself exploring the missions (64). Melville arrived in Honolulu the same month. But while in late August Melville signed on the naval frigate *United States*, Cheever was only about to begin his whaling career. Not quite a year and a half after arriving in the Sandwich Islands (today's Hawaii), Cheever took passage (not the same as signing on, as Ishmael explains in "Loomings") in the whaler *Commodore Preble*, Captain Lafayette Ludlow, on September 23, 1844 (Cluff 2001, 67). The voyage of the *Commodore Preble* lasted eight months after Cheever joined her, arriving in Boston on May 20, 1845 (68).

Henry Cheever "knew whaling; more to the point, he knew whaling men," as Cluff states (67). But he could not have known method or men in the sense that either Dana knew droghing or Melville knew whaling, men with hides on their heads or their feet in gurry. Dana himself wrote, "No man can be a sailor, or know what sailors are, unless he has lived in the forecastle with them—turned in and out with them, eaten of their dish and drank their cup" (50). Nor would Cheever have wanted to claim that he shared the sentiments of the foremast hand. To Cheever the common sailor was an object of religious pity, not a shipmate to be embraced. Cheever's role on the voyage home was that of a man of the cloth evangelizing the crew of a Sabbath-keeping ship. Whaling lore was easy enough for Cheever to come by through observation, but honest sympathy for the tar-besmirched sailor is not to be looked for.[8]

As a frequent contributor to his brother George Barrel Cheever's religious paper, the *New York Evangelist*, it is easy for scholars to pin on him the authorship of the April 9, 1846, review of *Typee* that nearly sunk the breeching novelist's career (see review, page 201). Nothing if not vicious (to borrow Cheever's own diction), the review demonstrates the vicelike grip on morality maintained by evangelical Christians at mid-century, along with their ability to enforce censorship throughout the literary community. Fully justifying Melville's view of the narrow bigotry of the missionary mentality, Cheever's review initiated a series of sectarian attacks on Melville's novels that would reverberate throughout his career, even as Melville grew to be (as he demonstrated in *Clarel* in 1876) one of the great religious searchers of the century.

Cheever may have contributed further reviews of Melville's works to the *Evangelist* (see note 7), but he did not compete directly with Melville (or any other sea writer) until he gathered his material for *The Whale and His Captors*. And even then, Cheever could safely assume that Melville—having left travel writing behind in *Mardi* and whaling altogether in *Redburn*—would not be bringing his "savageism" to a narrative of a whaling voyage. Certainly there was room after Browne's *Etchings* for a demonstration of piety in the whale fishery. Cooper had taken a turn toward the pious sea story with *The Sea Lions*, but that was fiction and Cheever would be presenting himself as a "camera obscura" through which would be seen "a gallery of Daguerreotypes" of the craft of whaling, not without their "moral hints" (Preface).

In fact, his book was far more ambitious. Cheever did his homework: he studied Thomas Beale's essay on the natural history of the sperm whale (not the 1839 book, which he may not have been aware of). He plundered Scoresby extensively, but in a way that complimented his whaler-preacher role model. He knew Wilkes's *Narrative* of the U.S. Exploring Expedition, and he praised Browne's *Etchings* along with Francis Allyn Olmsted's *Incidents of a Whaling Voyage* (1841), probably plundering from both. And he was, after all, an eyewitness to eight months of whaling. In short, *The Whale and His Captors* really does have a strong claim to being at least as authentic as any other American book on whaling. If his intention in writing was to enforce the Sabbath at sea and not to break through the mask, it should be remembered that in Cheever's day those might have seemed equally imposing if antithetical tasks. Skepticism and style have elevated Melville's book far above Cheever's, but evangelical piety does not automatically disqualify Cheever as a whaling voice. If anything, it probably presents a more representative worldview of both whalemen and masters than does Melville's—however much Melville may personally have resented missions in his own experience and writing.

Several chapters of *The Whale and His Captors* saw early publication. Chapters VII, IV, VI, and VIII appeared in the *Evangelist* in 1849 (February 8 and March 8, 22, and 29, respectively). Chapters III and IV appeared in the *Christian Parlor Book* (1849), a Christmas annual.

"Cheever's Whale and His Captors" was noted in Harper & Brothers' full-page advertisement in the *Literary World* for December 29, 1849, purportedly listing all their publications for the year (Cheever is numbered 5).[9] "Melville's Redburn" appears a few titles below (number 21), as well as "Melville's Typee" (number 44) and "Melville's Mardi" (number 54). Neither *Omoo* nor Browne's *Etchings* made the list. An editorial in the same issue (547) of American books published between November 30 and December 22 lists Cheever's book but none of the Melville titles. Although *The Whale and His Captors* received nothing like the attention the *Literary World* had lavished on *Redburn*,[10] Cheever might reasonably have assumed that he had earned a place as the authority on American whaling for the next decade, sort of an American Scoresby.

But by the autumn of 1850, Cheever might have heard rumors—perhaps from J. T. Headley or other literary figures who had summered in western Massachusetts—that his old *Typee* nemesis was at work on a whaling story. Cheever himself was probably at work by now assembling his next book, *The Island World of the Pacific* (1850), a little troubled perhaps that Melville had returned to a South Pacific setting scene in *White-Jacket* (1850), but also relieved that that book began after Melville's sojourn in Hawaii and wouldn't compete directly with a collection of Cheever's island reminiscences. Properly a prequel to *The Whale and His Captors, Island World* would also be published by the Harpers and would have to share space on their list with the expurgated *Typee* and the unfathomable *Mardi*. Cheever's book came out within the year; Melville's disappeared. Maybe Melville had bottomed out. He had published three books within a span of months in 1849–1850, and now it had been nearly a year and a half and Melville had published only a couple of magazine pieces.

In their October 1851 issue, *Harper's New Monthly Magazine* published "The Town-Ho's Story," accompanied by this note: "From 'The Whale.' The title of a new work by Mr. Melville, in the press of Harper and Brothers, and now publishing in London by Mr. Bentley" (658).[11] It was official: *The Whale*—not *Etchings*, not *Incidents*, not *The Whale and This or That*, but just *The Whale*. And judging by "The Town-Ho's Story," it was as good as Hawthorne.

When he had reviewed *Typee* in 1846, Cheever was defending not only morality but also professional friends and acquaintances. He was not, however, defending his own place in the literary culture. This time, with the onset of *The Whale*, Cheever knew that he—as the reigning literary Christian whaleman—would be called upon to review the book and that this review would not only be defending morality and religion but also would define his own place among interpreters of the sea. We do not know with what eagerness or trepidation he undertook this role, but descriptions of Cheever as a hard-charging Valiant-for-Truth suggest the former. Thus it is puzzling that *two* very different reviews have variously been attributed to him. The first—and probably the *least* likely to express Cheever's response to what was published in November as *Moby-Dick; or, the Whale*—is the following from the *New York Evangelist*, November 20, 1851, which does not seem aware of either *Redburn* or *White-Jacket*:

Mr. Melville grows wilder and more untameable with every adventure. In Typee and Omoo, he began with the semblance of life and reality, though it was often but the faintest kind of semblance. As he advanced, he threw off the pretense of probability, and wandered from the verisimilitude of fiction into the mist and vagueness of poetry and fantasy, and now in this last venture, has reached the very limbo of eccentricity. From first to last, oddity is the governing characteristic. The extraordinary descriptive powers which Typee disclosed, are here in full strength. More graphic and terrible portraitures of hair-breadth 'scapes we never read. The delineation of character, too, is exquisitely humorous, sharp, individual and never-to-be forgotten. The description of Father Mapple's sermon is a powerful piece of sailor-oratory; and passages of great eloquence, and artistic beauty and force, are to be found everywhere. It will add to Mr. Melville's repute as a writer, undoubtedly, and furnishes, incidentally, a most striking picture of sea life and adventures.[12]

If Cheever wrote this *and* the *Evangelist Typee* review, he was either insincere or schizophrenic.

And yet, if Cheever did not write this review, who at the *Evangelist* did? If Cheever were not the actual editor making decisions about who reviewed what, who was? Surely his brother George would not have offered Melville's new book to anyone else, unless to prevent his brother having an apoplectic fit. It is theoretically possible that Henry initially penned an irresponsible review after only glancing at the book (his missionary eye caught by "The Sermon"). But, when oddity turned to blasphemy, there was just as much time to substitute a revised review as there was to submit a more characteristic one to the *Independent* (see the full review below)—they came out on the same day.[13] If Cheever recognized (or appreciated) that his own book was among Melville's sources, he didn't indicate it in either review. He should have seen his book named in the "Extracts" (who wouldn't look to see if they'd been cited?), but he's not likely to have recognized his own contribution to "The Gam," since he would have no reason to suspect that Melville might not be writing from an experience similar to his own—especially since Cheever used the term to refer to a meeting of whales as well as of whale ships.

The first half of the *New York Independent* review could have been a paraphrase of that in the *Evangelist*. But then the reviewer—whom we have no reason to doubt was Cheever—turns on the author with the mortal quickness of Moby Dick himself:

The writer evinces the possession of powers that make us ashamed of him that he does not write something better, and freer from blemishes. And yet we doubt if he could, for there is a primitive formation of profanity and indecency that is ever and

Introduction

anon shooting up through all the strata of his writings; and it is this which makes it impossible for a religious journal heartily to commend any of the works of this author which we have ever perused. Let his mind only turn on the poles of truth, and be fixed with the desire to do good rather than to tickle and amuse by the exposure of his foolish vagaries, and few could do more than the author of Moby-Dick to furnish instructive literary aliment for the Sons of the Sea.

The Judgment day will hold him liable for not turning his talents to better account, when, too, both authors and publishers of injurious books will be conjointly answerable for the influence of those books upon the wide circle of those immortal minds on which they have written their mark. The book-maker and the book-publisher had better do their work with a view to the trial it must undergo at the bar of God.[14]

The purpose of sea fiction for Cheever, obvious from *The Whale and His Captors* and stated here obliquely, is "instructive literary aliment" for sailors. But the "poles of truth" phrase must have struck Melville like a whale's flukes: Who on earth in 1851 knew more about the poles of truth than the author who had written "The Needle"? Extrapolating from the same phenomenon that Melville draws on (from Scoresby), in chapter XVIII Cheever writes more explicitly, "There is an analogy to this in the mind of a Christian under a storm of trial—a mind that has been once thoroughly magnetized by the grace of God, and stamped with the law of DIVINE POLARITY, making it to turn always to that POLE-STAR OF BETHLEHEM, the great magnet of the regenerated soul."[15]

Both Cheever and Melville were struck by the weirdly coincidental reports of the sinking of another whale ship by a sperm whale that were circulating the same month *Moby-Dick* was published. On November 2, the *New-York Daily Tribune* reprinted the story of the sinking of the *Ann Alexander*, which had taken place on August 20, 1851, in the South Atlantic. Melville's response to Duyckinck's sending him a clipping (it might have been from another paper) of the disaster is typically playful: "I make no doubt it *is* Moby Dick himself, for there is no account of his capture after the sad fate of the Pequod about fourteen years ago.—Ye Gods! What a Commentator is this Ann Alexander whale. What he has to say is short & pithy & very much to the point. I wonder if my evil art has raised this monster."[16]

Cheever savored the coincidence and connected the two (without rancor or judgment) in the revised edition of *The Whale and His Captors*: "A recent instance, which puts almost all former exploits of the whale and perils by the whale fishery into the shade, is furnished in the destruction of a New Bedford whale ship by the malice aforethought of a sperm whale, who may have been the prototype or twin-brother to the notable 'Moby Dick'" (note F, continued in Cheever's appendix).

Perhaps by 1853 Cheever could afford a little generosity. *The Whale and His Captors* would continue to be reprinted until well after the Civil War, both in America and Great Britain, while Melville's reputation as a popular novelist collapsed with the publication of *Pierre, or the Ambiguities*. Cheever's *The Island World of the Pacific*[17] also was kept in print for the next twenty years. A third book in Cheever's trilogy, *Life in the Sandwich Islands*,[18] lacked the publicity, appeal, or publisher's support of the Harper publications. But for the rest of the century, at home and abroad, Cheever was the voice of the American whale fishery.

Robert D. Madison

Professor of English, Emeritus, U.S. Naval Academy

NOTES

1. Richard Henry Dana Jr., *Two Years Before the Mast and Other Voyages*, edited by Thomas L. Philbrick (New York: Library of America, 2005), 31. Philbrick's edition is particularly useful for its substantial chronology of Dana's life and, exceptionally for Library of America volumes, the book is actually handy enough that it's pleasant to hold and read—a characteristic of the Harper's Family Library format in which *Two Years Before the Mast* first appeared in 1840. Note that the cited page numbers refer to this edition.

2. Evert A. Duyckinck to George L. Duyckinck, November 15, 1847. Quoted in Steven Olsen-Smith, *Melville in His Own Time* (Iowa City: University of Iowa Press, 2015), 30.

3. Herman Melville, *Moby-Dick; or, the Whale*, edited by Charles Feidelson Jr. (Indianapolis: Bobbs-Merrill, 1964), 156 (the last line in chapter 24, "The Advocate"). Some Melvilleans keep copies of *Moby-Dick* in immediate proximity, with only a little less reverence than copies of *Walden* are stored up by Thoreauvians or bits of the true cross carried about in Rome. Feidelson's edition is a good candidate for such a copy, with its decent size print and distilled annotation. Feidelson's "whale-ship" was Yale University.

4. Charles A. Madison (no relation), *Irving to Irving: Author-Publisher Relations 1800–1974* (New York: R. R. Bowker Company, 1974), 26. A print run for a Cooper novel might be two to three thousand copies, depending on the ups and downs of Cooper's reputation at the moment. The Danas might well have expected that Harpers could not sell more than a thousand copies of his book and might have viewed an offer of royalties after a thousand copies to be valueless. When the book sold ten times that number in the first year, the Danas realized their error—but blamed the publisher.

5. *Notes on Life and Letters* (Garden City, NY: Doubleday, Page & Company, 1925), 56.

6. Harper and Brothers would continue to publish substantial accounts of whaling, both in *Harpers New Monthly Magazine* and in book form. Cf. "Aboard a Sperm Whaler," *Harper's New Monthly Magazine* 8:47 (April 1854), 670–674; "Huntsmen of the Sea," *Harper's New Monthly Magazine* 4:293 (October 1874), 650–662; William M. Davis, *Nimrod of the Sea; or, the American Whaleman* (New York: Harper & Brothers, 1874); and William Henry Giles Kingston. *Shipwrecks and Disasters at Sea* (London and New York: George Routledge and Sons, 1875). The first of these is an oddity for Harpers, with its opening sentence, "We dare say the reader is sufficiently familiar with the many-times told story of the Greenland Whale-fishery, but we may be permitted to doubt whether he knows much about the sperm-whale, and its capture in the far-off South Seas" (670). This sort of assertion might have been acceptable before 1840 or so, but the author obviously hadn't kept up with Harpers' list. This derivative piece at least has the courtesy of acknowledging two of its sources: "We refer the reader who desires to know more of the peculiar habits of the sperm-whale to the books of Herman Melville, the American sailor-author, and of Mr. Bennett" (670). As it turns out, the article was lifted from *Chambers's Journal of Popular Literature, Science, and Arts* 1:4 (January 28, 1854), 52–55.

7. *Leviathan: A Journal of Melville Studies* 3:1 (March 2001), 61–71. Cluff seems to have missed Keith Huntress's "Melville, Henry Cheever, and 'The Lee Shore'" in the *New England Quarterly* 44:3 (September 1971), 468–475. Huntress leans toward the idea that Cheever penned *all* of the reviews of Melville's books that appeared in the *Evangelist*: *Typee* (April 9, 1846), the revised *Typee*, *Omoo* (May 27, 1847), *White-Jacket* (May 23, 1850), *Moby-Dick* (November 20, 1851), and *Israel Potter* (March 21, 1855). Huntress cites Hugh Hetherington's *Melville's Reviewers: British and American 1846–1891* (Chapel Hill: University of North Carolina Press, 1961), 47, 83, 179, 207–208, 244.

It can be difficult for readers of Cheever and Melville to keep the Scoresbys straight. William Scoresby the elder (1760–1829) was a noted whaleman in the Greenland Whale Fishery. His son, William Scoresby Jr. (1789–1857), sailed with his father as mate at the age of seventeen. It was the son who became the noted authority on the northern fishery and wrote *An Account of the Arctic Regions, with a History and Description of the Northern Whale-Fishery* (1820) and *Journal of a Voyage to the Northern Whale-Fishery* (1823). Both Melville and Cheever plundered Scoresby exhaustively, with Cheever usually acknowledging his borrowings directly while Melville did so only half the time. The latter refers to Scoresby by name in "Cetology," "Moby Dick," "Of the Less Erroneous Pictures of Whales, and the True Pictures of Whaling Scenes," and "Measurement of the Whale's Skeleton." But in "Cetology," Melville also assigns a detail from Scoresby (the use of the narwhale's tusk) to fictional messmate Charley Coffin. In "The Mast-head," Melville mentions the father's invention of the crow's nest but references his source (the son's 1820 book) as the "fire-side narrative of Captain Sleet": *A Voyage among the Icebergs, in quest of the Greenland Whale, and incidentally for the re-discovery of the Lost Icelandic Colonies of Old Greenland*. In "The Whale as a Dish," Melville writes of Scoresby as "Zogranda, one of their most famous doctors," who "recommends strips of blubber for infants, as being exceedingly juicy and nourishing." In "Ambergris," Scoresby appears as "Fogo Von Slack," who has written "a great work on Smells, a text-book on that subject." Finally, Melville draws inspiration from a single passage of Scoresby for two inventions: "Fitz Swackhammer," the supposed author of a work entitled *Dan Coopman*, and Scoresby himself as "Dr, Snodhead, a very learned professor of Low Dutch and High German in the college of Santa Claus and St. Potts, to whom I [Ishmael] handed the work for translation." Scoresby had cited a work titled *Den Koopman*, not naming any author (Edinburgh: Archibald Constable & Co., 1820, 2:151). In each case, Melville's reference is to Scoresby Jr.

That Scoresby left whaling to preach probably endeared him to Cheever and alienated him from Melville—hence, perhaps at least in part, the satire. To complicate further, Cheever cites Scoresby's *Memorials of the Sea*—but Scoresby published three books with that title, the original one in 1835 and two later: one subtitled "Mary Russell" (excerpted from the 1835 edition) and the other "My Father." The original is an Increase Mather sort of affair with examples of remarkable providences arising from keeping the Sabbath at sea; it was reprinted by Longman in 1850 with the subtitle "Sabbaths in the Arctic Regions"; if actually published at the end of 1849, this could be the edition known to Cheever. Cheever could well have known Scoresby first through Leslie, Jameson, and Murray's *Narrative of Discovery and Adventure in the Polar Seas and Regions . . . and an Account of the Whale-Fishery* (New York: J. & J. Harper, 1833 et sequitur), which became number 14 in Harper's Family Library. Two of Cheever's illustrations ("Whaling Implements" and "Right Whale staving a Boat") are recycled from this volume.

8. The usual biographical sources—*Appleton's Cyclopædia of American Biography* (1874) and the *Dictionary of American Biography* (Supplement, also 1874)—join *The Congregational Year-Book, 1898* (Boston: Congregational Sunday School and Publishing Society, 1898, 17) and the Andover Theological Seminary *Necropolis, 1896-97* (Boston: Beacon Press, 1897), 240-241, in listing Cheever in the various roles of "associate editor" (1843-1844), "assistant editor" (1850-1852), and "editor" (1849-1852) of the *New York Evangelist*, of which (according to the same sources) his brother George was "principal editor" after 1845, having previously been a "corresponding editor" (*A Sketch of the Life of the Rev. Geo. B. Cheever, D.D., Pastor of the Church of the Puritans* [New York: Hall, Clayton, & Co., 1861], 16; the name on the masthead of the *Evangelist* is W. H. Bidwell as "Editor & Proprietor"). At the time Cheever wrote *The Whale and His Captors* (that is, when he revised previously published chapters and assembled them into a book), he lived at 17 Eldridge Street and was pastor of the Free Congregational Church on Chrystie Street, New York City (1848-1849), but he moved on to Greenport in 1852. In 1856 he was installed as pastor in Jewett City, Connecticut, where he married Jane Tyler (the

daughter of Dr. Lucius Tyler, a Yale graduate) in 1857; in 1861 he moved to Worcester, Massachusetts, where he made his home for the rest of his life (Duane Hamilton Hurd, *History of New London, Connecticut* [Philadelphia: J. W. Lewis & Co., 1882], 408). While he was actively publishing his own travel books, he acted as literary executor for U.S. Navy chaplain and California diplomat Walter Colton (1797–1851), editing the latter's *Land and Lee, Ship and Shore, The Sea and the Sailor*, all published by A. S. Barnes in 1851.

9. Volume 5 (July through December 1849), 576.

10. November 17; 5 (July through December 1849), 418–420.

11. Volume 3 (June to November 1851), 658–665.

12. Reprinted in Brian Higgins and Hershel Parker, *Herman Melville: The Contemporary Reviews* (New York: Cambridge University Press, 1995), 379.

13. J. Ross Browne was probably in Europe or the Levant.

14. Reprinted in Higgins and Parker, *Herman Melville: The Contemporary Reviews*, 379. Compare the language and theme to the unsigned *Evangelist* review of the revised Harper & Brothers *Typee* (July 5, 1849):

> This work is pretty well known—its virtues and its vices both conspire to give it notoriety. Its literary merit is not to be questioned. It exhibits a spirit and grace irresistible to most readers, and depicts the loveliest scenery in the world with true poetic genius. And its degraded moral tone, its slanderous attacks upon missionary labors and character, and its unquestionable falsehood from beginning to end, are quite as undeniable. If it had pleased Mr. Melville to use his fine powers to add to the stock of our information, and to open our sympathies for these far off tribes, he might have secured a permanent fame; as it is, he must be content with the brief notoriety which the production of a splendid piece of fiction can bestow. He will probably live long enough to discover the difference between what he has, and what he might have had. (108)

15. Scoresby's *Journal of a Voyage to the Northern Whale Fishery* (1823). Cf. Wilson L. Heflin, "The Source of Ahab's Lordship over the Level Loadstone," *American Literature* 20:3 (November 1948), 323–327. Is Cheever's own experience also a reshaping of the Scoresby passage?

16. November 7, 1851. *Correspondence*, ed. Lynn Horth (Evanston and Chicago: Northwestern University Press and the Newberry Library, 1993), 208–209.

17. New York: Harper & Brothers, 1850, which acknowledged that the author had read *White-Jacket* by June.

18. New York: A. S. Barnes, 1851.

A NOTE ON THE TEXT

This edition follows the text of the 314-page 1850 impression of the stereotyped Harper and Brothers edition of *The Whale and His Captors* entered for copyright in 1849. Additional material is drawn from the subsequent 356-page expanded American edition (printed at least as early as 1853, as digitized at the University of Michigan's Making of America website), which employed the original plates for the main body of its text. The present edition does not reproduce advertisements bound at the end of the 1850 impression, which feature "Abbott's Histories."

A presentation copy from Cheever's sister Elizabeth B. Cheever bearing the imprint 1849 is known (*fide* Peter Harrington, London). Copies with this date are exceedingly uncommon and may not have been offered to the public.

The volume was reprinted in Britain in 1850 by Sampson Low as the 304-page *The Whaleman's Adventures*; a presentation copy from the publisher to Cheever is in the American Antiquarian Society's collection. The first British edition was edited by William S. Scoresby Jr., author of Melville's sources, *An Account of the Arctic Regions, with a History and Description of the Northern Whale Fishery* (1820) and *Journal of a Voyage to the Northern Whale Fishery* (1822).

A 240-page London edition was published by Nelson in 1851 under the original American title.

All editions seem to have been reprinted through the 1860s, with an impression of the 356-page edition being printed in Boston by D. Lothrop in 1886.

The focus of the present edition is a text as it was known by Melville or evidenced subsequent interaction with his works. Egregious (by 1850 standards) errors of spelling and punctuation have been silently corrected, but in general wide leeway has been given to Cheever's preferences.

There she blows! There she blows!
Man the boats! For nothing stay!
Such a prize we must not lose!
Lay to your oars! Away! away!

THE WHALE AND HIS CAPTORS;

OR,

THE WHALEMAN'S ADVENTURES,

AND

THE WHALE'S BIOGRAPHY.

AS GATHERED ON THE HOMEWARD CRUISE
OF THE "COMMODORE PREBLE."

BY REV. HENRY T. CHEEVER.

With Engravings.

Oh, the rare old Whale, mid storm and gale,
In his ocean home will be
A Giant in might, where might is right,
And King of the boundless Sea.

NEW YORK:

HARPER & BROTHERS, PUBLISHERS,
82 CLIFF STREET.

1850.

PREFACE

This book is simply what its title indicates, the mind of the author pretending to be only the camera obscura through which the rays from Nature and Nature's living scenes have passed uncolored to the canvass. It may be that some who were with the writer, and others too, experienced and old in whaling life, may like to glance through this gallery of Daguerreotypes, and by their help recall to mind scenes of which, if they can not say, like many in this vocation, *Quaeque ipse miserrima vidi*, yet with equal truth, *Quorum pars magna fui*.

To them, the author is sure it will be pleasurable to review life-passages that were fraught with no ordinary interest in passing, and to compare the glimpses and sun-paintings found here with their more subtle images in the brain, which memory loves to be retracing in the downhill of life.

And if it be true, what the philosophic Latin poet Lucretius touches so beautifully,

Suave mari magno, turbantibus aequora ventis,
E terra, magnum alterius spectare laborem —

It is a view of delight to stand or walk upon the shore side, and to see a ship tossed upon the sea; or to be in a fortified tower, and to see two battles join upon a plain; or it is sweet, from a post of safety, to review the labors of other men beyond the seas — if there be truth in this, the writer may hope his book will not be barren of interest to many, who, having never experienced the reality of the life which is here delineated, may now behold it safely from afar off.

Hoping also that there are moral hints and lessons herewith interwoven, that will catch the eye and touch the heart of the casual reader, like sober threads of green in tapestry of gold, this book is honestly commended to the purchase and perusal of all classes, by the

AUTHOR

Introduction

The mighty whale doth in those harbors lye,
Whose oyle the careful merchant deare will buy.
—Old English Poem.

From very early times it is probable that Northwest Indians, Esquimaux, and Norwegians were in the habit of capturing whales in their rude way, in order to supply themselves with fat and food. There is a curious tradition extant of one Ochter, a Norwegian, who, as long ago as King Alfred's time, "was one of six that had killed sixty whales in two days, of which some were forty-eight, some fifty yards long." But the Biscayans are believed to have been the first people who prosecuted the whale fishery as a commercial pursuit, so far back as the twelfth century. In the north of Europe and all around the Bay of Biscay whale's tongues were among the table delicacies of the Middle Ages.

When this branch of industry failed with them, by reason of whales ceasing to visit the Bay of Biscay, the English and Dutch, taught by the Biscayans, 'who were best experienced in that facultie of whale-striking,' took it up in the Northern Seas, where the gigantic game was then every where found in vast numbers by navigators in search of the northern passage to the Indies. By the middle of the seventeenth century, the Dutch had built the considerable village of Smeerenburg, on the Isle of Amsterdam, along the northern shore of Spitzbergen, within only eleven degrees of the North Pole, where the unbroken night is from September to March, and the day from March to September. This was the great rendezvous of Dutch whale ships, and it being their practice to boil the blubber on shore, it was amply provided with boilers, tanks, and all the apparatus then used for preparing the oil and bone.

This fishing colony of the frozen zone, an incidental fruit of those daring adventures after a northeast route to India, was founded nearly at the same time with Batavia in the East, and it was for a considerable time doubtful which of the two would be most important to the mother country. When in its most flourishing state, near 1680, the Dutch whale fishery employed two hundred and sixty ships and fourteen thousand seamen. This singular village and Bay of Smeerenburg, where there were seen at one time by the Dutch navigator Zorgdrager no less than one hundred and eighty-eight vessels, afford, perhaps, the most remarkable instance on record of what commerce can do against unyielding laws of Nature, and over obstructions which it would seem impossible to surmount. But how soon does Nature, if ever temporarily displaced, resume her sway. Now that the whales have long since deserted those parts, even the site of the old Arctic colony is hardly discernible, and the English branch of the Greenland whale fishery is all that is prosecuted in those seas, and that with very moderate success.

The first person that is recorded to have killed a whale among the people of New England was one William Hamilton, somewhere between 1660 and 1670. In the town records of Nantucket, there is a copy of an agreement entered into in the year 1672, between one James Lopar and the settlers there, "to carry on a design of whale fishing." But whether the first proper whaling harpoon used in America was wrought there or on Cape Cod can not be ascertained. From this time onward, whenever whales were descried in the bay or offing from the rude look-outs constructed along shore, notice was instantly spread, and they were attacked by boats then manned mostly by the Indians, who early evinced an aptitude and fondness for this business. Shore-whaling seems to have reached its height by 1726, during which year eighty-six whales were taken, eleven in one day. It was continued with declining success up to 1760, and for seventy years preceding that date not a single white man is known to have lost his life in the hazardous pursuit.

As early as 1700, they began to fit out vessels from Cape Cod and Nantucket to "whale out in the deep for sperm whales." These gradually crept along, emboldened by experience, north to the Labradors and south to the Bahamas, where New Providence became famous as a whale-fishing station, through the skill and daring of New England enterprise, while, as Burke said, but in the gristle, and not yet hardened into the bone of manhood.

By the year 1771, New England, through her adventurous whale fishery, was both in the North and South Atlantic Oceans, commanding the admiration of the world, and eulogized by the highest eloquence of the British Parliament. From the year 1771 to 1775, Massachusetts alone employed in it annually three hundred and four vessels, of twenty-seven thousand eight hundred and forty-six tons burden. The quantity of oil brought into Nantucket yearly at the time of the breaking out of the Revolutionary war, was thirty thousand barrels.

Stimulated by their success, both France and Great Britain now entered anew into this lucrative enterprise; Louis XVI, himself fitting out six ships from Dunkirk on his own account, in 1784, which were furnished with experienced harpooners and able seamen from Nantucket. In 1790, France had about forty ships employed in the fishery, but the wars consequent upon the French Revolution at once swept them all, and the whaling fleet of Holland also; as did the War for Independence likewise suspend this lucrative branch of the commerce of New England. By reason of it, no less than one hundred and fifty of her vessels were either captured or lost at sea, and great numbers of her seamen perished.

In 1788 Great Britain had the honor of opening the Pacific to the sperm whale fishery, through the Amelia, Captain Shields, fitted out at vast expense by Mr. Enderby, of London. Her unprecedented success started numbers on her track both from New England and Old, and by 1820 the whole South Pacific and Indian Oceans were traversed by intrepid whalemen; and in the seas of China and on the coasts of Japan they were drawing the line and striking the harpoon into those mammoth denizens of the deep.

Prostrated, however, by the Revolutionary war, the New England branch of the whale fishery had hardly recovered its former prosperity, when the last war with Great Britain, from 1812 to 1815, again broke it up. But upon the restoration of peace its recovery was rapid; so that by 1821 there were owned in Nantucket alone (which had lost during the war twenty-seven ships), seventy-eight whale ships, and six whaling brigs. In 1844, the entire American whaling fleet amounted to six hundred and fifty ships, barks, brigs, and schooners, tonnaging two hundred thousand tons; and they were manned by seventeen thousand five hundred officers and seamen. At the same time, the English whale fishery, which in 1821 employed three hundred and twenty-three ships, was reduced to only eighty-five. But the New Holland branch of the English whale fishery was rapidly growing, the proximity of those whaling ports of Australia to some of the most productive cruising grounds enabling the ships fitted out there to perform three voyages while the English and Americans are performing two. The number of whale ships from French, German, and Danish ports, at the same time, was between sixty and seventy.

The estimated annual consumption of the American whaling fleet was $3,845,500. Value of the annual import of oil and whalebone in a crude state $7,000,000, increased by manufacturing to $9,000,000. The number of vessels in the American whale fishery the present year, 1849, as gathered from the "Whaleman's Shipping List," is estimated at six hundred and ten, or one hundred and ninety-six thousand one hundred and thirteen tons, nearly one tenth of the navigation of the Union. Receipts of sperm oil the last year, 1848, one hundred and seven thousand nine hundred and seventy-six barrels, at an import value of $3,455,232. Receipts of right-whale oil in the same time, two hundred and eighty thousand six hundred and fifty-six barrels, at an import value of $3,429,494. Whalebone, two million three thousand six hundred pounds, worth $508,762. Crude value of the whale fishery in 1848, $7,393,488.

The average yearly quantity of sperm oil taken for nine years has been one hundred and forty-two thousand two hundred and forty-two barrels; of right-whale oil, two hundred and fifty-five thousand four hundred and fifty-six barrels; of bone, two million three hundred and twenty-four thousand five hundred and seventy-eight pounds. Average yearly value for nine years, $8,098,360. There was a falling off in 1848, from the previous year, of thirteen thousand barrels of sperm, thirty-three thousand barrels of right whale, and one million pounds of bone. Eighteen years ago it was estimated, by taking into account all the investments connected with the American whale fishery, that property to the amount of $70,000,000 was involved in it, and that seventy thousand persons derived from it their chief subsistence; a valuation which should be much augmented rather than diminished at the present time.

the WHALE & *his captors*

The New Bedford district now supplies to the whale fishery one hundred and two thousand three hundred and five tons. All other ports, including sixty-six ships, or twenty-three thousand tons from Nantucket, give ninety-three thousand eight hundred and eight, in all one hundred and ninety-six thousand one hundred and thirteen tons. The exports of oil to foreign ports, in 1848, from New Bedford, were seventeen thousand and ninety-three barrels.

To those who are in quest of definite information concerning the various cruising grounds and the times of finding whales there, the closing chapter of the Annals of the United States Exploring Squadron is the most satisfactory of any thing to be found. It should be printed in pamphlet form, and kept in the chart-box of every whaler. Other interesting matter, of a miscellaneous character, pertaining to the whale fishery, is to be found in the appendix to a work of J. R. Browne, called "Etchings of a Whaling Cruise," and in a volume entitled "Incidents of a Whaling Voyage, by F. A. Olmsted."

Without superseding or conflicting with either of those entertaining books, the course pursued in the present volume is an independent one, whereby it is aimed to finish the complement of whaling literature, and supply what was wanting, in order to put the reading public in possession of a full-length portraiture of the whaleman as seen in the actual pursuit and garb of his perilous occupation. Personal narrative and incident, other than what bears directly upon this, are therefore omitted, together with those minute descriptions of whaling implements, outfits, modes, customs, and sea-usages to be found elsewhere. Neither does it enter into our purpose to portray a sailor's life and manners in the forecastle or before the mast, alow or aloft, for this is a department of marine literature in which books are so numerous, both in the form of the novel and the sea journal, that little remains to be told. In adventures, however, almost every whaleman's voyage is an original, certainly so to himself. We begin, therefore, at once, with the peculiar lights and shadows of a homeward cruise in the Pacific and Atlantic, from the Sandwich Islands to Boston, in the good ship Commodore Preble, Captain Lafayette Ludlow.

In a voyage of two hundred and thirty-six days there will always be lights and shadows, good and evil, pleasures and displeasures, interlocking one another. To the author the comforts of this long voyage

A Polar Right Whale on the Ice.

far exceeded its discomforts, by the constant blessing of Providence, making it eminently conducive to the recovery of health, and through the personal kindness of a skillful captain and esteemed friend. Would that every wanderer in quest of health could be cheerfully returning homeward under circumstances as favorable!

> Now, little book, with prosperous tide and gale,
> I'll pledge thee to a voyage round the world.
> Buoyant and bounding like the polar whale,
> That takes his pastime, every joyful sail
> Here to the freedom of the wind unfurl,
> While right and left the parted surges curl!

the WHALE *&* his *captors*

II

Coral Island of Rimatara

Happy they were, and without a care,
Who had made their home forever there;
Happy they were, and calm and free,
Living upon their island-home,
Whose beach was girt with a silvery sea,
That sprinkled it ever with starry foam.
Their life was a moving melody,
Their season a long serenity.
— Story.

The first view we have of the Commodore Preble is as she is lying off and on the lone island of Rimatara, in quest of the fresh supplies which whalemen covet in order to keep at bay the scurvy. This is one of those fascinating South Sea Islands, which, on their first discovery by Europeans in the latter part of the last century, quite turned the heads of many, and at once started so much speculative nonsense and sentimentality about primeval innocence and bliss embosomed in the Pacific.

A coral rock, by gentle Nature made
Verdant and beautiful, through tropic sun,
And fertilizing rain, and grateful shade;
Placed far amid the melancholy main.

It is about seven miles long, one and a half or two wide, and lies in 152° west longitude, and 22° 45′ south latitude; about five hundred miles southwest from Tahiti. It is properly, perhaps, one of the Society Island group, being a mere pile of corallite and wave-washed coral sand. We came in sight of it on Tuesday afternoon, a blue hummock on the bosom of the ocean, and ran on until we discovered, to our great delight, what could not be mistaken for a meeting-house and a

The Commodore Preble taking Supplies at Rimatara.

white flag flying on a post near by, to indicate the friendliness of the natives, and induce us to stop for trade.

The sea broke so high upon the northeast and southwest points of the island, and, indeed, all along shore, that our captain did not deem it prudent to attempt landing that night. We therefore stood off until twelve o'clock midnight, and then tacking, were up with it again by ten o'clock next morning, on the leeward side.

The island presented a beautiful appearance, being thickly wooded to the water's edge, and elevated in some parts into gentle hills, crowned with all the various and luxuriant growth of the tropics. Canoes soon launched out through the boisterous surf, and came alongside of us, having two or three lads and men in each, much fairer-skinned and better looking than the majority of Hawaiians.

The captain's boat anchored off the reef, while the natives brought their articles of trade in their pigmy canoes. By four in the afternoon he had procured a boat-load of pigs and cocoanuts, with which returning to the ship, we stood off again until next morning, when the captain gave orders for two boats.

One of our sailors by the name of Johnson, that had lived on Ta-

the WHALE *&* his *captors*

hiti, and could talk a little in their tongue, had told the natives the day before that there was on board a missionary, or a missionary's friend, from Hawaii, and there was accordingly sent off through him, on a slip of paper, very legibly written by the native teacher, a Rimatara letter, of which the following is a literal translation:

"Dear Friend and Father,—

"May you be saved by the true God. This is our communication to you. Come thou hither upon the shore, that we may see you in respect to all the words of God which are right with you. It is our desire that you come to-day.

"From Teutino and his brethren."

Eager to know something more of a people from whom came so cordial an *aloha*, and

My very heart athirst
To look on Nature in her robe of green,

I made ready to go ashore. The breakers were not formidable enough, though beating with fearful violence, to make me forego the novelty of setting foot on a coral South Pacific island, and the pleasure of a stroll among the trees after seven weeks at sea. Taking, therefore, a life-preserver, I ventured into one of the little canoes that came alongside the boat, and was paddled and handed by a narrow cleft, through roaring breakers and ragged rocks that threatened instant destruction, among which a common boat could hardly live a moment. Those frail canoes, however, only nine and eleven feet long, carried safely through, one by one, all that ventured ashore.

Immediately on our landing, the natives gathered around and formed a ring, naturally curious, like savages every where, to notice every thing, and I not less so to observe their own eager attitudes, expressive gestures, and fine looks. The women have an uncommonly pleasing aspect of countenance, clear skin, but a shade or two darker than a dark brunette, black eyes, hair, and eyebrows, and a captivating beauty of form, and bashful turning away when looked at, that is not a little attractive. Their nostrils are not so negro-like, nor their lips so thick as those of the Hawaiians, but still they bear to them a close resemblance. Many of the little girls and maidens were truly beautiful, and would be deemed paragons, even in the artificial state where beauty is not left so much to itself, but has to be busked, bustled, and corseted by omnipotent fashion.

I soon made my way to the island king, Temaeva, who sat apart from others upon a block of coral, and leaning on a staff, his only dress being a shirt and *kihei* (mantle). He was a benevolent-looking, well-made man, having the port and presence of a king, and, if that were all,

> With Atlantean shoulders fit to bear
> The weight of mightiest monarchies.

He offered me his hand with much apparent cordiality, and immediately led the way to his house in the interior. The path was at first rugged as the volcanic clinkers of Hawaii, over heaps and swells of broken and sharp coral, overgrown with huge roots of the Kamani and Koa trees, in the borrowed terms of Wordsworth,

> A growth
> Of intertwisted fibres serpentine,
> Up-coiling, and inveterately convolved.

This barrier passed, there was a subsidence and inclining of the island inward, and the path went through a meadow of bulrushes, in time of rain flooded. The soil was a rich black loam. Next came beds of wet *kalo* (Arum esculentum), very luxuriant and large, beyond which were the houses of the king and native missionary teachers, the chapel, school-house, and principal settlement. These were prettily-made buildings of *kamanu* posts, wattled between, lined on both sides with a good coat of whitewashed plaster, and thatched on the roof with grass. Being clustered tastefully together, they make a very pleasing appearance outside.

The chapel and house of the king were furnished with flooring and settees. In the former was a round pulpit, very much like those seen in popish cathedrals, wherever is seen at all what popery is by no means fond of—the pulpit. They had been built eleven years, it being more than twenty, we were told, since the island was first Christianized by native missionaries from Tahiti. They were all surrounded by a low paling of posts driven slightly into the ground, merely to keep out

The WHALE & *His captors*

hogs; while cocoanut trees and giant bananas were dropping their fruits all around. The whole scene, in every feature, was most pleasingly corroborative of the representations quoted by Harris in "The Great Commission," to show the temporal utility of missionary exertions in the South Seas. "Instead of their little, contemptible huts along the sea-beach, there will be seen a neat settlement, with a large chapel in the center, capable of containing one or two thousand people; a schoolhouse on the one side, and a chief's or the missionary's house on the other; and a range of white cottages a mile or two long, peeping at you from under the splendid banana-trees or the breadfruit groves. So that their comfort is increased and their character elevated."

Soon after reaching this little metropolis of the island, the king had baked pig and delicious kalo placed upon a massive rude table, and plates of English crockery, with knives and forks. A blessing was asked by the native teacher, and I was invited to eat. It was, in their view, an important piece of courtesy, which a recent breakfast rather unfitted me for; yet I ate, with compliments, of the mealy kalo, and tasted of the pig, while the king was taking huge morsels that would almost sink a common man.

The wine of this feast was the delicious milk of young cocoa-nuts just from the tree; and I will venture to say that Hebe never poured such nectar into the goblets of the gods. It was more like that which Eve made ready once in Eden, as the poet tells, wherewith to entertain their angel guest:

With inoffensive must and meathes,
From many a berry and from sweet kernels pressed,
She tempers dulcet creams; nor them to hold
Wants her fit vessels pure; then strews the ground
With rose and odors from the shrub unfumed.

This entertainment over, we repaired to the teacher's, where again was served up the same, with the addition of banana made into a *poi*, of which the king ate freely. I was here presented with a couple of rolls of white *kapa* by the good woman of the house. After surveying the premises, getting a specimen of the king and teacher's handwriting, and giving them a card to certify any other chance ship of their hospitality, I returned to the shore by another path, through a dense wood, coming out of it on the windward side of the island, by the old church and grave-yard, where Temaeva pointed out the tomb of a former wife, having the date of her death rudely cut in a coral slab.

The cocoa-nuts passed were numberless, shedding their fruit by thousands; also lofty and straight pandanuses, *kukuis*, and *milo* trees. Following round the shore to the point at which we had struck off into the woods, we found the captain there busy trading. I pleased myself a while with looking at those mixed and motley groups, and trying to communicate with the harmless Arimatarians, and then went off to the boat through the outrageous surf, inly wishing I could leave with them some substantial and enduring testimony of good will.

The king and his wife, together with the captain, came, one by one, soon after, and we all pulled off to the ship, where the king seemed highly gratified with his entertainment and presents. He is manifestly king but in name, having to promise a recompense even to the men that brought him off to the boat in their canoe. The Gospel has abolished all tyranny, and, as the sailor interpreted it, all there are for themselves, and without distinctions. They are four hundred all told, and live, according to their own telling, in much peace, being visited two or three times a year by whale ships for recruits, whose trade just keeps them (the adults) with a single cloth garment, or *kihei* a piece.

A roughly-made schooner, of kamanu wood (much like our mahogany), was on the stocks, for which they were very anxious to get tar, oakum, and a compass. No white missionary, we were told, has ever resided upon the island, but all their imperfect Christianization and acquaintance with the arts have been effected by native teachers from Tahiti. White men have stopped on the island occasionally, but they say they do not want them, unless they know the language and have some trade.

I could not leave this secluded and lovely island, though but the stopping-place of a day, and ere long, I hope, to mingle with humanity in a wider and more populous field, without a feeling of sadness, I hardly know why. But so it is in the voyage of life, especially in that of a traveler, sailing down the stream of time, we hail a friendly bark, or touch here and there at a pleasant landing-place upon its banks, pluck a few fruits and flowers, exchange good wishes and kind words

the WHALE *&* HIS *captors*

with the friends of a day, truly love and are loved by some congenial hearts, both drop and take some seeds of good and evil, to spring up when we are in our graves, and then we are away; the places that now know us know us no more forever, and the faces that now smile upon us we never see again. Who can help sighing as he thinks of it, and wishing to leave, wherever he goes, some durable evidence that an immortal spirit has passed that way!

Oh, at what time soever thou
(Unknown to me) the heavens wilt bow,
And, with thy angels in the van,
Descend to judge poor careless man,
　　Grant I may not *like puddle lie,*
In a corrupt security,
Where, if a traveler water crave,
He finds it dead, and in a grave;
　　But as the *clear running spring*
All day and night doth flow and sing;
And though here born, yet is acquainted
Elsewhere, and, flowing, keeps untainted—
So let me all my busy age
In thy free services engage.
And though (while here) of force I must
Have commerce sometimes with poor dust,
Yet let my course, my aim, my love,
And chief acquaintance be above;
So when that day and hour shall come
In which thyself will be the sun,
Thou'lt find me dressed and on my way,
Watching the break of thy great day.

How different now our reception here by Islanders that had been blessed with the Bible, from that which a whale ship had while sailing along in this same Pacific in the year 1835, from barbarians that had never received the Gospel. A large number of natives came off, as to us, for purposes of trade. No treachery was suspected, and all for a while went on amicably. But, upon a signal from a chief, the natives sprang for the harpoons, whale-spades, and other deadly weapons at hand, and a desperate contest immediately ensued. The captain was killed by a single stroke of a whale-spade; the first mate also, soon after. The second mate jumped overboard and was killed in the water, and four of the seamen lost their lives. A part of the crew ran up the rigging for security, and the rest into the forecastle.

Among these last was a young man, the third mate, by the name of Jones, the only surviving officer. By his cool intrepidity and judgment, after a dreadful encounter, the ship was cleared of the savages, the chief killed, and many of his companions, both of those on board and those who came alongside to aid in securing the ship.

Jones now became the captain, buried the dead, dressed the wounded, put the ship in order, and made sail for the Christianized Sandwich Islands with the surviving crew. With a skill and self-possession worthy of the man that could accomplish such a rescue, and with a favoring Providence, he navigated the bereaved whaler to Oahu, where the survivors were hospitably entertained. The ship, however, had to be sent home, the voyage being completely broken up for want of the necessary officers, and thousands of dollars lost to owners and underwriters.

I remember once to have listened to the narrative of a captain who was wrecked in the Pacific on a sunken rock, and for fourteen days and nights himself and crew, twenty-two in number, were exposed in their boats, and had quite given up hope of ever again reaching the land. But on the morning of the fifteenth day after the loss of their ship, they found their boats nearing an unknown island. They were almost spent, and saw the shore, which was guarded by a reef, lined with natives, whether cannibals or Christianized they could not tell.

While their lives were in doubt, and they were questioning whether a worse death by savage violence did not await them than if they had perished at sea, one of the natives came out toward them through the surf, holding in his hand a book, and cried, with a loud voice, "Missionary! missionary!" An answering shout of recognition and beckoning from the poor mariners immediately brought the natives, through the waves, to their aid, by whom they were carried on shore in their arms, supplied with food, and generously entertained with more than human, with Christian kindness.

It so happened, according to the captain's statement, that this was

the WHALE & *his captors*

an island whose inhabitants had been first brought to the knowledge of Christianity by the brother of this captain, who had been some years before cast away on this very island, and, with one other of the ship's company, was saved. They were taken by the natives to be offered up as a sacrifice to their gods. But while on their way to the place where human victims used to be sacrificed, they remembered the tradition that a god should come to them from the sea.

Overruled, doubtless, by a divine impulse, they now entertained the white man as a god, and he instructed them concerning the only true God and Savior. They invited the missionary from another island, and in Heaven's blessing upon his instructions was read the secret of all their after-kindness to the white men who visited or were cast upon their shores. All whalemen may see in this contrast, as we have to our joy in the Commodore Preble, what a difference there is between islands that have, and that have not the "BOOK."

It is THE BOOK which has brought it to pass that the adventurous, weary whaleman can now traverse the entire Pacific, and land with impunity at most of its lovely islands, and be supplied on terms of equity with all he needs. Let, then, those that owe to it the most, be loudest in their praises, and warmest in their love, and most careful in their obedience to the BOOK OF BOOKS.

It was the reasoning of one of this great family of South Sea Islanders (with whom our ship has just had such pleasant intercourse), soon after he came into possession of the BIBLE:

When I look at myself, I find that I have hinges all over my body. I have got hinges to my legs, my jaws, my feet, my hands. If I want to lay hold of any thing, there are hinges to my hands, and even to my fingers, to do it with. If my heart thinks, and I want to make others think with me, I use the hinges to my jaws, and they help me to talk. I could neither walk nor sit down if I had not hinges to my legs and feet. All this is wonderful. None of the strange things that men have brought from England in their big ships are at all to be compared to my body. He who made my body has made all those clever people, who made the strange things which they bring in the ships; and he is God, whom I worship.

But I should not know much more about him than as a great hinge-maker, if men in their ships had not brought the book which they call the Bible. That tells me of God, who makes the skill and the heart of man likewise. And when I hear how the Bible tells of the old heart with its corruption, and the new heart, and a right spirit, which God alone can create and give, I feel that his work in my body and his work in my heart fit each other exactly. I am sure, then, that the Bible, which tells me of these things, was made by him who made the hinges to my body. I believe the Bible to be the word of God.

The men on the other side of the great sea used their skill and their bodies to make ships and to print Bibles. They came in ships, and brought iron hoops, knives, nails, hatchets, cloth, and needles, which are very good. They also brought rum and whisky, which are very evil. They moved the hinges of the jaws, and told lies and curses, which are abominable. At last some came and brought the Bible. They used the hinges of their bodies to turn over its leaves and to explain God's blessed word. That was better than iron-ware and stuff for clothing. They were the servants of the living God, and my heart opened to their words as if it had hinges too, like as my mouth opens to take food when I am hungry. And my heart feels satisfied now. It was hungry, God nourished it; it was thirsty, God has refreshed it. Blessed be God, who gave his word, and sent it across the sea to bring me light and salvation!

Now we say that this unsophisticated native thinker, working thus all by himself at the great theological argument from evidences of design; could hardly have done better had he been going to school to Calvin or Chalmers all his days. He might have written in his Polynesian Bible the lines which are said to have been found on the blank leaf of a copy of the Scriptures belonging to a great English poet. And, ah! how much better had it been for the world if Byron had loved *his* Bible as there is reason to believe the unknown Tahitian did his.

> Within this awful volume lies
> The mystery of mysteries:
> And bless'd, forever bless'd are they
> Who read to hope, and read to pray.
> But better had he ne'er been born,
> Who reads to doubt, or reads to scorn.

III

Raising and Cutting-In Whales

Here leviathan,
Hugest of living creatures, on the deep
Stretch'd like a promontory, sleeps or swims,
And seems a moving land; and at his gills
Draws in, and at his trunk spouts out, a sea.
—Milton.

For the first time in our now ten weeks' passage from the Hawaiian Islands, on this New Zealand Cruising Ground, we heard, day before yesterday, that life-kindling sound to a weary whaleman, THERE SHE BLOWS! The usual questions and orders from the deck quickly followed. "Where away?" "Two points on the weather bow!" "How far off?" "A mile and a half!" "Keep your eye on her!" "Sing out when we head right!" It turned out that three whales were descried from aloft in different parts, and in a short time, when we were deemed near enough, the captain gave orders to "Stand by and lower" for one a little more than half a mile to windward.

Three boats' crews pulled merrily away, glad of something to stir their blood, and with eager hope to obtain the oily material wherewith to fill their ship and make good their "lay." The whale was going leisurely to windward, blowing every now and again two or three times, then "turning tail," "up flukes," and sinking. The boats "headed" after him, keeping a distance of nearly one quarter of a mile from each other, to scatter (as it is called) their chances.

Fortunately, as the oarsmen were "hove up," that is, had their oars a-peak, about the place where they expected the whale would next appear, the huge creature rose hard by the captain's boat, and all the harpooner in the bow had to do was to plunge his two keen cold irons, which are always secured to one tow-line, into the monster's blubber-sides. This he did so well as to hit the "fish's life" at once, and make him spout blood forthwith. It was the first notice the poor fellow had of the proximity of his powerful captors, and the sudden piercing of the barbed harpoons to his very vitals made him caper and run most furiously.

The boat spun after him with almost the swiftness of a top, now diving through the seas and tossing the spray, and then lying still while the whale sounded; anon in swift motion again when the game rose, for the space of an hour. During this time another boat "got fast" to him with its harpoons, and the captain's cruel lance had several times struck his vitals. He was killed, as whalemen call it, that is, mortally wounded, an hour before he went into "his flurry," and was really dead or turned up on his back.

The loose boat then came to the ship for a hawser to fasten round his flukes; which being done, the captain left his irons in the carcass and pulled for the ship, in order to beat to windward, and, after getting alongside, to "cut him in." This done, and the mammoth carcass secured to the ship by a chain round the bitts, they proceeded to reeve the huge blocks that are always made fast for the purpose to the fore and main mast head, and to fasten the cutting-in tackle. The captain and two mates then went over the sides on steps well secured, and having each a breast-rope to steady them and lean upon. The cooper then passed them the long-handled spades, which he was all the time grinding and whetting, and they fell lustily to work chopping off the blubber.

First came one of the huge lips, which, after they had nearly severed close to the creature's eye, was hooked into by what they call a blubber hook, stripped off, and hoisted on board by the windlass. It was very compact and dense, and covered with barnacles like Brobdignag lice.

Next came one of the fore-fins; after that the other lip, and then the upper jaw along with all that peculiar substance called whalebone, through which the animal strains his food. It is all fringed with coarse hair that detains the little shrimps and small fry on which the creature feeds. The bones, or, rather, slabs of whalebone radiate in leaves that lie edgewise to the mouth, from each side of what may be called the ridge-pole of the mouth's roof, forming a house almost big enough for a man to stand up in. Outside it is crowned with what they call a

View of a Whale Ship in the Process of "Cutting in."

bonnet, being a crest or comb where there burrow legions of barnacles and crabs like rabbits in a warren, or insects in the shaggy bark of an old tree.

Next came the lower jaw and throat, together with the tongue, which latter alone must have weighed fifteen hundred or two thousand pounds; an enormous mass of fat, not, however, so firm and tough as the blubber. Whalers often have to lose it, especially from the northwest whale, it being impossible to get it up on deck detached and alone, because it would not hold, and it is generally too large and heavy to raise along with the throat.

After this was hoisted in, the rest of the way was plane sailing, the blubber of the body being cut and peeled off, in huge unbroken strips, as the carcass rolled over and over, being heaved on by the windlass, then hooked into by the blubber hooks, and hoisted in by the men all the time heaving at the windlass.

As often as a piece, nearly reaching to the top of the main mast, was got over the deck, they would attack it with great boarding-knives, and cutting a hole in it at a place nearly even with the deck, thrust in the strap and toggel of the "cutting blocks," that they might still have a purchase on the carcass below. Then they would sever the huge piece from the rest, and lower it down into "the blubber-room" between decks, where two men had as much as they could do to cut it into six or eight pound pieces and stow it away. It was from nine to eleven inches thick, and looked like very large fat pork slightly colored with salt-petre.

The magnificent, swan-like albatrosses were round us by hundreds, eagerly seizing and fighting for every bit and fragment that fell off into the water, swallowing it with the most carnivorous avidity, and a low, avaricious greed of delight, that detracted considerably from one's admiration of this most superb of birds, just as your veneration for one whom the coloring of a youthful imagination has made a little more than human, is not a little abated by finding him subject to the necessities and passions of poor human nature. Gonies, stinkards, horsebirds, haglets, gulls, pigeons, and petrels, had all many a good morsel of blubber. For at any time in these seas, though eight hundred or a thousand miles from shore, the capture of a whale will allure thousands of sea-birds from far and near. Sharks, too, appeared to claim their share; but it was not until after a man had been down twice on the wave-washed carcass, to get a rope fast to a hole in the whale's head, or I should have trembled for his legs.

Before the blubber was all off, the huge entrails of the whale burst out like barrels, at the wounds made by the spades and lances. I hoped the peeled carcass would float for the benefit of the gonies and other birds. But no sooner was the last fold of blubber off, the flukes hoisted in, and the great chain detached, than it sank plumb down. About the same time two ships bore down to speak us, the Henry of Sag Harbor, and the Lowell of New London. Their captains came on board to congratulate us on our success, and "learn the news." They had just arrived on the ground, and had not yet taken any whales.

Soon after we had finished cutting in, about eight o'clock in the evening, the wind increased almost to a gale, making it impossible to try out that night. But to-day, while the ship is lying to, the business has begun in good earnest; the blubber-men cutting up in the blubber-room; others pitching it on deck; others forking it over to the side of the "try-works;" two men standing by a "horse" with a mincing

the WHALE & *his* captors

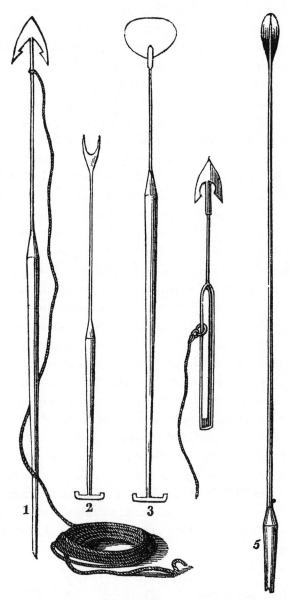

1. Hand Harpoon.   2. Pricker.   3. Blubber Spade.
4. Gun Harpoon.   5. Lance.

Whaling implements.

knife to cleave the pieces into many parts for the more easy trying out, as the rind of a joint of pork is cut by the cook for roasting: the boat-steerers and one of the mates are pitching it into the kettles, feeding the fires with the scraps, and bailing the boiling fluid into copper tanks, from which it is the duty of another to dip into casks.

The decks present that lively though dirty spectacle which whalemen love, their faces all begrimed and sooty, and smeared with oil, so that you can not tell if they be black or white. A farmer's golden harvest in autumn is not a pleasanter sight to him, than it is to a whaler to have his decks and blubber-room "blubberlog," the try-works a-blazing, cooper a-pounding, oil a-flowing, every body busy and dirty night and day. Donkey-loads of Chilian or Peruvian gold, filing into the custom-house at Valparaiso and Lima, or a stream of Benton's yellow-boys flowing up the Mississippi, or bags of the Californian dust riding into San Francisco, have no such charms for him as cutting in a hundred-barrel whale and turning out oil by the hogshead.

The whale now taken proves to be a cow whale, forty-five feet long and twenty-five round, and it will yield between seventy and eighty barrels of right whale oil. This is about the ordinary size of the New Zealand whale, a mere dwarf in comparison with that of the northwest, which sometimes yields, it is said, three hundred barrels, ordinarily one hundred and fifty, or one hundred and eighty.

Though so huge a creature, a very small part of its bulk appears out of water, and that bending with the undulations of the waves; nor do you have so fair a view of this immense mass of organized matter, as of a ship afloat in comparison to one on the stocks. To have a just idea of its greatness, it should be seen on dry land. As is usually the case, the observed reality of this mammoth animal, prodigious as it is, hardly comes up to the preconceived vague idea of it, still less to the poetic notion of

That sea-beast
Leviathan, which God of all his works
Created hugest, that swim the ocean stream.
Him haply slumbering on the Norway foam,
The pilot of some small night-foundered skiff,
Deeming some island, oft, as seamen tell,

the WHALE & *his* captors

With fixed anchor in his scaly rind,
Moors by his side under the lee, while night
Invests the sea and wished morn delays.

They used to tell some big "fish stories" in Milton's day, and I have
no doubt they had something to do in his mind with the creation of
that image of Satan on the burning lake.

With head uplift above the wave, and eyes
That sparkling blazed; his other parts beside,
Prone on the flood, extended long and large,
Lay floating many a rood; in bulk as huge
As whom the fables name of monstrous size,
Titanian or earth-born, that warred on Jove:
Forthwith upright he rears from oft the pool
His mighty stature: on each hand the flames,
Driven backward, slope their pointing spires, and rolled
In billows, leave in the midst a horrid vale.
Then, with expanded wings, he takes his flight
Aloft *incumbent on the dusky air,*
That felt unusual weight.

IV

New Zealand Cruising Ground

Oh, the whale is free, of the boundless sea;
  He lives for a thousand years;
He sinks to rest on the billow's breast,
  Nor the roughest tempest fears.
The howling blast, as it rushes past,
  Is music to lull him to sleep:
And he scatters the spray in his boisterous play,
  As he dashes—the King of the deep.
—Sea Song.

The recent capture of one right whale, getting fast to another, and pursuit of several more, and the sight of them blowing all around, close at hand and at a distance, naturally puts one upon inquiring into the habits and resorts of this great sea-monster. It is of the class mammalia, order cetacea, warm-blooded, bringing forth its young alive, generally one at a time, and giving them suck. It is not, therefore, a fish, is without scales, breathes the air through enormous lungs, not gills, and respires by what is called its spout or blow-holes, a kind of nostrils, or, in other words, two apertures situated on the after part of its head and neck, through which is forcibly expelled all the water taken into the mouth in the act of feeding and breathing, and all the warm air and vapor of the lungs.

The form of the spout serves to distinguish at a distance the kind of whale, whether right whale (Balæna mysticetus) or sperm (makrocephalus). The right whale, having two large orifices on the top of the back part of its head as it lies along in the water, the spout of vapor and water ejected is forced up perpendicularly till its power is spent, and it begins to fall over on both sides, looking then, at a distance, in shape like a Gothic elm parted into two branches. This can be easily perceived when the whale is either coming directly toward or going directly off from the ship, the *jets d'eau* being sometimes thirty or even fifty feet high. The sperm whale, on the other hand, has but one blowhole, and that a little on one side or corner of its head, from which the ejected stream of breath issues a little obliquely, and not straight up, as in the right whale. Being only the confined air of the lungs, and condensed into a white mist, it vanishes instantly.

Its propellers and means of defense are two fins, planted a little behind the head on each side, and the flukes of its tail, also, with which it sculls and attempts to strike its enemy. The juncture of these flukes with the main body of the whale is comparatively small, and a skillful whaler always tries to cut the tendons, like a hamstring, with his spade when the whale is violent. If successful in this, the flukes will be still, and the danger of approaching the whale greatly diminished. The natural working of them on their joints by the waves, after the animal is dead, will always carry the carcass directly to windward.

Of one that I have measured, the fins were five feet long each, and the flukes twelve feet across, horizontally. Of another the body was thirty-nine feet long and nineteen feet round, the head seven feet from its tip to the spout holes, three feet wide just behind the same, and three feet from the upper outside superficies to the roof of the mouth inside, making its entire head, with the mouth closed, seven feet in diameter, or twenty-one feet round. The length of another, which I have exactly measured, a sperm whale, was fifty-nine feet, and thirty round.

The ear of the whale is extremely small, and so hidden, like a mole's, that you would not find it without diligent search. Still the creature is thought by seamen to be quick of hearing as well as sharp of sight. The organ for the latter sense is about as large as the eye of an ox. The head of a right whale, when his mouth is open in feeding, or when he breaches, as I have sometimes seen him do quite out of water, is a most uncouth and formidable sight. It looks at a little distance like the black, rugged mouth of one of those lava caverns a traveler meets with on the Island of Hawaii. The huge lips close from below upward, and shut in, when the monster has got a mouthful, upon his immense whalebone cheeks, like the great valve of a mammoth bellows, or the water gates of a canal lock.

The sole living of this vast animal is thought to be upon a substance which I hear universally called by whalemen "right whale feed" (medusæ). It appears in the water like little red seeds of the size of mustard, which is intrapped by the hair that fringes the leaves of whalebone, as the whale swims along with mouth open. It is, in fact, a little red shrimp, sometimes seen floating on the surface in these seas alive, oftener dead, when it has the appearance at a distance of clots of blood, only yellower. I have seen it in both states, and as entangled in the hair of dead whales. The quantity necessary for the animal's support must be prodigious.

I can doubly appreciate now that amusing passage in the Holy War, where Bunyan says, "Silly Mansoul did not stick nor boggle at a monstrous oath that she would not desert Diabolus, but *swallowed it without chewing, as if it had been a sprat in the mouth of a whale.*" This feed is supposed to lie generally rather deep under water in these seas, as whales are often taken in greatest numbers where none of it is to be seen on the surface. In the Greenland and Arctic Seas it often covers miles and miles in extent, thick enough, it is said, to impede the course of a ship; and perhaps, in the economy of Providence, whales as well as sharks are but the scavengers of the great deep, to consume what would otherwise putrefy and decay.

A volume of the Family Library, on "Polar Seas and Regions," which I have been reading with great interest on shipboard, says, that the basis of subsistence for the numerous tribes of the Arctic world is found in the genus *medusa*, which the sailors graphically describe as sea-blubber. The medusa is a soft, elastic, gelatinous substance, specimens of which may be seen lying on our own shores, exhibiting no signs of life, except that of shrinking when touched. Beyond the Arctic Circle it increases in an extraordinary degree, and is eagerly devoured by the finny tribes of all shapes and sizes. By far the most numerous, however, of the medusan races are of dimensions too small to be discovered without the aid of the microscope, the application of which instrument shows them to be the cause of a peculiar color, which tinges a great extent of the Greenland Sea. This color is olive-green, and the water is opaque compared to that which bears the common cerulean hue.

"These olive waters occupy about a fourth of the Greenland Sea, or above twenty thousand square miles, and hence the number of medusan

the WHALE & *his captors*

animalcula which they contain is far beyond calculation. Mr. Scoresby estimates that two square miles contain 23,888,000,000,000,000; and as this number is beyond the range of human words and conceptions, he illustrates it by observing, that eighty thousand persons would have been employed since the creation in counting it. This green sea may be considered as the Polar pasture ground, where whales are always seen in greatest numbers. These prodigious animals can not derive any direct subsistence from such small invisible particles; but these form the food of other minute creatures, which then support others, till at length animals are produced of such size as to afford a morsel for their mighty devourers.

"The genus *cancer*, larger in size than the medusa, appears to rank second in number and importance. It presents itself under the various species of the crab, and, above all, of the shrimp, whose multitudes rival those of the medusa, and which in all quarters feed and are fed upon. So carnivorous are the propensities of the northern shrimps, that joints of meat hung out by Captain Parry's crew from the sides of the ship were in a few nights picked to the very bone, and nothing could be placed within their reach except bodies of which it was desired to obtain the skeleton. Many of the zoophytical and molluscous orders, particularly *Actinia sepia*, and several species of marine worms, are also employed in devouring and affording food to various other animals."

We learn, then, that the law of mutual consumption holds throughout the wide domain of the deep. And Byron was literally correct when saying, in his apostrophe to the Ocean,

> Even *from out thy slime*
> *The monsters of the deep are made.*

The internal anatomy of a whale is to me a subject of great curiosity, and I wish it were in my power to report a full and accurate, leisurely *post-mortem* of the subjects we have discussed. But a few clinical notes, roughly taken by the bed-side, as the whalemen have been operating between wind and water with their professional spades and lances of dissection, are all I have to exhibit. From the barrel-like size of the protruding intestine of the last we have dissected, or more properly peeled, it is reasonable to infer by the law of relative proportions on which Agassiz constructs a fish from a single scale, that the great aorta of one of the largest kind of whales can be but little less in diameter than the bore of the main pipe of the Croton water-works; and the water roaring in its passage through that pipe must be inferior in impetus and velocity to the blood gushing from the whale's great heart, when his pulse beats high in the conflict with his captors.

In Dr. Hunter's account to the Philosophical Society of the dissection of a small whale cast upon the coast of Yorkshire, this aorta measured a foot in diameter. In that case, fifteen or twenty gallons of living blood are ordinarily thrown out of the heart of a large whale at a stroke, with an immense velocity, through the great bore of a blood-vessel, or rather blood aqueduct, a foot or two in diameter.

How it is, then, that, with such a prodigious current of blood constantly flowing and needing, oxygenization by the air, the whale can remain under water so long, respiration suspended (sometimes, in the case of a sperm whale, an hour and a half), it was difficult to conceive, until dissection discovered that in the cetaceous animals, the arterial blood, instead of passing into the venous circulation, the ordinary way, has interposed, by the Creator's providence, a structure which is nothing less than a grand reservoir for the reception of a great quantity of arterial blood, which, as occasion requires, is emptied into the general circulation, and thus for a time supersedes the necessity of respiration. It may be that the accidental piercing, now and then, of the walls of this great penstock of arterial blood, by the harpoon or lance, has something to do with the whale's occasional sinking after being killed, a phenomenon not yet satisfactorily explained.

Until within a few years this gigantic game has been every where so abundant that whalemen have used no means to keep their rich prizes from sinking; but when one has gone down worth $1500 or $2000, or even $3000, they have taken it as a whaleman's fortune, and have gone to capturing others instead. In some voyages they say more whales have been sunk than have been saved. The useless devastation thus caused among these huge denizens of the deep has been very great. One practical whaleman calculates the number of whales killed in one season on the northwest coast and Kamtschatka at 12,000.

Would whalemen go provided with India-rubber or bladder buoys, ready to be bent on to harpoons and darted into a whale's carcass as soon as "turned up," or when he is perceived to be going into "his flurry," we are persuaded that many thousands of barrels of oil might be saved, and not a few poor voyages would be made good ones. According to Commander Wilkes's Narrative of the United States Exploring Squadron, the Indians of the northwest coast take quite a number of whales annually, by having their rude fish spears fastened to inflated seal-skin floats, four feet long and one and a half or two feet broad, that keep the whale on the top of the water, and allow him to fall a comparatively easy prey. The same thing used to be effected by the Indians of Cape Cod, having their fish spears fastened to blocks of wood, in lieu of which sperm whalemen now use what is called a "drag." Now that whales are getting scarce, we think it impossible but that Yankee sense and forehandedness will soon see to this, and go prepared against such disheartening catastrophes as losing their game by its sinking, after unsurpassed skill and daring have made it fairly their own.

If owners knew how much might be saved by it, they would never let a ship go from port without buoys to hold up dead whales, and long hawsers to lay-to with by them in gales of wind. The Commodore Preble has lost, in the course of this voyage, seven by sinking after they were "turned up," and three from alongside in rugged weather, because without a long and strong hawser to secure them by to windward while lying-to. Six of our boats were stove in one season on the northwest coast, some of the crew were badly hurt, and the men got so afraid of a whale, that some of them would hide away when the order was given to lower.

The only cause I have ever heard assigned for the right whale's sinking so often, is having the air-vessel which Nature is thought to provide this animal with, pierced by the lance or harpoon. Any one can see that a few buoys fastened to them would counterweigh this tendency to sink. I have even heard of their being hauled up when out of sight by four boat's crews pulling upon the tow-lines that were fast to the harpoons buried in the sinking carcass.

Till we know more of the natural history of the whale than we yet do, its sinking so apparently without law can not be certainly accounted for. One whaleman says that he has known a whale of the largest size, which, in cutting him in, proved to be a dry-skin, that is, the blubber containing a milky fluid instead of oil, and yet the whale floated as light as a cork. Again, he has killed a whale with a single lance, and he sunk like a stone, and another has sunk after lancing a hundred times.

An ingenious Frenchman, I am told, in these seas, once rigged swivels in the heads of his boats, and had bladders and other gear to float dead whales; but he succeeded with it all so poorly, that, in mortification and despair, when he put into one of the ports of New Zealand, he went out into the woods and shot himself with a brace of pistols through both his eyes. I think some quick-witted Yankee would do better to give his attention to experimenting in this line; and, even if the whales would not be killed or floated, he would not be such a fool as to blow his own brains out. It is a true saying of Massinger:

Who kills himself t' avoid misery, fears it,
And at the best shows a *bastard* valor;

which, forasmuch as the crime is becoming popular nowadays, it would not be amiss to put a stop to, by enacting a law, as they once did in ancient Rome, to expose the body of every suicide naked in the market-place after death.

V

The Whale's Physiology
and Natural History

Spout! spout! spout!
The waves are purling all about,
Every billow on its head
Strangely wears a crest of red.
See her lash the foaming main
In her flurry and her pain.
　　Take good heed, my hearts of oak.
Lest her flukes, as she lies,
Swiftly hurl you to the skies.
　　But lo! her giant strength is broke.
Slow she turns, as a mass of lead;
The mighty mountain whale is dead.
—Whaler's Song.

There are some points in the whale's physiology, and in the way of
disposing of the blubber, not noted in previous chapters, which are so
well described in parts of a sailor's yarn that I have found in a loose
number of the Sailor's Magazine, of which most excellent periodical
we have several on board, that I will take from it here and there, with
corrections, what may be wanting to complete the integrity of our description. Although it is difficult to describe the head of a right whale
without the assistance of a drawing, yet a tolerably correct idea may
be obtained of it, by comparison with known shapes and objects, and
by accurate dimensions.

　It is curiously adapted to the habits of the animal, and is unlike
any other head in nature. Its general shape is not unlike a flat-soled,
round-toed shoe, the sides being straight, and the widest part, or heel,
joining the body. The lower jaw is, say, eight or ten feet wide, where
it joins the body, and grows narrower toward the nose, so that when

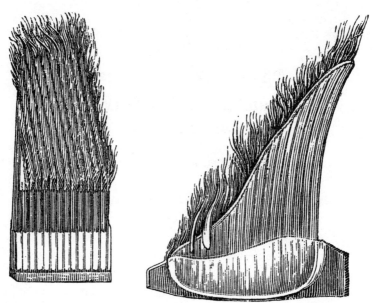

Perpendicular View of the Whalebone.   Side View of the Whalebone.

the jaw-bones are cleaned from the flesh they form a bluntly-pointed arch, and are often preserved and used as gateposts; many of them may be seen, about New Bedford and Nantucket, applied to this use. The skull or crown bone (for there is no upper jaw) is a single bone, rounded on its roof or top, about four or five feet wide at the neck, and gradually lessening to the nostrils or blow-holes, which are at its outward extremity. To this bone is attached the whalebone of commerce, which is in slabs averaging about a quarter of an inch thick. The longest are nearest the body, and are eight or ten inches wide where they join the skull, and are in a large whale six or eight feet long, narrowing to a point as they approach the lower jaw.

They hang perpendicularly from the crown to the jaw, with their thickest edges out; they are set about half an inch apart, something like the slabs of a Venetian blind made very close. The inner edge of each slab has a fringe of hair about an inch long, so that, on looking into the cavity of the head, the sides of it appear as if lined with felt or hair-cloth. Upon the lower jaw lies the enormous tongue, which is a mass of fat containing four or five barrels: it appears like a large cushion of white satin, so exceedingly soft and delicate is it. The lips

the WHALE & *his* captors

are attached to the sides of the lower jaw, and extend nearly the whole length of the head on each side. Except when feeding, they are closed over the sides of the head, their upper edges fitting to the skull or crown, and the whole head appears as a solid mass; but when it takes its food, the whale unfolds the lips, and they drop upon the surface of the water.

The food of this whale, as we have already observed, is a species of shrimp, of a blood-red color. Some of them are very minute, and few are found more than half an inch long; these float in immense shoals on the surface of the ocean, and sometimes color the water for miles. When the whale is disposed to break his fast, he rushes through a field of shrimps with open mouth, until he has received myriads of the little animals; then, with the lips thrown open, the water is forced out between the slabs which I have described, leaving the shrimps attached to the hairy strainer within; by means of the tongue they are collected, and the delicate mouthful is conveyed to his capacious stomach.

When "cutting in a whale," as the carcass rolls over by the power of the windlass, the lips, which are composed entirely of hard blubber, are cut off and hoisted on board as they present themselves. The crown bone is also disjointed from the body, and is hoisted in with the whalebone attached to it. A very large head produces a thousand pounds. The tongue and the fins are also saved; so that when the carcass is turned adrift, after being properly stripped, very little oily matter falls to the share of the birds, who make a terrible clamor, however, in quarreling for that little.

The "blubber-room" is a space under the main hatch, between decks, capable of receiving the blubber of two or three whales; into this every piece is lowered as it comes from the whale: these are called "blanket pieces," and some of them weigh one or two tons. As they are piled one on another, the pressure of their own weight, with the motion of the ship, which is never at rest, causes the oil soon to exude, and, mixing with the blood, more or less of which comes in with each piece, the blubber-room soon presents an indescribable mess.

Into this odorous retreat it is the duty of one man immediately to descend with a cutting-spade, to commence cutting the "blanket pieces" into "horse pieces;" these are about a foot square, and by means of a pike or fork, are pitched up on deck for mincing, and taken to the "mincing horse," a small table secured to the rail of the ship, where a boy, with a short-handled hook, holds the piece to keep it from sliding, while the mincer, with a two-handled knife, slashes it nearly through into thin slices, which just hang together; the piece then becomes a "book," and is pitched into a large tub ready for boiling.

A fire is now kindled in the arches under the pots, which are two or three in number, firmly set in brick work, and each will contain a hogshead of oil. A small quantity of oil is first put in each, and, soon as it becomes heated, fresh blubber is added, until the pots are full, when a portion from each is bailed out with a large ladle into a copper cooler, from whence it is received into casks and stowed below. The operation of boiling continues day and night until the whole is finished, and sometimes, when whales are plenty, the fires are not put out until the ship is filled.

With such an intense fire over a wooden deck and frame for weeks together, and with tarred cordage and canvass above, both of which would burn like tinder, it may seem strange that so few ships take fire. Close attention and untiring vigilance can alone prevent it. If the "pen" under the works, which should be kept full of water, happened to spring a leak in the night without being observed, a short time only would be sufficient to envelop the ship in flames. Sometimes, too, a pot full of boiling oil will burst, without any apparent cause, and let its contents into the fire beneath. Several ships have been lost by such an accident.

Frequently the oil in a pot rises at once and boils over, communicating fire to the others: this is generally checked by means of covers which are at hand to smother the flame; but, though not an uncommon occurrence, it is attended with considerable danger. The color of the oil depends much upon the mode of boiling it. Unless the pots are kept perfectly clean, and no sediment permitted to adhere to the bottom, the oil will be dark and of inferior value. It is necessary, therefore, that one man be constantly employed in stirring the mass, while it is the duty of another to skim out the scraps as fast as they are "done:" these are used for fuel, no wood being necessary after the fire is started.

The blubber on a fat whale is sometimes, in its thickest parts, from fifteen to twenty inches thick, though seldom more than a foot; it is

the WHALE *&* H*is* c*aptors*

of a coarser texture and much harder than fat pork. So very full of oil is it, that a cask closely packed with the clean raw fat of the whale will not contain the oil boiled from it, and the scraps are left beside: this has been frequently proved by experiment.

Both the sperm and right whale are usually of a jet black color, but not unfrequently the right whale is found with irregular spots of a milky whiteness, very like those on a pied horse. The skin of both kinds is similar. Outside of the sensible skin, which has no peculiarity, there is a coat of something resembling fur, very close and compact, and the fibres united by a glutinous matter, so as to render it about as hard as the rind of a new cheese: this is termed the "black skin," and is about half an inch thick. Still outside of this is a very thin and delicate skin, which, when first detached from the body, whence it is easily stripped, very nearly resembles a glossy black silk; and when the whale basks in the sunbeams on the surface of the water, its smooth outer covering glistens as if it were from the looms of France or Italy, so much is it like the shining silk.

Soon as the business of the voyage is fairly commenced by taking the first whale, the appearance of the ship and her crew wofully changes for the worse. The decks, which have hitherto been kept scrupulously clean, are now covered with oil, and it is only by keeping a thick coat of sand scattered over them that the crew are enabled to get about without slipping. The smoke from the try-works blackens every face, so that the watch on deck resembles a party of colliers. Each rope, too, exposed to its influence, is coated with lamp-black, and the clothing of the men saturated with oil. Even the sails, which on the passage were of a snowy whiteness, receive their share of defilement; for, as they are handed every night, the men, as they spring aloft from the try-works with besmeared hands and clothes, can not furl them without leaving a mark wherever they touch.

Your ship, perhaps, has been thoroughly scrubbed and cleansed, crew cleared of "gurry," and all again is ship-shape and tidy, when, just after dinner, as all hands are on deck, the welcome cry is raised, "There she blows!" "Where away?" says the captain, hailing the man aloft. "About two points on the lee bow, sir." There she blows! There she blows! is shouted again, and echoed back by a dozen voices all agog. The mate, if lively, is soon aloft. "What do you make them,

Launch the harpoon! Laugh at fear!
Plunge it deep, the barbed spear!
Strike the lance in swift career!
Give her line! Give her line!
Down she goes through the foaming brine.

Mr. ——?" says the captain, mounted on a thwart in the quarter boat, and scanning the horizon with the most eager interest. "I can't make 'em out yet, sir. There's three or four of 'em; and they're going quick to windward."

Presently there sings out one from the foretop-gallant yard, "There goes flu-u-u-kes—flukes." This is always decisive, for the right whale, after breathing or blowing a few moments on the surface, pitches down head foremost into the deep, and as the head descends, the tail or flukes rise with a graceful curve above the water, and for a moment are seen in nearly a vertical position, and then slowly disappear. All now in your ship is eagerness and engrossment in the motions of your game, and every man is intent at his station. The tubs of lines have just been put into the boat; the harpoons and lances adjusted in their proper places, ready for action.

"Lower away!" at length cries the mate, and every boat is instantly

The WHALE *&* His *captors*

resting on the water, manned by their respective crews. "Give way, my lads!" is the next you hear, and the boats are leaping as if alive toward the point where the whale was last seen. All orders are now given in a low tone; every man is doing his utmost, and the boats are springing over the smooth swells, each striving to be headmost in the chase. "Now we rested, with our oars apeak," says a sailor, narrating an actual scene like this, "for the whales, who had gone down, to break water again. Presently they were up and blowing all around, and very much scattered, being alarmed by the boats, so that it was impossible to get near enough for a dart. But at one time five of the monsters rose close to our boats. The mate motioned us all to be silent, when we could have fastened to one, and the only reason, as we supposed, why he did not, was because he was so frightened.

"The whale now ran to the southward, and every boat was in chase as fast as we could spring to our oars. The first mate's boat was headmost in the chase, ours next, and the captain's about half a mile astern. The foremost now came up with and fastened to a large whale. We were soon on the battle ground, and saw him struggling to free himself from the barbed harpoon, which had gone deep into his huge carcass. We pulled upon the monster, and our boat-steerer darted another harpoon into him. 'Stern all!' shouted the mate. 'Stern all, for your lives!' We steered out of the reach of danger, and peaked our oars.

"The whale now ran, and took the line out of the boat with such swiftness that we were obliged to throw water on it to prevent its taking fire by friction around the loggerhead. Then he stopped, and blindly thrashed and rolled about in great agony, so that it seemed madness to approach him. By this time, however, the captain came up and boldly darted another harpoon into his writhing body. The enraged whale raised his head above the water, snapped his horrid jaws together, and in his senseless fury lashed the sea into foam with his flukes. The mate now, in his turn, approached near enough to bury a lance deep in his vitals, and shouted again, at the top of his voice, 'Stern all!' A thick stream of blood, instead of water, was soon issuing from his spout-holes. Another lance was buried; he was thrown into dying convulsions, and ran around in a circle; but his flurry was soon over; he turned upon his left side, and floated dead. We gave three hearty cheers, and took him in tow for the ship, which was now about fifteen miles off."

This towing of captured whales is no boy's play; although it is one of the pleasantest parts of a whaleman's duty, it is also often the most laborious, and fraught, too, with danger when the ship is distant and nightfall at hand. Under a fierce equatorial sun, to row for hours, perhaps right to windward or in a dead calm, with a carcass of seventy tons' weight dragging astern, will blister the hands and strain the muscles of the hardiest whaleman, and wearied nature will sometimes give out. But it is cheerfully endured for the end in view, of cutting in, and trying out, and stowing down a "hundred barreler," that will net to the ship three thousand or fifteen hundred dollars, according as it is a sperm or a right whale. If money makes the mare go, so does oil the crew of a "blubber hunter," from the green cabin-boy to the sable doctor.

VI

Different Cruising Grounds
and Northwest Whaling

Thou didst, O Lord! create the mighty whale,
    That wondrous monster of prodigious length:
Vast are his head and body, vast his tail;
    Beyond conception his unmeasured strength.
When he the surface of the sea hath broke,
    Arising from the dark abyss below,
His breath appears a lofty stream of smoke,
    The circling waves like glittering banks of snow.
—Anon.

It will be readily surmised that none but a genuine son of the sea, a veritable Cape Horner, "homeward bound," in the great South Pacific, could make these characteristic rhymes, and many other rude but expressive ones, which there is not room to transcribe here. The sailor that made them says of himself, in the course of some doggerel staves of autobiography,

I twice into the dark abyss was cast,
Straining and struggling to retain my breath;
Thy waves and billows over me were past;
Thou didst, O Lord! deliver me from death.

Different practised whalemen tell me of twelve or fourteen different species of this great sea monster: right, sperm, black-fish, humpback, razor-back, fin-back, grampus, sulphur-bottom, killer, cow-fish, porpoise, nar whale, scrag whale, and elephant whale. In the attempt to capture one of the latter kind, a New London ship, not long since, lost eleven men, including the first mate. The first four of this catalogue only are much sought after for their oil; now and then some of the others are taken by chance. The razor-back is sometimes one

{ 43 }

hundred and five feet long, but not so large round as the right whale, bearing about the same comparison to the latter that a razor-faced fellow you now and then meet with among men does to a fair, round alderman. The porpoise, as every one knows, is harpooned from a ship's bow, hauled on board, and its carcass eaten by the name of "sea beef." Its oil, like the ship's slush, is a perquisite of the cook's.

The fin-back, so called from a large fin on the ridge of its back, looking just like the gnomon of a dial, is a large whale found all over the ocean, and, could it be taken, would add greatly to the productiveness of the whale fishery. It often comes near a ship with a ringing noise, in spouting, like the sound of bell-metal, but it can seldom be so closely approached by a boat as to dart a harpoon; and when it is struck, it is said to run with such amazing swiftness as to part the line before it can be let out, or compel to cut it loose. Its spout at a distance, especially near the Falkland Islands, where I have seen them in great numbers, flashes up from the ocean just like smoke from the breech of a gun fired in a frosty morning. I have seen the horizon thus, for an extent of many miles, all smoking with them, and the ocean all alive with their gambols. It is not a thing beyond the reach of probability that this hitherto unmolested sea-rover may yet be brought within the all-powerful grasp of predatory man by swivels or air-guns, that shall fire harpoons into him, or poisoned arrows from a distance.

The places where the right whale is now most sought by the adventurous American whaleman are, in the Atlantic Ocean, what are called Main and False Banks, between Africa and Brazil, the parts around the Falkland Islands and Patagonia, and the region of ocean in mid-Atlantic, in the vicinity of the Island of Tristan d'Acunha; in the Southern Ocean, south of the Cape of Good Hope, there are the uninhabited Crozettes Islands, St. Paul's, and other parts of the Indian Ocean; in the Pacific Ocean, there are the New Zealand cruising ground, the New Holland, Chili, and the Northwest, from the coast of America clear over to Kamtschatka.

This last is now the great harvest-field of American whalers from May to October; and it will be likely to last longer than any other, because they are prohibited by the Russians from bay whaling, which destroys the cows about the time of calving. Almost all ships fill up there. Some have even *thrown overboard* provisions to make way for

the WHALE & *his* captors

oil. The havoc they make of whales is immense. There are ships that took, during the last season, twenty-five to even thirty-three hundred barrels in a few months. I have heard of one ship that sunk twenty-six whales after she had killed them; of another that killed nine before she saved one; of another that killed six in one day, and all of them sunk; of another that had three boats stove and all the men pitched into the sea, without any one's being lost. This forced trial of hydropathy is, indeed, so common an occurrence, that whalemen make nothing of it.

Those huge northwest whales are more vicious, and less easily approached after they are struck, than the whales of other latitudes. It is considered no disgrace to be run away with by one of those jet-black fellows, found in forty-five or fifty degrees north; and many an old whaler, who has made his boast that never yet did a whale run off with him, has been compelled to give in beat when fast to one of these "Northwest Tartars."

One captain says he has seen instances of the most wonderful strength and activity in these whales, greater than he ever saw before in either right or sperm. He was once fast to a large cow whale, which was in company with a small one, a full-grown calf. They kept together, and after a time the captain hauled his boat up between them. When they were both within reach, he shoved his lance "into the life" of the cow, at which she threw her flukes and the small part of her body completely over the head of the boat without touching it (although they were half drowned with the water she scooped up), and the full weight of the blow, intended for the boat, fell upon the back of the other whale. He sunk immediately, going down bent nearly double, and, the captain thinks, must have been killed by the blow. The same person has seen a stout hickory pole, three inches in diameter and six feet long, broken into four pieces by a blow from a whale's tail, and the pieces sent flying twenty feet in the air, and that, too, when no other resistance was offered than that of the water upon which it floated.

The first whale this man struck there turned him over in two different boats, and afterward "knocked them into kindling wood," while spouting blood in thick clots, and yet this whale lived four hours after, showing its great tenacity of life. He came up alongside the boat, and

He came up alongside of the Boat, and turned it over with his Nose
as a Hog would his Eating trough.

turned it over with his nose, as a hog would his eating-trough, and
then with his flukes deliberately broke it up. Of course the crew had
to take to Nature's oars, and they all marvelously escaped unhurt, although one of them was carried sitting upon the whale's flukes several
rods, till he slid off unharmed from his strange sea-chariot. This man
could say, in one of the sailor's rude rhymes whom we have already
quoted,

> Although he furiously doth us assail,
>> Thou dost preserve us from all danger free
> *He cuts our boat in pieces with his tail,*
>> *And spills us all at once into the sea.*

This northwest cruising ground was first visited in the spring of
1836 by two or three of the Chili whalers, who saw, indeed, numerous whales, but gave it as their opinion that the fishery could never be
prosecuted there with any success, by reason of constant and dense
fogs. The following year several more of the Chili fleet started to the
northward, "between seasons," and, looking further to the north and

The WHALE *&* HIS *captors*

westward, found better weather, and made a good cruise. During the three years following few ships were found there; but upon the almost entire failure of the southern whale fishery, the right whalemen were forced to turn their prows to those inhospitable seas, and the *northwest*, as all men know, became a very El Dorado to the intrepid American whalers. This cruising ground extends properly from the thirty-fourth to the fifty-ninth degree of north latitude, and from the coast of America, in west longitude say one hundred and thirty, to the meridian of one hundred and seventy east longitude, or about fifty degrees. The largest whales are said to have been found between fifty and sixty degrees north latitude, and from one hundred and forty-five to one hundred and eighty degrees west longitude. At the Fox Islands, in latitude fifty-two degrees north, sperm whales of the largest size have been found as well as right, and near the peninsula of Alaska they are very numerous.

Intelligence from the northern whaling ground of latest date shows that the Arctic Ocean has been entered at Behring's Straits by our intrepid American whalemen. Captain Roys, of the bark Superior, from Sag Harbor, is thus reported in the Sandwich Island Honolulu Friend: "I entered the Arctic Ocean about the middle of July, and cruised from continent to continent, going as high as latitude seventy, and saw whales wherever I went, cutting in my last whale on the 23d of August, and returning, through Behring's Straits, on the 28th of the same month. On account of powerful currents, thick fogs, the near vicinity of land and ice, combined with the imperfection of charts and want of information respecting this region, I found it both difficult and dangerous to get oil, although there were plenty of whales. Hereafter, doubtless, many ships will go there, and I think there ought to be some provision made to save the lives of those who go there, should they be cast away."

During the entire period of his cruise no ice was seen, and the weather was ordinarily pleasant, so that the men could work in light clothing. In most parts of the ocean there was good anchorage, from fourteen to thirty-five fathoms, and a part of the time the vessel lay at anchor. The first whale was taken at twelve o'clock at night. It was not difficult to whale the whole twenty-four hours, it being so light that it was easy to read in the cabin at midnight. The whales were quite tame, but different from any Captain Roys had ever before taken. He captured three different species, one of the largest yielding two hundred barrels of oil. The first species much resembled the Greenland whale, affording one hundred and sixty or seventy barrels. The second was a species called Polar whale, a few of which have been taken before on the Northwest Coast; and the third was a small whale peculiar to that ocean. The last three whales which were taken yielded together over six hundred barrels.

It is the opinion of Lieutenant Maury, of the United States National Observatory, that all the whales in the Pacific Ocean have particular resorts at certain seasons of the year, where the whalers may generally expect to find them, just as the shad, salmon, herring, and other fish are periodically found. He is endeavoring to work out this conclusion, and to fix the localities of whales' resorts by a comparison of the logs of a vast number of whalers. It is easy to see that, if he should succeed, it will be of great importance to the whaling interest, as it will reduce the expense of outfits by shortening the time of voyages, and making their results more sure and speedy.

If we inquire into the probable duration of this Northwest whaling, including this Arctic opening, there seems good reason to believe, from the extent of ocean it embraces, greater than all the other cruising grounds together, that it will continue good at least twenty or twenty-five years from its commencement. An experienced captain thinks that as there is not, nor is likely to be, any bay whaling on this cruising ground, the whales will be less constantly hunted, and nearly all the calves born will arrive at an age when they can take care of themselves before the old whales are encountered in the summer season by their sworn enemy, man. He estimates that by three hundred ships capturing or mortally wounding forty whales each, twelve thousand whales are killed in a season; and as many of these, perhaps full half, are cows with calf, the number of whales to be born and arrive at maturity, in order to make up for this sweeping destruction among them, must be not less than eighteen thousand. He thinks, therefore, that the poor whale, chased from sea to sea, and from haunt to haunt, is doomed to utter extermination, or so near it, that too few will remain to tempt the cupidity of man.

The history of the sperm whale fishery, from the first, when only

The WHALE & His captors

five and six months were necessary to complete a cargo upon the Brazil ground, and fifteen upon that of Chili, to its present almost entire abandonment as a separate business, confirms this calculation. Before the end of the present century, therefore, judging from the past, is it likely that the hunting of whales on the sea will be any more prosecuted as a business than the hunting of deer on the land? In one part of the world they have been driven to the deepest recesses of Baffin's Bay, and in another to the very confines of the Pacific, and off to the icebergs of the antarctic zone. "Whether their mammoth bones in some distant century shall indicate to the untaught natives of the shores they now frequent that such an animal *was*, or whether, lurking in the inaccessible and undisturbed waters north of Asia and America, the race shall be preserved, is almost a problem."

> They roamed, they fed, they slept, they died, and left
> Race after race to roam, feed, sleep, then die,
> And leave their like through endless generations:
> So HE ordained, whose way is in the sea,
> His path amid great waters, and his steps
> Unknown!

VII

The Whale's Biography and Incidents in the Capture

The whale he shall still be dear to me,
　　When the midnight lamp grows dim;
For the student's book, and his favorite nook,
　　Are illumined by aid of him.
From none of his tribe could we e'er imbibe
　　So useful, so blessed a thing.
Then hand in hand we'll go on the land,
　　To hail him the Ocean King.
—Sailor's Song.

In continuing our inquiries into the peculiarities of whales and incidents of whaling, it is to be remarked of the great right whale (Balæna Mysticetus), that, like the hugest of all land animals, its disposition is mild and inoffensive. It never shows fight except when wounded, and then in an awkward and blind way, that proves it is not used to war either offensive or defensive. Its immediate recourse is to flight, except when it has young to look out for, and then it is bold as a lion, and manifests an affection which is itself truly affecting. It grazes quietly through the great deep, never using its prodigious strength to seize or lord it over other inhabitants of the seas, but strains its insect-like food through its admirably contrived apparatus of bone and hair, that strikingly evinces His beneficence and wise design,

　　　Whose creating hand
　Nothing imperfect or deficient left
　Of all that he created.

It makes one think of the couplet we used to read, when boys, in the New England Primer:

> Whales in the sea
> God's voice obey.
> Even the mute fish that swim the flood,
> Leap up, and mean the praise of God.

I have heard of one of these whales with a cub, when driven into shoal water, being seen to swim around its young, and sometimes to embrace it with her fins, and roll over with it in the waves, evincing the tenderest maternal solicitude. Then, as if aware of the impending peril of her inexperienced offspring, as the boat drew near, she would run round her calf in decreasing circles, and try to decoy it seaward, showing the utmost uneasiness and anxiety. Reckoning well that, the calf once struck, the dam would never desert it, the only care of the harpooner was to get near enough to bury his tremendous weapon deep in its ribs, which was no sooner done than the poor animal darted away with its anxious dam, taking out a hundred fathoms of line. It was but a little time, however, before, being checked, and the barb lacerating its vitals, it turned on its back, and, displaying its white belly on the surface of the water, it floated a motionless corpse.

The huge dam, with an affecting maternal instinct more powerful than reason, never quitted the body till a cruel harpoon entered her own sides; then, with a single tap of her tail, she cut in two one of the boats, and took to flight, but returned soon, exhausted with loss of blood, to die by her calf, evidently, in her last moments, more occupied with the preservation of her young than of herself.

The habits and living of the sperm whale are quite as different from those of the right as is its structure. Its head is enormously large and unshapely, and furnished with an immense under jaw, that is armed with two rows of mammoth teeth, forty-eight and fifty-four in number. It seizes its prey with these teeth, having no whalebone sieve or strainer, like what has been already described in the right whale, and it is supported principally by the squid, otherwise called cuttle-fish, or Sepia Octopus, of which one sperm whale that we have lately captured disgorged pieces as long as the whale boat, before going into its flurry.

From what I have observed myself and have been told by others, it appears that when this whale is inclined to feed, he goes to a certain depth below the surface, and there remains in an oblique position, as quiet as possible, opening his vast elongated mouth like a great bag-net, until the lower jaw hangs down perpendicularly, or at right angles with the body. The roof of his mouth, the tongue, and especially the teeth, being of a glistening white color, must of course present a remarkable appearance, which seems to be that which attracts his prey. When a sufficient number of other fish, or quantity of the squid, as the case may be, are within the mouth, he rapidly closes his jaw and swallows the contents.

When this creature is fatally struck or killed while in the act of feeding, the whalemen will soon know the items of its last bill of fare; for, while the waters around are purpled with its gore, and a crimson tide is flowing from its spiracles, portions of its lance-lacerated lungs and the contents of its capacious stomach also are being vomited at the mouth. The sea, too, will be lashed by its mighty tail with a sound that may be heard in calm weather for miles like thunder.

It is painful to witness the death-agony of any creature, even the smallest that God has given life to, much more that of one in which life is so lively and tenacious, and animating so vast a bulk. And though it be true what the dramatic poet said,

> The sense of death is most in *apprehension,*
> And the poor beetle that we tread upon,
> In *corporal* sufferance feels a pang
> As great as when a giant dies,

yet I am not one that can coolly observe the last agony of so mighty an organized creature as the whale with as little emotion as some persons feel at the crushing of a reptile or the writhing of a worm; nor do I believe that the suffering in the one case is as great as that in the other. But it is painful enough to see any thing forcibly bereft of the boon of life, the gift of Him that made us all,

> Who gives its luster to the insect's wing,
> And wheels his throne upon the rolling worlds.

Cowper's principle in regard to animals and insects is the right one:

> The sum is this: if man's convenience, health,
> Or safety interfere, his rights and claims

Are paramount, and must extinguish theirs.
Else they are all—the meanest things that are—
As free to live, and to enjoy that life,
As God was free to form them at the first,
Who in his sovereign wisdom made them all.

The substance called ambergris, and highly prized in perfumery, is obtained from the sperm whale, being formed, it is thought, in that state of the system which calls for a cathartic. A peck of Morrison's or Brandreth's pills, or the homeopathic dose of a pound of calomel and jalap, would probably remove obstructions in the creature's abdominal viscera, and prevent the formation of ambergris concretions, with undoubted benefit to the whale's corporation from the drastic operation, though it might be a loss to the perfumer and the Asiatic gastronomer, inasmuch as we learn from the Materia Medica that in Asia and parts of Africa ambergris is not only used as a medicine and a perfume, but considerable use also is made of it in cooking, by adding it to several dishes as a spice. A great quantity of it also is constantly brought by the pilgrims who travel to Mecca, probably to offer it there in fumigations, like as frankincense in the worship of the Church of Rome.

A costive whale, when struck by the harpoon, will often throw up or discharge this substance, and it will be found floating about him. It is said to have been a Nantucket whaler that thus accidentally ascertained the origin of a substance which had been known before vaguely as an unaccountable product of the sea. Pieces have been picked up by sailors about a dying whale worth twenty dollars; and masses of it have been found of from sixty to two hundred and twenty-five pounds' weight, floating on the surface of the ocean, in regions much frequented by the sperm whale. We have not been so fortunate as to light upon any. It is a pity that nine tenths of the mineral drugs in use could not be employed to purge the ambergris out of the huge intestines of sick whales, rather than to turn the stomachs, and irritate the bowels, and loosen the teeth, and produce caries in the bones of men.

If the gigantic denizens of the deep were as much physicked, doubtless there would be full as much sickness among them as among the human mammalia on the land. As it is, it is quite clear that they are subject both to disease and deformity, some having been taken that were entirely blind, both eyes being completely disorganized, and the orbits occupied by fungous masses protruding considerably; rendering it certain that the whale must have been deprived of vision for a considerable space of time, yet not so as to incapacitate him for feeding, blind whales being found as fat as the seeing ones.

The deformity referred to is a crookedness of the lower jaw, which old whalers say is caused by fighting. Sperm whales have been seen to fight by rushing, head first, one upon the other, their mouths at the same time wide open, their object appearing to be to seize their opponent by the lower jaw. For this purpose they frequently turn themselves on the side, and become, as it were, locked together, their jaws crossing each other, and in this manner they strive vehemently for the mastery, with a force compared to which not even Milton's wars of the angels

> Could merit more than that small infantry
> Warred on by cranes; though all the giant brood
> Of Phlegra with the heroic race were joined
> That fought at Thebes and Ilium, on each side
> Mixed with auxiliar gods; and what resounds
> In fable or romance, of Uther's son,
> Begirt with British and Armoric knights.

The size of a sixty foot right whale, which is, perhaps, that of the average, can be somewhat clearly apprehended by Captain Scoresby's estimate of its weight at seventy tons, or the weight of three hundred fat oxen, of which the oil in a fat subject will be nearly thirty tons. Some whalemen judge it does not attain its full size until twenty-five years, by certain notches which they think they can observe in the slabs of whalebone. But this can not be clearly ascertained. The natural life of the animal is undoubtedly much longer. Analogy would lead to the inference that it might be as long lived as the elephant, to which it bears a resemblance in certain other particulars besides its size.

The calf of a large right whale at birth is about fourteen feet long, and weighs a ton. The milk of the cow is then very abundant. I have heard those who have seen it say, that when the mammæ of a nursing cow whale are cut, the flow of milk will whiten the ocean. The ascertained fact that it brings forth its young only one at a time, or at most two, and probably once a year, or after a period of nine or ten months' gestation, together with the rapid decrease of their numbers by slaughter on every cruising ground in the ocean where whalers have found them, to the number often of hundreds at once, would seem to be evidence of its slow growth and long life.

The only natural enemies it is known to have are the sword-fish, thrasher, and killer. This latter is itself a species of whale that has sharp teeth, and is exceedingly swift in the water, and will bite and worry a whale until quite dead. When one of them gets among a *gam* or school of whales, he spreads great consternation, and the timid creatures fly every way like deer chased by the hounds, and fall an easy prey to whale-boats that may be near to avail themselves of the opportunity. I have heard a captain detail with great interest a scene of this kind, in which the killers and harpooners were together against the poor whales, and the killers actually succeeded in pulling under and making off with one prize which the whalemen thought themselves sure of.

In the United States exploring squadron, on board the Peacock, as we learn from the narrative of Commander Wilkes, they witnessed a sea-fight between a whale and one of these enemies. The sea was quite smooth, and offered the best possible view of the combat. First, at a distance from the ship, a whale was seen floundering in a most extraordinary way, lashing the smooth sea into perfect foam, and endeavoring apparently to extricate himself from some annoyance. As he approached the ship, the struggle continuing and becoming more violent, it was perceived that a fish, about twenty feet long, held him by the jaw, his spoutings, contortions, and throes all betokening the agony of the huge monster.

The whale now threw himself at full length upon the water, with open mouth, his pursuer still hanging to his under jaw, the blood issuing from the wound, and dyeing the sea for a long distance around. But all his flounderings were of no avail; his pertinacious enemy still maintained his hold, and was evidently getting the advantage of him. Much alarm seemed to be felt by the many other whales about. These "killers" are of a brownish color on the back, and white on the belly, with a long dorsal fin. Such was the turbulence with which they passed, that a good view could not be had of them to make out more nearly the description. These fish attack a whale in the same way that a dog baits a bull, and worry him to death. They are endowed with immense strength, armed with strong, sharp teeth, and generally seize the whale by the lower jaw. It is said the only part they eat of them is the tongue.

The sword-fish and thrasher have been also seen to attack the whale together, the sword-fish driving his tremendous weapon into the belly of the whale from beneath upward, and the thrasher fastened to his back, and giving him terrific blows with his flail. The thrasher not having any power to strike through the water, it has been observed by all who have witnessed these strange combats, that it seems to be the instinctive war policy of the sword-fish to make his attack from below, thus causing the whale to rise above the surface, which, under the prick of the cruel sword of his enemy, he has been known to do to a great height, the unrelenting thrasher meanwhile holding on like a leech, and dealing his blows unsparingly through the air with all the force of his lengthy frame, sometimes twenty feet.

From a statement made by a Kennebec shipmaster in 1818, and sworn to before a justice of the peace in Kennebec county, Maine, it would seem that the notable sea serpent and whale are sometimes found in conflict. At six o'clock in the afternoon of June 21st, in the packet Delia, plying between Boston and Hallowell, when Cape Ann bore west southwest about two miles, steering north northeast, Captain Shubael West, and fifteen others on board with him, saw an object directly ahead which he had no doubt was the sea serpent, or the creature so often described under that name, engaged in fight with a large hump-back whale that was endeavoring to elude the attack.

The serpent threw up his tail from twenty-five to thirty feet in a perpendicular direction, striking the whale by it with tremendous blows rapidly repeated, which were distinctly heard and very loud for two or three minutes. They then both disappeared, moving in a west southwest direction, but after a few minutes reappeared in shore of the packet, and about under the sun, the reflection of which was so strong as to prevent their seeing so distinctly as at first, when the serpent's fearful blows with his tail were repeated and clearly heard as before.

Combat between a Whale and the Sea Serpent.

They again went down for a short time, and then came up to the surface under the packet's larboard quarter, the whale appearing first and the serpent in pursuit, who was again seen to shoot up his tail as before, which he held out of water some time, waving it in the air before striking, and at the same time, while his tail remained in this position, he raised his head fifteen or twenty feet, as if taking a view of the surface of the sea. After being seen in this position a few minutes, the serpent and whale again sunk and disappeared, and neither were seen after by any on board. It was Captain West's opinion that the whale was trying to escape, as he spouted but once at a time on coming to the surface, and the last time he appeared he went down before the serpent came up.

Between all these natural foes and its predatory human enemy, the great mammoth of ocean seems doomed to extinction. But I have no scruple at confessing that, since I have become closely acquainted with the habits of the great right whale, how quietly it grazes through the great pasture-ground which God has ordained for it and fitted so well to be its home, and since I have observed the hazards that have to be encountered and the perils to be surmounted in its capture by men, and have coupled with this the consideration of the various other sources from which the human family can now be supplied with oil, whether for burning or the arts, I begin to be somewhat doubtful about the lawfulness and expediency of the whale fishery. As an old whaleman once said in his own way, "Whales has feelings as well as any body. They don't like to be stuck in the gizzards, and hauled alongside, and cut in, and tried out in them 'ere boilers no more than I do."

This may seem foolish, and let it go for what it is worth. But if the business can not be successfully pursued without the flagrant violation of the Sabbath now caused by it, and the consequent disastrous effect upon the moral and religious characters of those engaged in it, no well-grounded Christian will be in doubt as to its *un*lawfulness and *im*morality. Whale ships, almost without exception, desecrate the Lord's day by taking their game and making way with it just as on any common day. They pay no practical regard whatever to the great law of the Sabbath, seeming utterly to forget the combined prophecy and principle,

> Who resteth not one day in seven,
> That soul shall never rest in heaven!

But of this more hereafter. Meanwhile, let me say to any seamen that may chance to read these pages, hold fast to the Sabbath; claim it of your employers as a right; stipulate beforehand that it shall be yours for rest, religious reflection, and worship, and refuse on principle to desecrate it by any other labor than may be necessary for the safety and proper working of the ship.

> Wanderers on the dark blue sea!
> As your bark rides gallantly,
> Prayer and praise become ye well,
> Though ye hear no temple bell.
> The Sabbath hours which God has given,
> Give ye to worship, rest, and heaven!

the WHALE & *his captors*

VIII
Atlantic Ocean Mammoths and Monsters

In the free element beneath me swam,
Flounder'd, and dived, in play, in chase, in battle,
Fishes of every color, form, and kind;
Which language can not paint, and mariner
Had never seen; from dread Leviathan
To insect millions peopling every wave:
Gather'd in shoals immense, like floating islands,
Led by mysterious instinct through that waste
And trackless region, though on every side
Assaulted by voracious enemies,
Whales, sharks, and monsters, arm'd in front or jaw,
With swords, saws, spiral horns, or hooked fangs.
— *World Before the Flood.*

False Banks, Atlantic Ocean, lat. 36° S., lon. 46° W.
Since doubling Cape Horn, Providence has been propitious in the
offer of whales. We lowered off the notable Cape itself, when in sight
of the islands called Diego Ramirez. Although so near to that formidable out-jutting barrier of Nature, between two great oceans, which
the reports of weather-beaten mariners have made the abiding-place
of storms, it was the loveliest day we had known since leaving the
southern tropic; the sky cloudless, the sun genially warm, its place in
the heavens away off to the north of us, and the ocean nearly calm.
The short night, too, was one of surpassing splendor, the whole southern hemisphere lit up with all the glorious lamps, never seen by those
who dwell at the north, the Magellanic clouds, and the sightly constel-
lation of the southern cross, and a brilliant though small comet visible in the southwest, its tail pointing upward to the zenith, and about
twice as long as the belt of Orion.

In the afternoon a school of sperm whales passed us, making for

the Pacific with all the speed of flukes and fins. They showed themselves a few minutes about a quarter of a mile off, and three boats
were soon lowered in pursuit; but they never let us see them again, it
being the habit of the sperm whale to stay under water much longer
than the right whale. Poor fellows! they will find keen human enemies
enough where they were going, and not unlikely the blubber sides of
one or more of them are already headed up in the hold of some ship,
and biding their time to fill honorable lamps with light ten thousand
miles off.

We have felt the cold this side the American continent, in the rude
Atlantic, more than ever in that other ocean, which does not belie its
name, or even than at the pitch of the Cape, in sixty degrees south. A
few days ago, just after breakfast, I had the pleasure of climbing the
mizzen rigging to witness the capture of our first Atlantic whale. The
ocean was in its stillest, loveliest mood, its breast heaving only like a
sleeping infant's; the morning sun most glorious; the sky without a
cloud, and that glimmer of reflection from the molten steel mirror
beneath, which I remember being so much struck with the first time
I ever saw the sublime sight when a boy.

The two whales proved, as was thought, to be a cow and a yearling
calf, perhaps a steer of the second year. They were putting their heads
together as in love, or to rub off the crab-lice and barnacles that adhere by millions to the top and sides of their heads. The calf was soon
struck, and made little ado of being killed, not going into a flurry, or
sounding long, or making the water foam, fly, or splintering the cedar
with strokes of his tail, and "spilling the men," as they sometimes do.

The one thought to be the dam prudently made off a mile and a half
to windward, while we got the cub alongside the ship about eleven
o'clock. His proportions were respectable for a youngling—thirty-
nine feet long and nineteen feet round; his head seven feet from its
tip to the spout-holes, and three feet wide just behind the same, and
three feet thick to the inside roof. The thickest of the blubber was
eight inches. His fins were each five feet long, and he was six feet
across the throat. They rifled him of his blubber and bone in the way
already described, and some time before evening the refuse scrap-
matter of his blubber was burning brightly under the try-works, and
affording all the fuel for trying out.

the WHALE & *his* *captors*

Just after sundown that evening, while we were lying to, and the try-works were blazing, there was seen going slowly by the ship, a rod or two off, a large sun-fish. The captain cautiously lowered his boat, and, paddling lightly, was up with him, and had effectually darted his cruel iron before danger was suspected. Finding it impossible to hoist him into the boat or warp him along, they made fast another iron, and came to the ship with the tow-line, which the men at once reeved round a block, and soon merrily hauled him in, singing the while a sailor's song.

We found our prize a singular-looking ichthyological wonder as ever was seen. His form is that of an ellipse, or like an elliptical shield, about four and a half feet in the longest diameter, three feet across, and one foot thick. His mouth is small and round, like a sea-porcupine's, and sucking constantly with great force like a sucker. His eye is large as a bullock's, and very prominent. He has two curious fins to scull with—one on his belly, or one rim of the ellipse, the other on his back, or the other rim of the ellipse—and a sort of steering oar in the middle of one of the sides. He moves edgewise through the water. He is covered to the depth of three or four inches on both sides with a white elastic case, like the meat of a cocoanut, and very much resembling the sturgeon's nose that boys put into balls to make them bounce well.

Under this case lies some excellent white meat, which has been dug out and served up into very fine chowder, and has supplied all hands, fore and aft, with several excellent meals, that relish nobody can tell how that has not been as long at sea without any thing fresh. The liver of this sun-fish contains a large quantity of yellow oil, which is thought to be excellent as an external unguent or embrocation for the rheumatism.

The next morning our captain made fast to another much larger right whale, turned him up dead about half past ten, after a hard fight, and in less than twenty minutes the huge carcass sunk bodily, with all the irons in it—a dead loss of more than a thousand dollars, which could easily have been prevented, had there been buoys or floats to have bent on to harpoons, and darted into him as soon as dead.

A few days after this mortifying event, we had much better success in the capture of a large bull whale, of the sperm kind, worth to the ship at least twenty-five hundred dollars. The captain's boat was also fast to another, that ran off very swiftly upon being struck, along with the rest of the school, making the deep to boil like a pot, and terrifying all his comrades by the extravagant and mad antics which the prickings of those cruel irons naturally goaded him to. They would have been glad enough, I have no doubt, to help their brother whale in his *pilikia*, and as it was they greatly endangered the lives of all his pursuers. But after being lanced several times, and dragging the lone boat quite out of sight from the mast-head, and tiring them all out, he was cut loose from, and left with two harpoons buried in his blubber sides. They will probably prove the death of him in a few days, and waste his oil upon the ocean like thousands before.

I was feeling not a little anxiety for the captain and boat's crew, pursuing thus alone and out of sight, amid a horde of infuriated and frightened whales, all the time fastened to one of them by those great harpoons, and momently liable to be struck and upset. It was a pleasurable relief to hear them announced from the masthead as returning, though I could not help pitying that they should have to come back with only their labor for their pains; and, when seemingly in the very arms of victory, after all the hazard and toil of the chase, to be compelled to abandon the lawful prize, which perhaps an hour's longer holding to would have made all their own. But such, time and again, is a whaleman's fortune. To him, emphatically,

> There's many a slip
> 'Tween the cup and the lip.

From the conduct of those whales, from what I have before observed, and from what others that know tell me, it is evident that the societies of these great sea monsters seldom go to war, but live together in cordial and happy amity, and render each other all the help in their power when in distress. They read to predatory and contentious man the same lesson that Milton derives from the concord of the fallen angels:

> O shame to men! devil with devil damn'd
> Firm concord holds; men only disagree
> Of creatures rational, though under hope

The WHALE *&* His *captors*

Of heavenly grace; and, God proclaiming peace,
Yet live in hatred, enmity, and strife
Among themselves, and levy cruel wars,
Wasting the earth, each other to destroy:
As if (which might induce us to accord)
Man had not hellish foes enow besides,
That, day and night, for his destruction wait.

IX

Episodes in the Fortunes of Whalemen

There she lies! there she lies!
Like an isle on ocean's breast;
"Where away?" west southwest,
Where the billows meet the skies.
Port the helm! trim the sail!
Let us chase this mighty whale.
—Whaler's Song.

The mortifying event referred to in the last chapter of losing our whale by sinking, after all the toil and hazard incurred in its capture, is paralleled only by a like occurrence in the fortunes of another whaleship on these very False Banks some two or three years ago, which I will give, partly in the words of one who was himself an actor in the scene described, being one of the hands in the captain's boat.

Upon getting into a "gam" of whales, this boat, together with that of one of the mates, pulled for a single whale that was seen at a distance from the others, and succeeded in getting square up to their victim unperceived. In a twinkling the boat-steerer sprang to his feet, and, as he darted his second harpoon, the bow of the boat grounded on the body of the whale, but was instantly "sterned off," and before the whale had sufficiently recovered from his surprise to show fight, the "cedar" was out of the reach of his flukes.

The captain, who now took his place in the bow of the boat, seized his lance, and the oarsmen again shot the boat ahead, but before he could plunge the lance the whale pitched down and disappeared. The line attached to the harpoon, being of great length, is coiled very carefully and compactly in a large tub in the centre of the boat; from thence it passes to the stern, and around a post called the loggerhead, firmly secured to the frame of the boat; and it is used for checking the line by friction as it runs out, a "round turn" being taken for that purpose. From the loggerhead the line passes along the whole length of the boat between the men, and leads out through a notch in the bow to the harpoons, two of which are always attached to the line's end.

Soon as the whale disappeared, the line commenced running through the tub so rapidly, that, as it rubbed around the loggerhead, sparks of fire flew from it in a stream. As the different coils run from the tub, they sometimes, when not well laid down, get "foul" or tangled, in which case there is great danger, for, in attempting to clear it, a turn will get by accident around an arm or a leg. As any one can see, there is little hope for the unhappy man thus entangled, for, unless the line be cut instantly, either the limb is lost or the man goes overboard.

A few years since, one of the most active and energetic of our whaling captains was thus taken overboard by the line, and had the singular good fortune to survive to tell the story. The whale was sounding very swiftly when the line became entangled. The boat-steerer, who was at his post in the stern of the boat, tending the line, instantly threw the turn off the loggerhead, and the tangled part ran forward and caught in the bow. The captain was seen to stoop to clear it, and then at once disappeared. The boat-steerer seized the hatchet, which is always at hand, and chopped the line, with the faint hope that when it slackened the captain could extricate himself.

The accident being so sudden and dreadful as almost to stupify the amazed crew, neither of them spake a word, but each eye was fixed upon the sea with fearful interest. Several minutes had elapsed, and the last hope was expiring, when an object was seen to rise to the surface a short ways from the boat, which, though exhibiting no sign of animation, was speedily reached, and the body of the captain, apparently lifeless, was lifted into the boat. It was evident that vitality was not extinct, and, to the joy of the little crew, symptoms of consciousness became visible in a few minutes, and the oars were lustily plied to reach the ship. By means of the usual remedies, the resuscitated captain was in a few days, in his own words, "as good as new."

In giving an account of the accident and his singular escape, he said that, as soon as he discovered the line had caught in the bow of the boat, he stooped to clear it, and attempted to throw it out from the "chock," so that it might run free. In doing this he must have caught a turn round his left wrist, and felt himself dragged overboard. He was perfectly conscious while he was rushing down, down, with unknown force and swiftness; and it appeared to him that his arm would be torn from his body, so great was the resistance of the water. He was well aware of his perilous condition, and that his only chance for life was to cut the line. But he could not remove his right arm from his side, to which it was pressed by the force of the element through which he was drawn.

When he first opened his eyes, it appeared as if a stream of fire was passing before them; but as he descended it grew dark, and he felt a terrible pressure on his brain, and a roaring as of thunder in his ears. Yet he was conscious of his situation, and made several efforts to reach the knife that was in his belt. At last, as he felt his strength failing and his brain reeling, the line for an instant slackened; he reached his knife, and instantly that the line again became taut, its edge was upon it, and by a desperate effort of his exhausted energies he freed himself. After this he only remembered a feeling of suffocation, a gurgling spasm, and all was over, until he awoke to an agonizing sense of pain in the boat.

But to come back from this digression, the whale to which our hero's boat was now fast took out a large portion of the line with great rapidity before it was deemed prudent to check it; then an extra turn was taken around the loggerhead, and the strain upon it became very great; for the whale, continuing to descend, would bring the bow of the boat down till the water was just about to rush over the gunwale and fill it, when the line would be "surged," or slacked out.

Sometimes, when the line is nearly spent, and there is great danger of losing the whale by having it all run out, the disposition to hold on has been fatally indulged too far, and the boat taken down. I have heard of one boat being thus lost on the "False Banks," and her whole crew drowned. And very lately the whaling bark Janet, of Westport, lost her captain and a boat's crew of five men, they being all carried down and drowned by the boat-line getting foul while they were fast to a whale.

In the present instance, before taking all their line, the whale began to ascend, and as it became slackened, the line was hauled in, "hand over hand," by the boat's crew, and coiled away by the boat-steerer.

The WHALE & *His captors*

The moment the whale came to the surface, "he went smoking off like a locomotive with an express." They held manfully to the line, and with oars peaked, ready to be seized in a moment, they dashed along in the track of the whale. Had they been fast yoked to a team of wild horses on a plank road, their rate of traveling could hardly have been quicker. Mile-stones, trees, and rails were all one in their Gilpin race; and, Mazeppa-like, as they dashed along at the heels of the monster, they could only see one white bank of foam, which rolled up before them higher than the bow of the boat, as if it would momently rush aboard.

The whale, in this instance, decided that their ride should not be altogether barren of variety, for they soon found themselves rushing into the midst of loose whales, who, having been disturbed by the other boats, were merrily fluking and snorting all around, and playing their mad antics and gambols. The other boats had also fastened, and as their whale, too, seemed to have a fondness for company, they were all in a muss together.

At length, as the first whale slackened his speed, they hauled up to him, and the captain darted his lance adroitly, which took effect. The second mate, who had kept as near as possible during the chase, now fastened with his barbed irons, and whichsoever way the harassed whale turned, he met an enemy. Weakened with the loss of blood, that was now jetted forth from his huge nostrils in torrents, the subdued monster soon became passive, and his captors lay off at safe distance to wait the last struggle. This was speedily over; for, after a few moments of convulsive writhing, there came the final spasm, which is always terrible to see. The surrounding waters were lashed into foam, and all previous exhibitions of power were as nothing compared with the incredible strength put forth in the flurry.

At last, leaping almost clear from the water, the whale pitched down head foremost, and as their lines tautened, they commenced hauling in hand over hand, expecting that he would die under water, and that the body would rise directly; but in this they were deceived. The strain upon the lines soon indicated that the whale was sinking, and it was all in vain they endeavored to check its downward tendency. It would sink like lead in spite of all their efforts, and they were obliged at last to cut the lines in order to keep the boats from going down with it. Thus they lost not only the fruits of many hours of severe toil, but a large quantity of line and the valuable harpoons also, besides the incalculable moral detriment and loss of spirits from such a disappointment.

Bad as this luck was, it was not attended with loss of life like the following I have met with in fragments of a sailor's journal, being a contribution to "The Sheet Anchor:" We were cruising, he says, somewhere between the latitude of thirty-six and thirty-seven degrees south, and the longitude of sixty-eight degrees east, in search of right whales. It was in the afternoon, and the ship was moving along under her top-gallant sails at the rate of about five knots the hour. The most hardened grumbler could not find fault with the day. At the fore and main top-gallant cross-trees were two men on the look-out for whales. It was now nearly four o'clock, when the man at the main sung out, "There she blows!" He repeated the cry regularly five or six times. All was now excitement among the officers and men. Every one was anxious to know if it was the kind of whale we wanted. The mate hailed the man at the mast-head, "Where away is that whale? What do you call her?"

"Right whale, sir, on the lee beam, two miles off; look out sharp for her!"

"Sing out when the ship heads for her!"

"Ay, ay, sir."

"Keep her away!" said the captain to the man at the helm. "Boy, hand me the spyglass." "Steady!" sung out the man at the mast-head. "Steady it is!" answered the wheel. The captain then started to go aloft. "Mr. A. (to the mate), you may square in the after yards, and then call all hands."

"Forward, there!" shouted the mate. "Haul the main-sail up and square the yards! Bill!" (to an old sailor). "Sir?" "Call all hands!" "Ay, ay, sir. All hands, ahoy!" shouted old Bill, in a voice like a tempest. "Stand by the boats!" In less than no time the deck was alive with men.

"Boat-steerers, get your boats ready!" In a moment, as it were, the boats were in readiness, the tubs put in, the lines bent on to the harpoons, and the crews standing by, ready to follow the boats down to the water, when the word came from the captain to lower away.

the WHALE *&* his *captors*

"There she blows!" sung out the man at the fore; "not half a mile off."

"Down helm!" shouted the captain. "Mr. A., brace up the mizzen top-sail. Hoist and swing the boats! Lower away!" Down went the boats, and down followed the crews. As the boats struck the water, every man was on his thwart, with his hand on the loom of his oar, and all at once the three boats were cutting their way through the water in the direction of the whale.

It was my duty to steer the mate's boat, and she happened to be the fastest puller, so that, although we all left the ship together, and for a few rods kept nearly head and head with each other, still we knew well enough that, as soon as the word came from the mate to "give way," we should drop the others in a moment. So we did not fret ourselves, but kept cool for a tight pull when the whale should show himself on the surface of the water again, which he did the moment after.

"Here she is!" cried the mate; "and not over ten rods from the boat. Now, my dear fellows, lay back hard! Spring hard, I tell you! There she blows! Only give way, my boys, and she is ours!" The boat bounded forward like a thing of life. "Spring like tigers!" said the mate, his voice sinking almost to a whisper. I looked over my shoulder to see what kind of a chance I was about to have, at the same time pulling at my own oar with all my might. We were going on her starboard quarter; just the chance I liked to fasten to a whale.

"Stand up!" shouted the mate; and in a moment I was on my feet, and in the next moment I had two harpoons to the hitches into her. "Stern! stern all!" sung out the mate, as he saw the irons in the whale. "Come here, my boy!" said he to me. We shifted ends; he to the head, and I to the stern of the boat. The whale started off like lightning.

"Hold on, line!" said the mate; and away we shot after her, like an arrow from the bow. The mate by this time had his lance ready. "Haul me on to that whale!" he shouted; and all hands turned to hauling line, while I coiled it away in the stern-sheets. We had got nearly up to the whale when she took to sounding, taking the line right up and down from the head of the boat. I had two turns of the line round the loggerhead, and was holding on as much as the boat would bear, when, all at once, another large whale, that we knew nothing about, shot up out of the water nearly her whole length, in a slanting position,

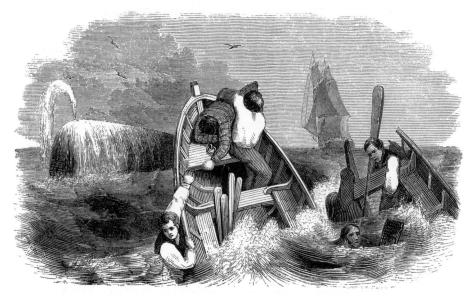

View of a Whale-boat crushed by a Whale.

hanging directly over the boat. I threw off the turns from the logger-head, and shouted to the men to "stern." But it was of no use; she fell the whole length of her body on the boat.

I heard a crash! and, as I went down, I felt a pressure of water directly over my head, caused, as I thought, by the whale's flukes as she struck. How long I was under water I know not; but I remember that all looked dark above me, and that I tried very hard to shove my head through in order to breathe. At last I succeeded; but what a sight was that on which I gazed when I found myself on the surface of the water! About a rod off was the whale that we were fast to, thrashing the water into a foam with his flukes, the ocean red with blood, and the crimson streams pouring from the wounds in the whale's sides made by the harpoons. In another direction I could see pieces of the boat floating around. At the distance of two or three miles, I could occasionally get a glimpse of the ship as I rode on the top of a swell, and not a human being in sight.

Not losing heart or hope, I struck out for a piece of the stern of our once beautiful boat a few rods distant. The crew came up one after another, catching at any thing they could see to help keep them afloat.

the WHALE *&* his *captors*

One poor fellow came paddling along with two or three oars under him, crying out that his back was broken. Another of the crew and myself got him on a piece of the boat that we had hold of. His thigh was broken, and he could not move his legs at all.

The second mate soon after picked us up in his boat, and so much had we been engaged in looking out for ourselves, that we did not perceive one of our number was missing. But alas! it was too soon found out. He was a young man, about seventeen years old, and did not belong to the boat, but went in the place of the midship oarsman, who was sick at the time. The whale fell directly over him, and probably killed him in a moment.

With what feelings we pulled around and around the spot where the boat was stoven, unwilling to believe, even after we knew there was no hope, that our shipmate was gone, never more to return! How silently we glided, alongside of the ship, and hoisted in our other poor shipmate, now lamed for life!

"Ah, that some of those people who look upon sailors as little better than brutes, and who know little or nothing of the kind feelings and strong affections that are hid under their rough outside, could have seen what I saw on board that ship. Even their hearts would melt; and they would find it is not always the polished and educated, the smooth-faced and handsome man, that has the warmest heart or the most generous feelings."

How true is all this, and how often has it been proved in my own intercourse with seamen. Under many a rough, pea-jacket bosom there beats a heart, which you will be feeling long for, and be slow in finding under the purple, and silks, and satins of fashion and frivolity. The poet Burns knew it when he sang so sweetly:

The *heart* aye's the part, ay,
    That makes us right or wrang:
Nae treasures, nor pleasures,
    Could make us happy lang.
It's no in titles nor in rank;
It's no in wealth like Lon'on bank.
    To purchase peace and rest:
It's no in making muckle *mair*,

It's no in books; it's no in lear,
     To make us truly bless'd.
If happiness hae not her seat
     And center in the breast,
We may be wise, or rich, or great,
     But never can be bless'd.

Conquest and Disposal of a Bull Whale

Ye gentlemen of England, that live at home at ease,
Ah, little do ye think upon the dangers of the seas!
—Ocean Song.

I love thee—when I see thee stand,
The Hope of every other land:
A sea-mark in the tide of Time,
Rearing to heaven thy brows sublime.
I love thee—when I contemplate
The full-orb'd grandeur of thy state:
Thy laws and liberties, that rise,
Man's noblest works beneath the skies;
To which the Pyramids are tame,
And Grecian temples bow their fame.
—Montgomery.

Brazil Banks, Atlantic Ocean, off the Rio de la Plata.
We are just now at work upon the carcass of a bull whale lately captured, a genuine makrocephalus, which I have found by measurement to be sixty feet long and thirty feet round. His lower jaw-bone is sixteen feet long, and it has forty-eight large teeth, some of them a foot long, three of which are broken off, and others much worn. There are also several very large scars on the outside of the jaw, and sundry other marks upon his person, that show him to have been in the wars. All these things, and the way in which he slued his flukes whenever the boat came near, were thought by his captors to prove him an old cruiser in these seas, and to have known a whale-boat, and, not unlikely, to have had a taste of cold iron before. It would seem, indeed, as if there could be very few sperm whales in the ocean of age, that have not been some time or other chased by a whaler, and their numbers

are getting so greatly reduced that the sperm whale-fishing alone will not be much longer attempted.

What goes under the name of the sperm whale's head is nearly one third of the monster's length. It is customary to sever this entirely at first, and let it tow astern, while the rest of the carcass is being stripped of its very valuable blubber. Utterly unlike the right whale, which has no teeth, the head of a sperm whale is square, the end of it something like the largest mill-log ever seen, sawed off straight. It is truly a prodigious mass of organized, compact matter, with which this animal has been known sometimes to butt like a ram against the sides of a ship and break it to pieces. They often go in this way "head on" to boats, but are generally pricked off and turned with a lance, or dexterously avoided.

From what may be called the top of the forehead to the roof of the mouth of this square-faced *sui generis* monster, it measured nine feet in a straight line, and there was a corresponding breadth and depth of forehead, so that, with its prodigious volume of brain (head matter), and so large a facial angle, the bust of this creature is most favorably commended to the fingers of phrenologists. Is it not a little surprising, that in the researches of comparative phrenology the cranium of the great sperm whale should be overlooked?

For the matter of room, a phrenologist might keep shop in it, and light it up, if he chose, with its own brains, and there point out to visitors by the lamp-light the places in the walls and ceiling where the different organs lay. It would be like a painter at Rome who should open his studio in the Parthenon; the celestial gods would be eying him from the ceiling; deified men and the infernals would be looking on him from all around. And if the aforesaid phrenologist and the favored artist should not alike become masters, under circumstances so imposing, it would be nobody's fault but their own.

But to finish the disposal of our present prize: the lower jaw, with the teeth all in it, was first separated by the sharp spades, in the hands of the officers, from the head, and hoisted in upon deck; then the upper jaw was separated from the mass of crown, forehead, and brains; then what whalers call the *junk*, or the mighty mass of blubber, separated from the *case*, which is the name they give to the brain-pan, *white horse*, integuments, and flesh of the head. The *junk* was hoisted in on

the WHALE & *his* captors

deck, weighing I will not say how many thousand pounds. The former captain of this ship on another voyage found a large barnacle in the center of a sperm whale's *junk*, that must have got there in the same way that stones, and deers' horns, and toads get into the solid heart of trees, by being lodged in the bark and then overgrown by it.

When old Captain Bunker, of New Bedford, of whom almost every body has heard, was on a cruise in the ship Howard, in north latitude thirty degrees thirty minutes, and east longitude one hundred and fifty-four degrees, he threw a harpoon into a large whale. But the whale was not captured, and the harpoon of course lost. It was about five years afterward, that, being precisely in the same latitude, and east longitude one hundred and forty, he made fast to a noble whale, and after a hard struggle succeeded in getting him alongside. And lo! when cutting him up, a harpoon, rusted off at the shank, was found fast anchored in the old fellow's "cut-water." "Hallo!" said Captain Bunker, jesting, "here is my missing old iron." What he said in joke proved to be very truth, for the blubber-kept harpoon was the identical one he had lost five years before, having on it the ship's name and his own private mark.

But to come back to our great subject of dissection now in hand, the *case* was raised partially out of water, so as to keep the waves from washing into it, and an incision was then made through the membrane of one of the ventricles of the head, into which they are now letting down great buckets as into a well, dipping them full of pure sperm, and whipping it up into hogsheads. It has a slight rose tint, and looks like ice cream or white butter half churned. There will be about fifteen barrels of these brains (?) alone (it turned out sixteen), and ninety or ninety-five barrels of oil in all. The sea has been all white on that side the ship with the spermaceti and blubber that have escaped. Thousands of albatrosses, gulls, and haglets have more than got their fill, so that they fly heavily and with difficulty, and will probably have to spend three or four days, if not weeks, in digestion, like the sloth. Sperm whalers are provided with large scoops, by which, in good weather, they save a great deal of what we are losing, some of the boys being out in a boat to dip it up.

The boat-steerers have been down upon the carcass four times to secure hooks and hawsers into the great holes they cut in the blubber from above. Eight or ten sharks are prowling round, of the picked-nose kind, some of them eight and nine feet long. They will come right up on to the whale's body with a wave, bite out great pieces of flesh, turn over on to their bellies, and roll off. Several of them have been harpooned, and two have gone off with irons in their backs, that do not seem to annoy them any more than a little splinter in the thumb of a wood sawyer.

The tenacity with which the shark holds to life, or, rather, life to the shark, is astonishing, and hardly to be credited by one who has not himself observed it. We have caught a number on this passage for their skin, which, cleansed and dry, is an excellent substitute for sand-paper, much used in whale ships to smooth and polish the various things they make up out of whale's bone and teeth. One that we hauled upon deck, after it was cut open, and the heart and all the internal viscera were removed, would still flap and thrash with its tail, and try to bite it off. The heart was contracting for twenty minutes after it was taken out and pierced with the knife. And, from what I have myself seen, I could not ridicule or deny a story that one has told me of a shark's being known to swim off, upon being thrown overboard, after it was opened, gutted, and had its tail chopped off. Sailors don't like them a bit, but kill them whenever they can; and there is little wonder, considering they are so likely to be themselves eaten by this greedy ranger through the paths of the sea.

To have done with our whale, it remains to finish bailing the case, and to cut out the blubber of the junk from the part of it called "*white horse*," which is a tough, stringy, and slightly elastic substance interposed with it, that contains little or no oil, and is as good as a cotton bale to shield a sperm whale's head from blows. Then follows the trying out, stowing down, overhauling, and coopering again the hogsheads of this valuable fluid, which they on land, who are turning night into day by means of its clear light, little know the hazard and labor of American whalemen in procuring. At the completion of the voyage this oil will be drawn from the casks, and, after a process of boiling and cooling, will be put into vats with a strainer which detains the spermaceti mixed with oil.

It is then a yellow viscous substance, which is afterward put into

The WHALE & *His captors*

strong canvass bags, and subjected to a screw press, and next to the pressure of the hydraulic engine, whereby the oily matter is all expelled, leaving the spermaceti in hard, concrete masses. This, after boiling with potash and purifying, is molded into those beautiful oil-less candles which are sold under the name of spermaceti.

The first manufactory of sperm candles in America was started in Rhode Island in 1750, by one Benjamin Crab, an Englishman. By the year 1761 there were eight in New England and one in Philadelphia. Owing to the increased influx of sperm, by reason of the energetic and widely-extended prosecution of the sperm whale fishery, the number of spermaceti candle manufactories is now greatly increased. In 1834 it was estimated that there were sixty of them constantly in operation, and the quantity of sperm candles then made was three millions of pounds.

For the well-deserved commendation of this branch of American industry, all persons in any way connected with it will be as pleased as we in the Commodore Preble have been at the way in which New England enterprise was toasted at the New England Society's last dinner in New York. There is an account of the Anniversary of the Pilgrims' Landing, and the festivities of the occasion, in a paper to which we have been treated from an outward-bound whale ship just fallen in with. How greedily we have devoured it, none but a news-hungry whaleman knows. "New England enterprise: It grapples with the monsters of the Pacific to illuminate our dwellings, and with the problems of science to enlighten our minds."

Now if the lines of commercial enterprise can be only kept from parting with the rectilinear of moral propriety and the law of God, our career of greatness as a nation is clear and glorious. The great future is before us, full of hope, if old Puritan principles be only at the head with modern New England enterprise.

Far, like the comet's way through infinite space,
Stretches the long, untraveled path of light
Into the depth of ages: we may trace, afar,
The brightening glories of its flight,
Till the receding rays are lost to human sight.

Conquest and Disposal of a Bull Whale

I love thee; next to Heaven above,
Land of my fathers! thee I love;
And rail thy slanderers as they will,
With all thy *faults*, I love thee still.

I love thee when I hear thy voice
Bid a despairing world rejoice,
And loud from shore to shore proclaim,
In every tongue, Messiah's name;
That name at which, from sea to sea,
All nations yet shall bow the knee.

XI

Authentic Tragedies and Perils
of the Whaling Service

At length his comrades, who before
Had heard his voice in every blast,
Could catch the sound no more.
For then, by toil subdued, he drank
The stifling wave, and then he sank.
And he, they knew, nor ship nor shore,
Whate'er they did, should visit more.
—Cowper's *Castaway*.

In this Daguerreotype gallery of Life and Adventures in a Whale Ship, it is but fair that our late experience of the bright side of whalemen's fortune, in the safe capture and stowing down of a noble hundred-barrel spermaceti, as told in the last chapter, should be set off by incidents of another character that are equally common. A writer in the London Quarterly, a few years ago, described an adventure in the pursuit of a whale, which, given here for substance with some additions, will be read with deep interest by all who are anywise familiar with the "hair-breadth 'scapes and moving accidents" in the ordinary career of whalemen.

One of a ship's company or officers in the North Pacific, near the close of a day that had been rather stormy, says that a school of young bull whales made their appearance close to the ship, and the weather having cleared up a little, the captain immediately ordered the mate to lower his boat, while he did the same with his own, in order to go in pursuit of them.

The two boats were instantly lowered, for they were unable to send more, having had two others "stove" the day before. They soon got near the whales, but were unfortunately seen by them before they could dart the harpoon with any chance of success, and the consequence was, that the school of whales separated, and went off with great swiftness in different directions. One, however, after making several turns, came at length right toward the captain's boat, which he observing, waited in silence for his approach, without moving an oar, so that the "young bull" came close by his boat, and received the blow of the harpoon some distance behind his "hump," and so near to the ship as to be seen by all on board.

The whale appeared quite terror-struck for a few seconds, and then suddenly recovering itself, darted off like the wind, and spun the boat so quickly round, when the tug came upon the line, that she was within a miracle of being upset. But away they went, "dead to windward," at the rate of twelve or fifteen miles an hour, right against a "head sea," which flew against and over the bows of the boat with uncommon force, so that she at times appeared to be plowing through it, making a high bank of surf on each side.

The second mate, having observed the course of the whale and boat, managed to waylay them; and when they came near to him, which they speedily did, "a short warp" was thrown, and both boats were soon towed at nearly the same rate as the captain's boat had been before.

The captain was now seen darting the lance at the whale, as it almost flew along, but he did not seem to do so with any kind of effect, as the speed of the whale did not appear in the least diminished, and in a very short time they all disappeared together, being at too great a distance to be seen with the naked eye from the deck. The officer ran aloft, and by the aid of a telescope could just discern from the masthead the three objects, like specks upon the surface of the ocean. At an alarming distance, he could just observe the two boats, with the whale's head occasionally darting out before them, with a good deal of "white water" or foam, which convinced him that the whale was still running. He watched with the glass until he could no longer trace them, even in the most indistinct manner, and then called to those on deck that they might take the bearing, by the compass, of the direction in which he had lost sight of them, so that they might continue to "beat" the ship up to that quarter.

It was now, says the story, within half an hour of sunset, and there was every appearance of the coming on of an "ugly night;" indeed, the wind began to freshen every moment, and an "awkward bubble"

Boat returning from the Search for Berry.

of a sea soon to make. I remained aloft until I saw the sun dip, angry
and red, below the troubled horizon, and was just about to descend,
when I was dreadfully shocked at hearing the loud cry of "a man overboard!" from all upon deck. I looked astern, and saw with horror one
of our men, by the name of Berry, grappling with the waves, and calling loudly for help.

The ship was soon brought round, but in doing so she unavoidably
passed a long way from the poor fellow, who still supported himself by
beating the water with his hands, although he was quite unacquainted
with the proper art of swimming. Several oars were thrown overboard
the moment after he fell, but he could not reach them, though they
were near to him; and directly the ship brought up, a Sandwich Islander, who formed one of the crew, leaped overboard and swam toward him, while at the same time the people on deck were lowering a
spare boat, which is always kept for such emergencies. I could be of no
service, except to urge their expedition by many calls, for it was only
the work of a few minutes.

The good Sandwich Islander struck out most bravely at first, but,
finding that he was some distance from the ship, and being unable to
see Berry on account of the agitated surface of the sea, actually turned
back through fear—finding, as he said, that the "sea caps" went over

his head. The men in the boat now plied their oars with all their strength, and were making rapidly toward the drowning young man, who now and then disappeared entirely from view under the seas which were beginning to roll. A sickening anxiety pervaded me, as my thoughts seemed to press the boat onward to the spot where the poor fellow still grappled, but convulsively, with the yielding waters.

The boat, urged by man's utmost strength, sprang over the boisterous waves with considerable speed, but they arrived half a minute too late to save our poor shipmate from his watery grave. I saw him struggle with the waves until the last, when the foam of a broken sea roared over him, and caused him to disappear forever! The boat was rowed round and round the fatal spot again and again, until night fell, and then she was slowly and reluctantly pulled to the ship by her melancholy crew. As they returned, the turbulent waves tossed them about as if in sport, making the boat rebound from the beating and dashing waters which flew against her bow.

The moment the unfortunate seaman disappeared, a large bird of the albatross kind came careering along, and alighted on the water at the very spot where the poor fellow was last seen. It was a curious circumstance, and only served to heighten our horror, when we saw the carnivorous bird set itself proudly over the head of our companion; and which also served to remind us of the number of sharks that we had so frequently seen of late, and of the horrible propensities of which we could not dare to think.

By the time we had hoisted in the boat it was quite dark; the wind, too, had increased to half a gale, with heavy squalls at times, so that we were obliged to double reef our topsails. We had lost one of our men who had sailed with us from England, the bare thought of which, in our circumstances, aroused a crowd of heartrending ideas. Our captain and second mate, with ten of the crew, had disappeared, and were by that time all lost or likely to be so, in the stormy night which had set in: being, too, several hundred miles away from land. We, however, kept beating the ship to windward constantly, carrying all the sail she could bear, making "short boards," or putting about every twenty minutes. We had also, since night fell, continued to burn lights, and we had likewise a large vessel, containing oil and unraveled rope, burning over the stern rail of the ship as a beacon for them, which threw out great light.

the WHALE *&* HIS *captors*

But, although all eyes were employed in every direction, searching for the boats, no vestige of them could be seen; and, therefore, when half past nine P.M. came, we made up our minds they were all lost; and, as the wind howled hoarsely through the rigging, and the waves beat savagely against our ship, some of us thought we could hear the shrieks of poor Berry above the roaring storm; others imagined, in their melancholy, that they could occasionally hear the captain's voice ordering to "bear up;" while the boats had been seen more than fifteen times by anxious spirits, who had strained their eyes through the gloom until fancy robbed them of their true speculation, and left her phantasmagoria in exchange.

There were not many on board who did not think of home on that dreadful night; there were not many among us who did not curse the sea and all the sea-going avocations, while with the same breath they blessed the cheerful fireside of their parents, which, at that moment, they would have given all they possessed to but see. But at the moment despair was firmly settling upon us, a man from aloft cried out that he could see a light right ahead of the ship, just as we were "going about," by which we should have gone from it.

We all looked in that direction, and in a few minutes we could plainly perceive it; in a short time we were close up with it, when, to our great joy, we found the captain and all the men in the boats, lying to the leeward of the dead whale, which had in some measure saved them from the violence of the sea. They had only just been able to procure a light, having unfortunately upset all their tinder through the violent motion of the boats, by which it became wet, but which they succeeded in igniting after immense application of the flint and steel, or their lantern would have been suspended from an oar directly after sunset, which is the usual practice when boats are placed under such circumstances.

After securing the whale alongside, which it was feared they would lose during the night, from the roughness of the weather, they all came on board, when the sudden end of poor Berry was spoken of with sorrow from all hands, while their own deliverance served to throw a ray of light amid the gloom.

They thought of his worth, but no words found birth,
  To tell of the love they bore him;

But the sea-bird's wail, and the stormy gale,
　　And the roar of the ocean wave,
Sung deep and long the funeral song
　　O'er the seaman's traceless grave.

In this connection, it is not unsuitable to give place to what an accredited writer in the Westminster Review relates of an incident, or, rather, a dread tragedy in the Greenland whale-fishery, which is almost too appalling and unparalleled, not to say impossible, to be believed:

One serene evening in the middle of August, 1775, Captain Warrens, the master of a Greenland whale ship, found himself becalmed among an immense number of icebergs, in about seventy-seven degrees of north latitude. On one side and within a mile of his vessel, these were of immense height, and closely wedged together, and a succession of snow-covered peaks appeared behind each other as far as the eye could reach, showing that the ocean was completely blocked up in that quarter, and that it had probably been so for a long period of time. Captain Warrens did not feel altogether satisfied with his situation; but, there being no wind, he could not move one way or the other, and he therefore kept a strict watch, knowing that he would be safe as long as the icebergs continued in their respective places. About midnight the wind rose to a gale, accompanied by thick showers of snow, while a succession of thundering, grinding, and crashing noises gave fearful evidence that the ice was in motion.

The vessel received violent shocks every moment, for the haziness of the atmosphere prevented those on board from discovering in what direction the open water lay, or if there actually was any at all on either side of them. The night was spent in tacking as often as any case of danger happened to present itself, and in the morning the storm abated, and Captain Warrens found, to his great joy, that his ship had not sustained any serious injury. He remarked with surprise that the accumulated icebergs, which had the preceding evening formed an impenetrable barrier, had been separated and disengaged by the wind, and that in one place a canal of open sea wound its course among them as far as the eye could discern.

It was two miles beyond the entrance of this canal that a ship made

The WHALE *&* HIS *captors*

its appearance about noon. The sun shone brightly at the time, and a gentle breeze blew from the north. At first some intervening icebergs prevented Captain Warrens from distinctly seeing any thing but her mast; but he was struck with the strange manner in which her sails were disposed, and with the dismantled aspect of her yards and rigging. She continued to go before the wind for a few furlongs, and then, grounding upon the low icebergs, remained motionless. Captain Warrens's curiosity was so much excited that he immediately leaped into his boat with several seamen and rowed toward her.

On approaching, he observed that her hull was miserably weather-beaten, and not a soul appeared on the deck, which was covered with snow to a considerable depth. He hailed her crew several times, but no answer was returned. Previous to stepping on board, an open port-hole near the main chains caught his eye, and on looking into it, he perceived a man reclining back in a chair, with writing materials on a table before him, but the feebleness of the light made every thing very indistinct. The party went upon deck, and having removed the hatch-way, which they found closed, they descended to the cabin.

They first came to the apartment which Captain Warrens viewed through the port-hole. A tremor seized him as he entered it. Its in-mate retained its former position, and seemed to be insensible to strangers. He was found to be a corpse, and a green damp mold had covered his cheeks and forehead, and veiled his eye-balls. He had a pen in his hand, and a log-book lay before him, the last sentence in whose unfinished page ran thus: "November 11th, 1762. We have now been inclosed in the ice seventeen days. The fire went out yesterday, and our master has been trying ever since to kindle it again without success. His wife died this morning. There is no relief."

Captain Warrens and his seamen hurried from the spot without uttering a word. On entering the principal cabin, the first object that attracted their attention was the dead body of a female, reclining on a bed in an attitude of deep interest and attention. Her countenance retained the freshness of life, and a contraction of the limbs alone showed that her form was inanimate. Seated on the floor was the corpse of an apparently young man, holding a steel in one hand and a flint in the other, as if in the act of striking fire upon some tinder which lay beside him. In the fore part of the vessel several sailors were found lying dead in their berths, and the body of a boy was crouched at the bottom of the gangway stairs.

Neither provisions nor fuel could be discovered any where; but Captain Warrens was prevented, by the superstitious prejudices of his seamen, from examining the vessel as minutely as he wished to have done. He therefore carried away the log-book already mentioned, and returning to his own ship, immediately steered to the southward, deeply impressed with the awful example which he had just witnessed of the danger of navigating the polar seas in high northern latitudes.

On returning to England, he made various inquiries respecting vessels that had disappeared in an unknown way, and by comparing these results with the information which was afforded by the written documents in his possession, he ascertained the name and history of the imprisoned ship and of her unfortunate master, and found that she had been frozen in thirteen years previous to the time of his discovering her imprisoned in the ice.

If this strange tale be true, we see that Coleridge's wonderful Rime of the Ancient Mariner may not be all fancy, but may have a substantial basis of fact. Witness the following verses, eliminated from it here and there:

And now there came both mist and snow,
    And it grew wondrous cold;
And ice, mast high, came floating by,
    As green as emerald.

And through the drifts the snowy clifts
    Did send a dismal sheen;
Nor shapes of men nor beasts we ken—
    The ice was all between.

The ice was here, the ice was there,
    The ice was all around;
It cracked and growled, and roared and howled,
    Like noises in a swound!

Alone, alone, all, all alone,
    Alone on a wide, wide sea!

And never a saint took pity on
     My soul in agony.

I closed my lips, and kept them close,
     And the balls like pulses beat;
For the sky and the sea, and the sea and the sky,
Lay like a load on my weary eye,
     And the dead were at my feet.

The cold sweat melted from their limbs,
     Nor rot nor reck did they;
The look with which they looked on me
     Had never passed away.

All stood together on the deck,
     For a charnel dungeon fitter;
All fixed on me their stony eyes,
     That in the moon did glitter.

But soon I heard the dash of oars,
     I heard the pilot's cheer;
My head was turned perforce away,
     And I saw a boat appear.

The pilot and the pilot's boy,
     I heard them coming fast!
Dear Lord in Heaven! it was a joy
     The dead men could not blast.

The boat came closer to the ship,
     But I nor spake nor stirred;
The boat came close beneath the ship,
     And straight a sound was heard.

Stunned by that loud and dreadful sound,
     Which sky and ocean smote,
Like one that hath been seven days drown'd
     My body lay afloat,
But swift as dreams, myself I found
     Within the pilot's boat.

O wedding guest! this soul hath been
      Alone on a wide, wide sea:
So lonely 'twas, that God himself
      Scarce seemed there to be.

Farewell, farewell! but this I tell
      To thee, thou wedding guest!
He prayeth well who loveth well
      Both man, and bird, and beast.

He prayeth best who loveth best
      All things both great and small;
For the dear God who loveth us,
      He made and loveth all.

XII

Yarns from the Experience
of Old Whalemen

Row! row! row!
In our vessel she must go,
Over the broad Pacific's swell,
Round Cape Horn, where tempests dwell;
Many a night and many a day,
Hence with us she must away,
Till we joyful hail once more
Old Nantucket's treeless shore.
—Whaler's Song.

Brazil Banks, latitude 24° S., longitude 40° W.
Some few years ago, in the same region of ocean where we are now cruising, and about the same month of the year, an old weather-worn and barnacled whale ship was working slowly along on a wind, homeward bound, or after another sperm whale, if one should heave in sight. Her try-works were sending up a smoke black as night in huge volumes, for they were trying out an eighty-barreler not long taken.

The deck was lined with casks, and the main hatches off, men engaged in the blubber-room cutting up the blanket pieces into horse pieces, ready for mincing; others piking the pieces from one tub to another, ready for the mincers; some tending the fires, some filling up casks with hot oil from the cooler; every man busy, and each at his place, but the decks confusedly strown with barrels, and tubs, and whaling gear, like a street with goods in it after a fire.

All at once, says an old whaler, in a yarn of random recollections of his youth, all at once, a voice clear as the lark, and to the ear of the whaleman far sweeter, rang through the ship, THERE SHE BLOWS! Again and again it is repeated, at regular intervals. Now the captain hails the mast head. "Where away is that whale, and what do you call her?"

"Sperm whale, sir, three points on the weather bow, not over two miles off."

"Get your boats ready; slack down the fires; and stand by to lower away!"

The boats' crews each stand by their own boat, some of the men help put in the tub of line, others lay down the boat-tackle falls in such a way that they will run clear. The boat-steerer bends on his harpoons, the gripes are cast clear of the boats, and now comes the word, "Hoist and swing!" In a moment the boats are hanging by their tackles, and clear of the cranes, ready for the word "Lower away!" The mates, in the mean time, were aloft, watching the movements of the whale, in order to judge how to pull for her.

Now comes the word, "Lower away!" In a moment all the boats are off, and in chase at a good speed, in order to see who will be up with the whale first. However, at this time, it did not make so much difference which boat pulled the best, as the whale peaked her flukes and went down before any boat came up with her. Now each boat-header uses his own judgment as to where the whale will come up next, for a sperm whale is almost always going some when she is down or under water. The whale was gone an hour, when we caught sight of the signal at the main, which said plainly that the whale was up. All eyes gaze eagerly around in all directions for the whale.

"There she is," cries one of the men, "not twenty rods from the chief mate's boat! There, he sees her!"

"Down to your oars, lads!" said the captain, in whose boat I was. "Give way hard!" Now, then, the little boat jumps again, sending the spray in rainbows from the bow. "Spring hard, my dear fellows; if she blows a dozen times more, the mate will fasten. There she blows! Oh, she's a beauty! a regular old sog! a hundred-barreler! There she lays like a log! Oh, what a hump! There she blows! Stand up, David! (the name of the mate's boat-steerer.) There goes one iron into her, and there he gives her the second one; he is fast solid. Now, then, my boys, let us be up among the suds. Stand up!" shouted the captain to me, as he laid his boat square on to her. In goes two more harpoons, and our boat is fast.

the WHALE *&* HIS *captors*

I thought I had seen large sperm whales, but this old chap beat them all; he cut and thrashed with his flukes a while, but did not take to sounding or running, as some whales do. The mate pulled up to lance him; but, let him go on as he would, the whale would head for his boat, and prevent his getting a chance at her with his lance. "Now, then, Mr. ——," said the captain to me, "you must kill that whale." The captain steered me this day, as he had done several times before, as we were short of a boat-steerer. We pulled up to her, and I set my lance into her life, as I thought, the whole length; she spouted a little thin blood. "You are not low enough," said the captain; "set your lance lower down; this fellow is deep, and you must lance lower."

The whale settled away under water after she felt the lance, and I kept a look-out for her, expecting she would break water near the head of the boat. Pretty soon I saw her whiten under water, and got my lance ready as soon as she should come to the surface; the next moment I was flying in the air, and a moment after was several fathoms under water. The whale came up head foremost, hitting the boat a tremendous knock under my feet, sending me all flying. The captain at the same time grabbed his steering oar, and overboard he went also.

Fortunately, I could swim well, and soon came up to blow; but I had hardly time to spout, before I found that I was in a very disagreeable situation. Putting out my arm to swim, I hit the whale on his head, and at the same time saw the boat three or four rods from me. I confess I did not feel exactly right; but it was no use for me to lay still, and be picked up like a squid; so I made a regular shove off with my feet against the whale's head, and struck out for the boat. I saw that all was confusion in the boat, and that the men did not notice me at all. I had on thick clothes, and found it hard swimming. Finally one of the men saw me, and stopped the boat, which some of them were steering away from me as fast as they could.

As I got in at the bow, I saw the captain come over the stern. "Hallo!" said he, "where have you been to?" "After the whale," said I. "And I have been after you," said the captain. We had a good laugh, wrung our hair, and started for the whale again. She lay still, with her jaws open, and head toward the boat; the rest of her body was under water, so that she gave no chance to kill. We lay still, watching her motions. All at once she let her jaws fly back, striking the boat in the bow, and smashing a hole through her. The boat began to fill; but, fortunately, we had a jacket ready, and stopped the hole up, and so we kept from filling, and pulled up to the whale again.

This time she headed the mate, and lay her whole length broadside toward us. We had nothing to do but to pull up and in lance, the whale laying perfectly still all the time. In twenty minutes she went into her flurry, and soon after lay fin out. We took her alongside the ship, and commenced cutting her in; but it took all the next day to get her all in. She measured over seventy-five feet in length, and between fifty and sixty feet round the largest part of the body; her jaw was seventeen and a half feet long, and her flukes seventeen feet broad. She stowed us down one hundred and twenty-five barrels of sperm oil.

In the vicissitudes of whaling fortune, a prize like this now and then offers itself to a ship, in the form of a dead whale afloat. Such a fortunate wind-fall once came to the Cremona, of New Bedford, in 1839, while cruising on the coast of Peru, in the latitude of three degrees south. Her master there fell in with two whaling ships belonging to the same port. Being old acquaintances, they were happy to see each other—compared notes—talked of old times; and whales being in sight all around, although rather shy, they agreed to keep company for the night, hoping for good luck on the morrow.

At early dawn the mast heads were manned, and the horizon carefully scanned in every direction; and the survey increased in interest and care as the hour of sunrise drew nigh. But no whales were in sight.

The wind was light, and they packed on all sail, steering to the northward, in company with the ships they had fallen in with the day before—the Orion being about five miles distant, broad off on the weather bow, and the Lupin about three points under the lee—not more than two or three miles off. Being in the northeast trade winds, and standing along to the northward, they all, of course, had the starboard tacks on board.

On board the Cremona, said her captain, in giving this account, we had our mast heads doubly manned; and at the main-top-gallant-head was stationed Webquish, a smart, active Gay Head Indian, who was a faithful sentinel on such occasions, with a restless eye, and a keenness of vision seldom surpassed by any of his race. All hands were

The WHALE *&* His *captors*

on deck, and expectation was exhibited in the grave demeanor and semi-smiling countenances of the crew.

It was about nine o'clock in the forenoon that Webquish, the Indian, who had been looking steadily in one direction for some minutes, called out that he saw some object afloat away to windward. It was bobbing up and down, and looked something like a boat, but he could not tell what it was.

This excited the curiosity of every man on board; and, as is usual in such cases, all made a spring into the rigging, with a view to run aloft, and get a squint at the mysterious object reported by Webquish. But I ordered them to remain on deck, and sent up my first mate—a man of good judgment and sharp eyes—with a spy-glass, to the fore-top-mast-head. He soon got sight of the object, and immediately reported that it was a *large dead spermaceti whale*.

This was an event, the announcement of which created quite a sensation on board the Cremona; and the question asked of each other was, whether we could secure it for ourselves? In order to do this, it was necessary not only to see it first, but to *get fast to it first*! From the favorable position of the Orion, being to windward, it was clear that the whale would inevitably fall a prize to her, if it should be seen by the look-out before it could be reached by our boats. It was a matter which required a little *management*.

I directed my mate, Mr. Hopkins, to come down to leeward, and keep the mast between him and the Orion, that he might not be seen from that ship, which might excite suspicions that something was in the wind; and, in the same manner, I went myself aloft to take a look at the object to windward—an object of much interest to us, as it was probably of great value.

The other ships quietly kept on their course. The Lupin, being to leeward, could not possibly see the whale; and on board the Orion, the look-out aloft seemed to be taking a nap, for no indications were given that the whale was seen from the ship. This gave us hopes that we might secure the prize; and all was animation on board the Cremona. The mate's boat, being the fastest, was got in readiness, and a good coat of tallow was applied to her bottom—a set of the best oars was selected—and all due preparation made for a race.

For nearly an hour we kept on our course, occasionally going a little to windward, but not in a manner to excite observation. By this time the dead whale was abaft the weather beam. And now, without heaving to or altering the ship's course, the boat was lowered to leeward. Mr. Hopkins and his stalwart and eager crew stepped into it, seized their oars—the word was given—and hurrah, whiz! away they darted toward the whale with the swiftness of an arrow.

We watched the boat with much interest and no little anxiety; for even now, if the prize should be discovered from the Orion, that ship would be filled away, and, running down before the wind, would be able to reach it before Mr. Hopkins could get fast to it with his harpoon. And this reflection seemed to add vigor to the arms of the boat's crew, for they pulled away heartily—with a right good will—and forced the boat merrily through the water. But their fears were groundless. For nearly half an hour they pulled with a degree of strength and skill seldom equaled, and were close on board the whale, and still neither the whale nor the boat was seen by the sleepy lookout on board the Orion!

Under these circumstances, I considered that maneuvering was no longer necessary, and gave the orders to tack ship, which enabled us to steer almost *directly for the whale*! This opened the eyes of the Orion; for our yards were hardly trimmed before that ship squared her yards, and came running down directly across our track, and in a few minutes the Lupin hauled her wind, and came creeping up to windward.

But it was of no use. The Orion was just in time to see Mr. Hopkins strike his harpoon into the whale, and take possession of the prize in the name of the good ship Cremona, of New Bedford! And it was not long before we had the whale alongside, and forthwith commenced "cutting in" upon this noble specimen of the class Mammalia, which proved to be an eighty-barrel whale, and was worth to us twenty-four hundred dollars. By the time we had made fast to our prize, the Orion was within speaking distance. Evidently chagrined at the success of our maneuver, she lavished no compliments upon our enterprise, and soon resumed her former course. In about an hour or so the Lupin came up to inquire the news, but soon made sail after the Orion; and before night, both were out of sight to the leeward, and our oil was mostly boiled out and cooling, to stow away below.

the WHALE *&* his *captors*

The fortunate captain of the Cremona thinks that in this instance, and others like it, the whale, having been harpooned and deprived of life, sunk, we know not why, and remained below the surface until its specific gravity had diminished, by the generation of gases within the animal tissues, to such a degree that it rose from indefinite depths below.

Multitudes of the right whale sink immediately after capture, as we have already learned, and are a dead loss; but this is seldom the case with the sperm; and the Cremona's lucky prize in this instance may have been a sperm whale that had to be abandoned by some other ship, after being mortally wounded and dying on the surface, without ever sinking.

In what is called shore whaling, where there are soundings, they fasten buoys, like as to an anchor, to the sinking right whales, and then watch the spot or the buoy, till the dead animal rises after the ex-piration of two or three days. It is probable that old age, reducing the whale to leanness, and any other cause that diminishes the animal's adipose or oily matter, tends to increase his specific gravity, and, con-sequently, the tendency to sink when killed.

A chase similar to that described above, but for a living whale, once came off in the South Pacific between four ships of different na-tions, becalmed together within the neighborhood of a mile, English, French, Portuguese, and American. The officers of the American ship were making preparation to visit their English neighbors. The men were amusing themselves below, or loitering about the decks, when the lookout on the mast head gave intelligence of a whale by the ex-citing and familiar cry of "There she blows!" "There she blows!" "Oh, she's a beauty!" "There she blows again!"

"Where away?" hailed the officer of the deck.

"West of south, heading east."

"How far, and what is she?"

"Three miles—a real sperm," was the reply.

The men of the American had not been idle during this dialogue. As soon as the first "There she blows" was heard, each man had sprung to his station in the boat. Stopping for a moment to have a keg of water placed in the stern sheets, the boat-steerer, who gives the account, sprung into the boat, and, casting all clear, they were soon under weigh. "Our neighbors also had been on the alert. A well-manned boat from each ship was in the chase.

"These ships laying somewhat in advance, we found they had the advantage of from fifteen to forty rods the start of us. Speaking a few words of encouragement to the men, we were soon passing over the water with a velocity which is hardly conceivable to a landsman. The American whaleman is the only man who never turns his head to look while in the chase of a whale—that part belongs to the boat-steerer. They are thus enabled to give their whole energy to the oar, laying themselves to the work with a hearty good will. Placing the palm of my left hand under the abaft oar, while with my right I guided the boat, and at each stroke threw a part of my weight against it, our boat would 'skim the water like a thing of life.'

"A few moments from the start brought us up with the Portuguese. The crews of the different ships witnessing the chase, the excitement was tremendous. Our shipmates cheered us as we came up with the first boat, and as we passed, the whale again made its appearance. Singing out to the men, 'There she blows! She's an eighty-barrel—right ahead. Give way, my boys!' &c., we were soon alongside the Frenchman. The Frenchman was too polite to oppose us, and we passed him with ease.

"The English boat was now about ten rods in advance, and the whale about one and three fourths of a mile. Now came the trial. The English boat was manned by the same number of stout, active hands as our own, and, seeing us pass the other boats, their whole strength and force were put to the oar. We gained on them but slowly; and such was the excitement of the race, that we were in danger of passing over where the whale had last 'blowed.' At this moment the English boat-steerer noticed the manner in which I had placed my left hand and weight against the oar. Instantly laying hold of his own in like manner, his first effort broke it short at the lock. Thus disabled, he gave us a hearty curse, and we shot past him like a meteor.

"We had been so excited with the race that we had lost sight of the whale. As luck would have it, at this instant she 'blowed' but a few rods ahead. In a moment we were fast, and 'all hands stern.' Soon she was in a 'flurry,' and in the course of an hour we were slowly returning

The WHALE *&* HIS *captors*

Exploit of an American Harpooner in Delego Bay.

to our ship. That whale stowed us down eighty-five barrels of oil, and shortened our voyage two months."

It is easy to see that there must be a thrilling excitement in the adventurous chase of game like this, that has a tinge of the romantic to young and eager minds. There was romance surely, as well as reality, in a whaling feat I have read of, that came off in Delego Bay, South Africa, a smooth nook of ocean much frequented a few years ago by whalers and ships from different nations. A mammoth whale rose and was observed in those still waters at the same moment, and about equidistant from an American and an English ship. From both the boats were lowered, manned, and off in an instant with the speed of the wind.

The English, at first ahead, perceiving their rivals gaining on them, wisely bore wide off from their common game, in order to keep the Americans out of reach of the whale. But when the two boats were nearly abreast, the English of course inside, one of the American sailors sprang from his seat, and with extraordinary agility hurled his ponderous harpoon right over the English boat. Thrown with unwonted force and precision, it struck the monster in a vital part, and was buried to the socket.

The English boat, thus strangely intercepted and balked of its prize, shrunk back under the warp of its Yankee rival. The waves were soon crimsoned with blood, and the daring American took possession of the mastered Leviathan, while Delego Bay echoed and re-echoed with shouts of applause.

All honor to whalemen, bold and brave! We will sing for them, in passing, Park Benjamin's song:

How cheery are the mariners
    Those lovers of the sea!
Their hearts are like its yesty waves,
    As bounding and as free.
They whistle when the storm-bird wheels
    In circles round the mast;
And sing when, deep in foam, the ship
    Plows onward to the blast.

What care the mariners for gales?
    There's music in their roar,
When wide the berth along the lee,
    And leagues of room before.
Let billows toss to mountain heights,
    Or sink to chasms low,
The vessel stout will ride it out,
    Nor reel beneath the blow.

GOD keep those cheery mariners!
    And temper all the gales
That sweep against the rocky coast
    To their storm-shattered sails;
And men on shore will bless the ship
    That could so guided be,
Safe in the hollow of His hand,
    To brave the mighty sea!

XIII

Peculiar Vocabulary and Hazards of Whalemen

A perilous life, and hard as life may be,
Hath the brave whaleman on the lonely sea;
On the wide water laboring, far from home,
For a bleak pittance still compelled to roam;
Few friends to cheer him through his dangerous life,
Or strong to aid him in the stormy strife;
Companion of the Sea and silent air,
The hardy whaleman has no envied fare.
—Anon.

Midway between the False and Main Banks,
Atlantic Ocean, lat. 34° 30' S., lon. 47° W. Homeward Bound.
I like the eagerness and activity, and can very well put up with the smell and dirt which having dead whales alongside makes in a whale ship. We are having enough of it just now. Though not myself head and ears over in blubber-juice like all the rest, nor *in* for any share of the profits, I am taking, perhaps, as curious and eager an interest in the process going on as any one on board. All the ordinary *muxing* and *skimshander* with which active ones keep themselves busy on board whale ships when there is no work to do, are laid aside now. The cooper's driver is merry a-going on the great oil casks; the decks are cluttered, and full of *gurry* and dirt; and every body and every thing is besmeared with oil, and will be so until a strong ley they make from the ashes of the scraps has washed all clean.

It is almost worth taking one cruise in a whale ship to see how they capture and dispose of their gigantic game, and to learn some odd things a man can never know otherwise. Had Noah Webster ever gone a whaling, he would have been able to add some five or six notable and genuine English words to his Dictionary, which may never be known off salt water unless we record them here.

Mux and *skimshander* are the general names by which they express the ways in which whalemen busy themselves when making passages, and in the intervals of taking whales, in working up sperm whales' jaws and teeth and right whale bone into boxes, swifts, reels, canes, whips, folders, stamps, and all sorts of things, according to their ingenuity.

Gurry is the term by which they call the combined water, oil, and dirt that "cutting in" a whale leaves on deck and below. The yellowish stuff

That creams and mantles on a standing pool,

and affords such a favorite, nice comparison, ready to hand, and hackneyed, for writers that want to express the odiousness of moral putrescence and stagnation, is nothing to this *sui generis* composition elaborated in the hold of a whale ship. Hereafter, if any one should wish to illustrate morals by physicals in a way particularly new and original, let him say that the filth and foulness of Mr. So-and-so's mind, or the daily scum and dregs of Mr. Slabbering Editor Such a One, or the hebdomadal black vomit of this and that member of the "Satanic Press," look and smell like *gurry.*

Gally, or *Gallow,* as it is found in Shakspeare, is the term by which they express a whale's being frightened. Thus you often hear "that whale's gallied," as they pronounce it.

Gam is the word by which they designate the meeting, exchanging visits, and keeping company of two or more whale ships, or a sociable family of whales. Thus we *gammed* two days on the New Zealand whaling ground with the Niantic of Sag Harbor. One day the captain of the Niantic spent with us, the next our captain spent on board the Niantic, the boats' crews *gamming* together at the same time in the forecastle, and the mates of the ships meeting and having a *gam* in the ship that was left of her captain.

These *gams* are very pleasant interludes in a whaleman's life, when abroad upon the desert ocean, without change of society or scene, a thousand miles from land. It is peculiarly grateful for a rusty and barnacled old ship, that has been absent thirty or more months, to have

The WHALE & *His captors*

a *gam* of a day with a fresh competitor just arrived out with all the news from home. Such a *gam* gives matter of talk and old newspaper reading for a month, and nobody can tell how pleasant it is but one that has experienced it. A shipmaster has a chance to exchange counsel, and tell stories, and let himself be familiar with somebody that's new, and he is always the milder, and better pleased with himself and all about him, for some days after such a *gam*.

The use of these words is not a little amusing at first to a stranger; but I have come to believe them as good and veritable English, and to have as fair a claim to be placed in our dictionaries as a thousand words that are spoken oftener in ears polite. I like to talk with old whalemen upon the hair-breadth escapes and perilous adventures of their hazardous warfare upon the monsters of the deep. It is a marvel that death, in its most appalling forms, is not oftener met with. Whalers, I think, have to look danger more full and steadily in the face than any other class of men except soldiers.

Danger, whose limbs of giant mold,
What mortal eye can fix'd behold?

Besides the multifarious ordinary perils of the sea, there is that incurred in lowering boats so often; then the risk of being run under and swamped in the lightning-like speed and evolutions of a seventy-foot whale immediately upon being struck; then the danger from a whale's flukes and fins, as the monster slues and slats them round, and makes the deep boil like a pot, to the slightest tap of which a whale-boat is hardly more than a bubble. Sometimes the mammoth brute comes up from the depths right under the boat, and takes it, with all on board, transversely into his huge mouth, that can be opened sixteen and twenty feet. To be sure, the monster does not swallow it, but he crushes it to pieces as if it were an egg-shell, and, not unfrequently, some of its crew at the same time, and this is always to be apprehended.

Sometimes a sperm whale will drive "head on" to his captors with such a speed and force that they can neither prick him off with the lance nor have time to sheer away. A blow that would beat in the oak ribs of a man-of-war would hardly, I suppose, give a bull-whale the headache. There are two cases I have heard of, one in the Atlantic and one in the Pacific, in which an enormous sperm whale, with malice aforethought, did thus run three several times full tilt against a whale ship, until his butting had battered in her sides, and the men had to abandon the ships a thousand miles from land. But three or four survived the peril in each case and got safe to land. One of them, then a boy, is now master of a whale ship, still grappling with dangers, and successfully prosecuting this adventurous trade.

I have known of one captain who was killed instantly in the bow of his boat, by the tap of a whale's fin upon his skull, when no one else was at all injured. To have legs and arms broken, ribs knocked in, and a whole crew scrabbling together in the water, is, as we have already learned, very common. There are few that have been long in the service but have been banged and broken in some way, and snatched often from the gaping jaws of destruction. They can tell of marvelous escapes and providential deliverances from the very throat of death, that make you think a whaler, of all men, ought to be living with his will made, and ready for a sudden summons.

We should naturally think so, and that a man's constant exposedness to sudden death would give a serious turn to his mind, and induce a cast of reflection and thoughtful regard to his latter end. But it is now a long time that the practical observation of men has taught me, that familiarity with danger and death seldom produces a softening, monitory effect, except upon the mind of a Christian, but rather induces a moral hardness and effrontery that steels the mind against lessons of mortality, and sheds an ominous gloom upon the prospects of the soul. I have talked with a good many whalemen and common sailors, and have observed the conduct of irreligious men in times of fatal epidemics and more than ordinary dangers, but I never yet have met with one *permanently* reformed and brought to repentance by seeing others drowned and die before his eyes, and by what would seem to be the natural consideration of danger in his own case.

So true it is, in the words of the preacher, *The heart of the sons of men is full of evil; madness is in their hearts while they live, and after that they go to the dead. As the fishes that are taken in an evil net, and as the birds that are caught in the snare, so are the sons of men snared in an evil time, when it cometh suddenly upon them.* As an old poet hath it,

Such is the state of every mortal wight!
In health our glories and our lusts we show;
We fill ourselves with every vain delight,
And will least think of that which may ensue.
But let us learn to *heed* as well as *know*,
That spring doth pass, that summer steals away,
And that the flower which makes the fairest show,
Ere many weeks may wither and decay.
The stoutest form that walks the earth to-day,
To-morrow with the dead may senseless lay!

XIV

Remarkable Events in the Annals of Whaling

O'er the deep! o'er the deep!
Where the whale, and the shark, and the sword-fish sleep:
On the craggy ice, in the frozen air,
Heedless of dangers if game be but there,
Encountering all the great whale to snare.
—Anon.

The prodigious speed and strength of the gigantic whale, and the resulting danger to his captors referred to, in general terms, in the last chapter, are practically illustrated by two remarkable incidents, occurring, the one in the English, and the other in the American whale fishery.

On the 28th of May, 1817, the *Royal Bounty*, an English ship, fell in with a great number of whales in seventy degrees twenty-five minutes north latitude, and longitude five degrees east. There was neither ice nor land in sight. The boats were manned and sent in pursuit, and after a chase of five hours, one of them, which had rowed out of sight of the ship, struck one of the whales. This was about four o'clock in the morning. The captain directed the course of the ship to the point where he had last seen the boats, and about eight o'clock got sight of one, which displayed the signal of being fast. Soon after, another boat approached the first, and struck a second harpoon; and by midday two more harpoons were made fast.

But such was the astonishing vigor of this whale, that although it constantly dragged through the water from four to six boats, together with sixteen hundred fathoms of line, yet it pursued its flight nearly as fast as a boat could row, and whenever one passed beyond its tail it would dive. All endeavors to lance it were therefore vain, and the crews of the loose boats moored to those that were fast, the whale all the time steadily towing them on.

Polar Whale dragging the Boats of the Bounty.

At eight o'clock in the evening a line was taken to the ship, with a view of retarding its flight, and topsails were lowered, but the harpoon drew. In three hours another line was taken on board, which immediately snapped. At four in the afternoon of the next day, thirty-six hours after the whale was first struck, two of the fast lines were taken on board the ship.

The wind blowing a moderately brisk breeze, the top-gallant-sails were taken in, the courses hauled up, and the top-sails clewed down; yet in this situation she was towed directly to windward, for an hour and a half, with the velocity of one and a half to two knots an hour, the whale all the while beating the water with its fins and tail, so that the sea around was in a continual foam. At length, near eight o'clock, after forty hours of incessant exertion, this tenacious assertor of his vast animal vigor and territorial rights was killed.

There is an instance given by Captain Scoresby where a Greenland whale was at last killed who had drawn out ten thousand four hundred and forty yards, or about six miles of line, attached to fifteen harpoons, besides taking one boat entirely under water, which disappeared and was never seen, the harpoons by which it was held to the whale probably drawing out under the immense pressure, and leaving it to sink, or to rise under the ice.

But the most dreadful display of the whale's strength and prowess yet authentically recorded was that made upon the American whale ship Essex, Captain Pollard, which sailed from Nantucket for the Pacific Ocean in August, 1819. Late in the fall of the same year, when in latitude forty of the South Pacific, a school of sperm whales were discovered, and three boats were manned and sent in pursuit. The mate's boat was struck by one of them, and he was obliged to return to the ship in order to repair the damage.

While he was engaged in that work, a sperm whale, judged to be eighty-five feet long, broke water about twenty rods from the ship, on her weather bow. He was going at the rate of about three knots an hour, and the ship at nearly the same rate, when he struck the bows of the vessel just forward of her chains.

At the shock produced by the collision of two such mighty masses of matter in motion, the ship shook like a leaf. The seemingly malicious whale dove and passed under the ship, grazing her keel, and then appeared at about the distance of a ship's length, lashing the sea with fins and tail, as if suffering the most horrible agony. He was evidently hurt by the collision, and blindly frantic with instinctive rage.

In a few minutes he seemed to recover himself, and started with great speed directly across the vessel's course to the windward. Mean time the hands on board discovered the ship to be gradually settling down at the bows, and the pumps were to be rigged. While working at them, one of the men cried out, "God have mercy! he comes again!"

The whale had turned at about one hundred rods from the ship, and was making for her with double his former speed, his pathway white with foam. Rushing head on, he struck her again at the bow, and the tremendous blow stove her in. The whale dived under again and disappeared, and the ship foundered in ten minutes from the first collision.

After incredible hardships and sufferings in their open boats, on the 20th of December the survivors of this catastrophe reached the low island called Ducies, in latitude twenty-four degrees forty minutes south, longitude one hundred and twenty-four degrees forty

the WHALE *&* his *captors*

minutes west. It was a mere sand-bank, nearly barren, which supplied them only with water and sea-fowl. On this uninhabited island, dreary as it was, three of the men chose to remain, rather than again commit themselves to the uncertainties of the sea. They have never since been heard from, the island being seldom visited.

On the 27th of December, the three boats, with the remainder of the men, put away together for the Island of Juan Fernandez, at a distance of two thousand miles. The mate's boat was taken up by the Indian, of London, on the 19th of February, ninety-three days from the time of the catastrophe, with only three living survivors.

The captain's boat was fallen in with by the Dauphin, of Nantucket, on the 23d of the same month, having only two men living, whose lives had been eked out only through that last resort of hunger in the wretched, which words shudder to relate! Out of a crew of twenty, five only survived to make the ear of the world tingle at their strange, eventful story.

There is one other instance of the immediate shipwreck of a whaler by the shock of those mighty leviathans, that of the Union, of Nantucket, Captain Gardner, which was totally lost, in the year 1807, between Nantucket and the Azores, by a similar concussion. A merchant brig, plying between Panama and one of the ports of Western Mexico, has lately met with the same disaster, but without loss of life, the passengers and crew being all rescued by an American whale ship.

Another form of the perils of whaling is illustrated in the following incidents, taken from an authentic communication in one of the religious newspapers of the day, which we insert here in order to complete this Daguerreotype Gallery of Life and Adventures in a Whale Ship.

A few years ago, the captain of a whale ship was on a cruise in the Pacific Ocean. There were three boats attached to the ship. Early one morning a whale appeared. Two boats were sent to capture it. They fastened to the whale, and were soon drawn by this monster of the deep out of sight of the ship. An hour or two passed along, when, suddenly, another whale rose in the water, but a few rods from the vessel. The temptation to attempt its capture was too strong to be resisted. The captain ordered the remaining boat to be lowered, and, leaving but one man and two boys to take care of the ship, sprang into the boat with the rest of the crew.

Soon the harpoon was plunged into the whale, and they were carried, with almost the speed of the wind, about fifteen miles from the ship. Then the whale plunged perpendicularly down into the depths of the ocean. It was not long ere they saw him, fathoms deep in the crystal waters, rushing up, with open jaws, to destroy the boat. By skillfully sheering the boat, the whale missed his aim, and, thrusting his mammoth head some fifteen or twenty feet into the air, he fell over upon his side, and again disappeared in the fathomless sea. Soon he reappeared in the almost transparent abyss, again rushing upward to attack the boat. Again he was foiled.

The third time he descended, and as he arose, with invigorated fury, he struck the boat in the center of the keel, threw it some fifteen feet into the air, and, scattering the crew and fragments of the boat over the waves, again plunged into the deep and disappeared. The captain and the crew were now in the water, clinging to the pieces of the demolished boat. They were fifteen miles from the ship, and could not be seen from its deck. The other boats were gone, they knew not where. Apparently, every chance of rescue was cut off, and nothing awaited them but a watery grave. It was twelve o'clock at noon. The hours of one, two, three, four, five, and six passed slowly away, and still they were floating, almost exhausted, upon the heaving billows of the Pacific. When the ship rose on the swelling seas, they could just catch a glimpse of her rolling spars.

"Oh! how fervently I prayed," said one of these mariners, when afterward relating the scene, "that God would in some way providentially interpose and save our lives! I thought of my wife, of my little children, of my prayerless life, of the awful account I had to render at the bar of God for grieving the Spirit and neglecting the Savior. All the horrors of this dreadful death were forgotten in the thought, that in one short hour I was to render up an account to God for years of ingratitude and disobedience. Oh! thought I, if I were only a Christian, what a solace would it be to me as I sink into this watery grave!"

The sun had now disappeared behind the distant waves, and the darkening shades of a dreary night were settling down over the ocean. Just then they descried, dim in the dusky distance, one of the absent boats returning to the ship. It was, however, far off, apparently beyond the reach of their loudest outcries. Impelled by the energies of

the WHALE *&* HIS *captors*

Right Whale staving a Boat.

despair, they simultaneously raised a shout, which blended with the wash of the waves and sighing of the breeze, and the boat continued on its way. Again they raised another shout, and it was also unavailing.

The shades of the night were deepening, the boat rapidly passing by them. Almost frenzied at their terrible condition, they raised another cry. The sound of that distant shriek fell faintly upon the ears of the boatmen, and they rested on their oars. Another shout, which almost lacerated their throats, was raised, and the boat turned in pursuit. They were taken from the water, and carried almost lifeless to the ship.

In another authentic instance, when a boat was chasing a whale, he suddenly turned to windward, and made directly for his pursuers, who were so excited by the chase as to be blind to danger. On, therefore, they madly rushed, without trying to avoid the infuriated

Picture of a Whale-boat thrown into a Whale's Mouth.

monster, so eager were they to plunge into him their irons, till the boat struck with such force upon the whale's head as to throw the oarsmen from their thwarts. At the same moment, the boat-steerer let fly his two harpoons into the mammoth body, which rolled over on its back; and before the boat could get clear of danger, being to the windward, a heavy sea struck it and threw them directly into the whale's mouth! All, of course, sprang for their lives, and they had barely time to throw themselves clear of the boat before it was crushed to pieces by those ponderous jaws, and its ejected crew were providentially all picked up by another boat.

Such are the dangers which are continually incurred in the whale fishery, equal almost to those of the field of battle. We often wonder that so many escape with their lives from a battle field; and we equally wonder that, comparatively, so few perish in this most hazardous pursuit. A boat, almost as frail as a bubble, approaches the side of a whale, slumbering upon the ocean, sixty or eighty feet in length, and a harpoon is plunged into his body. His efforts to destroy his tormentors or escape from them, as we have again and again learned, are terrific. The ocean is lashed into foam by blows from his enormous

the WHALE *&* HIS *captors*

flukes, which would almost dash in the ribs of a man-of-war. Often he rushes at the boat with lightning speed and with open jaws, and it is crushed like an egg-shell in his mouth.

In this frightful warfare many are maimed, and many lives are annually lost. But some whales are worth between two and three thousand dollars, and this is majestic game to hunt. He, however, who earns his bread through the perils and hardships of this pursuit, has truly a hard lot in life. He is but a transient visitor at his home. Amid the solitude of the ocean he passes the greater portion of his days; and if he survives the perils of his adventurous pursuit, the storms of the ocean, and the pestilence of different climes, he usually finds that the friends of his youth are all gone, and that he is almost a stranger at his own fireside. And yet this mode of life has its own joys and emoluments, for, if ordinarily successful, in the course of fifteen or twenty years a whaleman will lay up a moderate competence for the rest of his days, and meanwhile, notwithstanding the unfavorable influences which are often at work in the whale ship, many are forming noble characters.

Although it is no genial soil, yet virtue, humanity, true nobility, and the fear of God, *can* live and grow in a whale ship, both fore and aft. I have met them on this present voyage, and in some signal instances elsewhere, which it would be base ingratitude and a denying of God's grace not to acknowledge and give credit for. But who that knows it as I do, would choose a life in a whale ship, or life any where at sea! Who does not rather say, with one that knew whereof he spake,

> Eternal ocean! old majestic sea!
> Ever I love from shore to look on thee
> And sometimes on thy billowy back to ride,
> And sometimes o'er thy summer breast to glide;
> But let me live on land, where rivers run,
> Where shady trees may screen me from the sun
> Where I may feel, secure, the fragrant air;
> Where, whate'er toil or wearying pains I bear,
> Those Eyes which look away all human ill,
> May shed on me their still, sweet, constant light,
> And the hearts I love may, day and night,
> Be found beside me safe and clustering still.

Claims and Advantages of
the Sabbath in a Whale Ship

When the Sabbath's peaceful ray
O'er the ocean's breast doth play,
Though no throngs assemble there,
No sweet church-bells call to prayer,
Spirit! let thy presence be
Sabbath to the mustering sea.
—Mrs. Sigourney.

Atlantic Ocean, Commodore Preble, latitude 32° N.,
longitude 64½° W. Off the Bermudas.

A prime end in the preceding sketches of whaling life has been to prepare the way and secure attention for certain considerations upon the wholesale violation of the Sabbath in this business. By the Whaleman's Shipping List, at the commencement of 1844 or thereabouts, there were employed in the whale fishery, from the ports of the United States, six hundred and seventy-four vessels, five hundred and ninety-three of them then at sea, chiefly from New Bedford, Nantucket, Sag Harbor, New London, Stonington, and Newport.

Allowing for the average thirty souls to a ship, which is a moderate computation, there were then more than twenty thousand persons prosecuting this trade. The number has not diminished since, but has rather increased, until the present year, and it is an estimate much within bounds, that there are now actually employed in this business, from the ports of the United States, eighteen or twenty thousand men. Among them are men of divers trades and nations, but a large majority are citizens of the United States from remote inland and sea-port towns.

Their characters and relative degrees of intelligence and moral worth are different, as are their origin and education. Some are of vicious, low stock, vicious education, and an incurable addictedness to vice. Others are of good families, from religious communities, sons of Christians, and have been taught to fear God and keep his commandments. A few of them profess godliness. All of them are alike in this, that they are rational, accountable men, under obligation to keep God's law, and having man's natural right to and need of the Sabbath for rest and religious worship.

But what is the law to which they are all alike subjected in whale ships? With very few exceptions, to be stated in their place, it is a law that *acknowledges no Sabbath*, but compels them to labor alike on the seventh day and all days, in order to capture whales and fill their ship. I repeat it, for the information of those whom it may concern, *there is no Sabbath known in the whale fishery.*

As generally conducted, it makes eighteen or twenty thousand habitual Sabbath-breakers. Men are kept at the fore and main mast heads, boats are lowered, whales are taken and "cut in," and all the work incident thereto is done on the Sabbath just as much as on any day, and this without the pretence of a plea of necessity, as in working a ship, but solely in order to "fill up" as soon as possible, and return to port with a cargo, taken as it comes, it matters not how, whether in those sacred hours which the easy owner ashore has been spending at church, or in the busy week days which he devotes to the counting-room, or farm, or workshop.

Owners, too, know this when their ships go from port, are generally willing it should be so, are averse to have it otherwise. Owners, captains, officers, and men are alike the willing participators in this gross violation of the Lord's day, for the sake of the gain they think it brings them; else either of these parties, by asserting their right to the Sabbath, and refusing to own or sail in ships that violate it, could easily prevent it.

But while there is an individual participation in this sin, the guilt of it rests especially upon owners and captains, and it is they who are chargeable with it, and who are to be arraigned at the bar of public opinion, as they will be at the tribunal of Almighty God. It is they whom we charge with being at the bottom of a systematic and most gross violation of one of the plainest commands of the Decalogue, and with willfully involving a great many others, willingly or not, in the same sin.

The only pretexts of reason we have ever heard urged to defend it are, This is the business by which I get a livelihood for myself and family. If I neglect to take whales when God offers them, my family and employers will be likely to suffer for it. I am necessarily absent a long time from home, and I ought to use every means in my power to shorten that time, and secure a voyage for myself and owners. If I do not lower for whales when they are in sight, the Sabbath will be more desecrated by the men's grumbling than it would be by cheerful labor in taking whales. The business of whaling is of such a precarious nature, that, unless all chances are seized, successful voyages will not be made; therefore it is necessary also to use the Sabbath in this work when Providence presents the game. No one regards the Sabbath more than I do when ashore, but my business exempts me from the obligation of such a strict observance of it at sea.

Now to all these specious efforts at self-justification, which we have heard put forth at different times and by different persons, and to every other of a similar sort, it is enough to reply, first, that there is no lawful worldly calling, except that whose immediate end is to relieve human suffering, or minister instruction and comfort to the soul, which it is right to pursue on the Sabbath. *Six days shalt thou labor and do all thy work. But the seventh is the Sabbath of the Lord thy God: in it thou shalt not do any work, thou, nor thy son, nor thy daughter, thy man-servant, nor thy maidservant, nor thy cattle, nor thy stranger that is within thy gates. For in six days the Lord made heaven and earth, and all that in them is, and rested the seventh day: wherefore the Lord blessed the Sabbath day, and hallowed it.*

2. God has revealed no indulgence in favor of Sabbath whaling, any more than to Sabbath-breaking railroad companies, steamboat, canal, or stage lines, or Sunday manufactories. Show us a single Divine statute of limitation yielding the privilege of Sabbath violation in but one clear case, and we will yield the argument.

3. The assertion, that if the Sabbath is not improved for getting whales, the voyage will be likely to prove a failure, is a mere assumption, for prosperous voyages have been and may be made, and ships filled, without a whale being struck on the Lord's day. What has proved true in one instance, other things being equal, there is reason to believe would prove true in all.

The WHALE *&* His *captors*

4. The obligation of the Sabbath is universal, and extends to all men alike, on the sea and land. The Sabbath was made for man universally, as a worker, under all circumstances. By man, therefore, it is to be always kept. It was given to the race by God for rest and holy worship, and every individual of the human race, to whom the law comes, is bound so to use it.

5. The man who conscientiously takes care to have the Sabbath sanctified by himself, and family, and dependents, will be likely to have his family blessed and taken care of by the Sabbath's almighty Lord. *Godliness is profitable for all things, having promise of the life that now is and of that which is to come. In keeping God's commandments there is exceeding great reward.*

6. It is better to obey God and please him, than to attempt to please men and get the favor of owners by taking oil for them on the Sabbath, in direct violation of a positive law of God, made for the good of all men, and in harmony with the human constitution.

7. It were better, if need be, to have a voyage prolonged, and then come back with a clear conscience and God's blessing, than to return sooner a Sabbath breaker, with the ill-gotten gains of Sabbath whaling, and a conscience defiled or seared by sin.

8. If men grumble, and swear, and sin because I do not order boats to be lowered on the Sabbath day, it is *their* look-out and blame. If *I* have boats lowered, it is *mine*, and God will not hold me guiltless.

9. It is an unfounded presumption that a steady and well-grounded refusal to have nothing to do with Sabbath whaling *will* produce discontent among the men. Experience has proved that they like the rest of the Sabbath as well as any other men, and are glad enough to have it theirs for a constancy, though they would like now and then to improve any rare chance offered on that day as well as on any other.

10. If no look-out is kept for whales on the Sabbath, but the day is devoted to rest, they will not often be seen that day, so as to be an occasion of discontent. These two last propositions are drawn from the experience of this ship, the Commodore Preble, during its present Sabbath-keeping voyage, and will, I am well convinced, be found true of every ship that shall try the experiment. The captain became persuaded at the Sandwich Islands that he would be wrong and without

excuse to whale any more on the Sabbath, and with a new heart he resolved to do so no more.

He took one season afterward on the Northwest, but, for reasons which it were easy to mention, not the least of which was not being well officered or manned for Northwest whaling, the ship did not succeed so well as many others. Several boats were stove early in the season, some of the men got upset and frightened, towlines parted, and many things went ill; but, so far from repenting of his purpose to keep the Sabbath, he is more strong in it than ever, well persuaded and well content that, if God do not pay him in oil here, durable riches and righteousness are his in heaven.

It should be mentioned, in passing, to the honor of Lynn, that the only two whale ships, of which this is one, that hail from that port, now keep the Sabbath. The heaviest owner in them is a religious man, who says he does not want any oil taken on the Sabbath. There is another from New London, the Nantasket, Captain Smith, and others, it is to be supposed, with which the writer is not acquainted.

It is painful to have to record the pitifully different course of another captain from New Bedford, a professor of religion and esteemed a good man. He was convinced and felt that it was wrong to whale on the Sabbath, and when he last went from the Sandwich Islands to the Northwest Coast, he proposed in his mind not to. For two Sabbaths he held out, and on one of them saw whales. By the time the next Sabbath came round they had done but little; he felt uneasy, could not stay below or on deck with any comfort, his mind running upon whales.

At length, *to get relief,* instead of betaking himself more earnestly to prayer and the Word of God, he ordered his mate to send a couple of men aloft, and when they sang out for whales, he lowered his boats and his purpose to keep the Sabbath at the same time. Blubber came in in abundance, and with it came occupation and content, purchased, I need not say, how poorly. He soon filled up and went home, even throwing overboard some provisions to give place to oil.

This story of his experience he told himself, while all the time acknowledging it was not right, his principle and conscience not being strong enough to carry out his convictions of duty, and keep him from acknowledged sin. On the other hand, a pious sailor, recently

the WHALE *&* HIS *captors*

returned from a two years' voyage, says that thirty whales were taken by his ship's crew during their absence. Three of these, to his sorrow, were taken on the Sabbath. But in taking these three, five boats were destroyed and five men were seriously wounded, two having their limbs broken, and one his skull fractured. In taking the remaining twenty-seven whales on the other days of the week, only four boats were injured, and one man slightly hurt.

Now it needs not that we say positively of so easy a professor and loose a conscience as that of the New Bedford captain just now referred to, that such a man can not be a Christian, or to deny that he may be saved so as by fire. But certain it is, it were a pity for the world if the goodness in it, and fear of God, and practical regard to principle and duty, were no stronger than this man's. The devil might keep it for all such Christians a thousand years longer, and we don't know that he would want any better agents than such pliable professors, that seem to take gain for godliness, and make a "gospel of their maw."

Such men will do well to read and ponder the following extract from the Narrative of an Expedition to the Sources of the Mississippi, by Henry Schoolcraft: "No Sabbath day was employed in traveling. It was laid down as a principle to rest on that day, and whenever it overtook us, whether on land or on water, the men knew that their labor would cease, and that the day would be given them for rest. Such of them as felt an inclination, had the further privilege of hearing a portion of the Scriptures read or expounded, or uniting in other devotional rites. There were but a few hours of a single morning and a few hours of a single evening, of separate Sabbaths, at distant points, which were necessarily employed in reaching particular places; and the use of these appeared to be unavoidable, under the peculiar circumstances of our local position.

"It may, perhaps, be thought, that the giving up one seventh part of the whole time employed on a public expedition, in a very remote region, and with many men to subsist, must have, in this ratio, increased the time devoted to the route. But the result was far otherwise. The time devoted to recruit the men not only gave the surgeon of the party an opportunity to heal up the bruises and chafings they complained of, but it replenished them with strength; they commenced the week's labor with renewed zest, and this zest was in a measure kept up by the reflection that the ensuing Sabbath would be a day of rest. It was found, by computing the whole route, and comparing the time employed with that which had been devoted on similar routes in this part of the world, that *an equal space had been gone over in less time than it had ever been known to be performed by loaded canoes or (as the fact is) by light canoes before.* And the whole expedition—its incidents and results—has been of a character furnishing strong reasons for uniting in ascriptions of praise to that Eternal Power who hath been our shield from *the pestilence that walketh in darkness, and from the destruction that wasteth at noon day."*

We have become acquainted with the names or persons of nine men belonging to the Church, masters of whale ships, and but three of these keep the Sabbath. Some of the reasons for this desecration of the Lord's day by whale ships, or the causes of it, we will endeavor to give in another chapter; and we close this with a voice of good cheer to upright Sabbath-keeping whalemen, as heard in the stirring Mariner's Hymn by Mrs. Southey:

Launch thy bark, mariner!
    Christian, GOD speed thee!
Let loose the rudder bands—
    Good angels lead thee!
Set thy sails warily,
    Tempests will come;
Steer thy course steadily,
    Christian, steer home!

Slacken not sail yet
    At inlet or island;
Straight for the beacon steer,
    Straight for the highland:
Crowd all the canvass on,
    Cut through the foam—
Christian! cast anchor now—
    Heaven is thy home!

XVI

A Plea in Behalf of the
Sabbath for Whalemen

What says the prophet? let that day be bless'd
With holiness and consecrated rest.
Pastime and business both it should exclude,
And bar the door the moment they intrude;
Nobly distinguished above all the six,
By deeds in which the world must never mix.
Hear him again! he calls it a delight,
A day of luxury, observed aright;
When the glad soul, made heaven's own willing guest,
Sits banqueting, and God provides the feast.
—Cowper.

The all-inclusive cause which perpetuates and lies at the bottom of
Sabbath whaling, is that which upholds and furnishes the stimulus
to almost all other forms of Sabbath breaking, the odious slave-trade,
&c.—I mean the lust of lucre, that deified greedy Devil of gain that in
the end troubleth *his own house.* Whaling captains and owners are
seldom willing, for the honor of GOD or regard to his law, to forego the
profits which they think accrue from Sabbath whaling; and therefore,
once at sea on whaling ground, they are unwilling to stop and take
breath for a long Lord's day.

Oil got on the Sabbath burns as well, sells as well, and, they think,
spends as well as oil got lawfully on week days. Not to use the Sabbath
in their gainful business, they think, would be losing one seventh part
of their time, neglecting one seventh of their chances, keeping them
one seventh longer out, consuming one seventh more provisions, ex-
hausting one seventh more of patience and spirits, and perhaps, in
the end, leaving them with one seventh less of oil than ships that use

all days alike, and one seventh less of every thing but a good conscience and the favor of God.

To balance these, we have only to offer, without swelling the list, as might easily be done, with other items, that keeping the Sabbath would be likely to make whalers three sevenths better and more respectable men, three sevenths more easy and peaceful in their minds, and one seventh the longer lived than those who persist in profaning God's holy day; and it would make owners at home all the better Christians, or more likely subjects of the grace of God here, and with less to answer for at the great bar of judgment hereafter.

At present it is said by many whaling captains, that their owners absolutely require whaling on the Sabbath, as one of the conditions on which they give them command of their ships. It is also said that many of these ship-owners are members of evangelical churches in Nantucket, New Bedford, Fair Haven, Sag Harbor, New London, Warren, Newport, Stonington, and other places. Some owners say nothing to their captains on the subject; but if their ships do but return *full*, no inquiries are made how or on what days the oil was obtained.

Now and then a shrewd Yankee captain *guesses that his pious owners have no objections to his taking oil when he can get it*. A full ship fills the heart with joy, and lights up the countenance with an approving and benignant smile; while a half-filled ship often clouds the brow, deranges the spleen, obstructs the biliary ducts, and stops the joyful and generous action of the heart. Especially would this be so had the crew of the half-filled ship been permitted to rest one day in the seven, according to the commandment.

Occasionally a master, an officer, or a sailor hints that he would be glad to rest on the Sabbath, according to the dictates of his conscience; but this he may not do, except at the risk of losing his ship and being thrown out of employment, and he will therefore conclude that Sabbath whaling with him, at least, is a work of necessity.

Rev. Titus Coan, an honored missionary at the Sandwich Islands, who has had much to do practically with whalemen, says, with not less truth than with a justifiable irony, that there are some captains "who will consent to be very pious and hold religious meetings on the Sabbath *when there are no whales*. Of course, they always keep a man at 'mast head,' on the 'lookout' for the oil of joy to the whalemen, while the rest *look up* for 'an unction from the Holy One;' or, in other words, one man looks out for *worldly*, while the rest look up for *heavenly* good. Now should it so happen that the prayer of this MAST-HEAD MINISTER should be first granted, by raising a whale during divine service, and should he, from his lofty pulpit, cry out, 'There she blows!' then what a thrill of joy electrifies all his hearers! How soon the lesser desire yields to the greater! How quick and how thrilling the response from the quarter-deck, 'WHERE AWAY? LOWER THE BOATS! BEAR AHAND, BOYS!'

"Now the scene changes. Devotion does not *cease*, but it is turned into *another channel*. Prayer, reading, sacred melody, exhortation, all give place to the weightier matter of pursuing this MOVING SEA-GOD! *The object* of devotion thus changed, interest, zeal, fervor, energy, are all quickened and strongly developed.

"True, most irreligious men ridicule this kind of piety, and heartily despise its selfishness and inconsistency; and Lord's-day whalemen often complain that it is hard to maintain religion, and especially so to keep up divine service at sea. No doubt it *is* hard, and perhaps it is *impossible*, to exercise *true religion* in connection with Sabbath breaking.* The two can not be reconciled. No man can serve two masters. *Ye can not serve God and mammon.*"

*A clergyman was once invited to preach on board a whale ship. The hour for service having arrived, Captain —— said to the officer of the deck, "Mr. ——, call all hands aft." The crew were soon assembled in the cabin. An "old salt" remaining behind, the captain inquired, "Where is S——?" "Down in the hold, sir; says he won't come to meeting, sir." He was then called again, but to no effect. He had gone down into the blubber-hold, and there intrenched himself, like a giant in his castle or a lion in his lair. He was reasoned with, but all to no purpose. He refused to be routed. There, in his den, he sat; and in his den he growled defiance: "I won't come up!" On this the officer left him, and reported to the captain.

The clergyman now asked the liberty to go himself and invite the old man in the blubber-hold. This granted, he proceeded to the hatchway, and kindly invited the iron-hearted tar to come up and attend service. For a moment the old man was silent; but it was only the silence of a dark cloud while it gathers strength for a burst and a roar. At length he raised his stern brow, and, with a look of defiance, brawled out, "No! I won't go!"

A gentle effort was then made to soften his rigid nerves; but Jack was not to be taken either by storm or by stratagem. Again he roared out, "I tell you, no! I won't go there!" On being asked the reasons for his prejudice against religious services, he again thundered

Another reason why the taking of whales is prosecuted so generally on the Sabbath as well as other days is, the neglect of ministers in whaling ports to apply God's law to Sabbath whaling. Captains at the Sandwich Islands, who have been remonstrated with by faithful ministers there, have said, "We never heard our ministers at home preach so against Sabbath whaling." And it has even been intimated that a clergyman, who should be faithful in reproving for this sin, would not be endured long in any of our whaling ports.

Now, though a poor excuse, this, we believe, is in fact true. Whether, by reason of mere apathy or inattention, this form of Sabbath breaking not being before their eyes; or, holding, as some do, that we are only to preach principles, and let them apply themselves; or, as fearing to offend wealthy parishioners, whose support the Church can not well spare—from one or all of these reasons combined, ministers in whaling ports (unless we have been greatly misinformed) have had little or nothing to say upon the sin of Sabbath whaling; and their parishioners have, consequently, kept on owning and sailing in Sabbath-breaking ships, kept in countenance by their own minister's silence, which has (emphatically to them) spoken consent.

It can hardly help reflecting upon the fidelity of clergymen at whaling ports, in some of which there have been of late years powerful revivals of religion, that ship-masters, officers, and men, converted in those very revivals, have gone out upon the high seas organized companies of Sabbath breakers. Surely, if there be the least propriety in speaking of a *slave-holding Christianity*, this may as well be called a *Sabbath-breaking Christianity*. But no! there is no propriety in either, when we call things by their right names. There *can* be such a strange anomaly as *slave-holding, Sabbath-breaking Christians*, but there is no slaveholding or Sabbath-breaking *Christianity*. She alike eschews both, as utterly at war with her doctrines and requisitions. They are both alike an incubus *upon* her, not her offspring.

---

out, "I don't want any of Captain ——'s religion! One Sunday it is all preach and pray, and the next Sunday it is *work! work! Catch whales! catch whales!* No! I won't go aft to meeting; and that's all about it!" The result of this interview was reported to the captain, the services proceeded, and old Jack remained in the blubber-room.

—*The Sailor's Sabbath: a Tract.* By Rev. Titus Coan. Honolulu, Oahu. Published by the Hawaiian Tract Society.

the WHALE *&* his *captors*

At the best, they are but temporary moles and blemishes upon her fair person, which time, together with her own internal purity and energy of constitution, will soon wash off and make to disappear. They are deforming excrescences upon the noble tree of the American Church, which, unless they be soon cut off, may produce the vegetable gangrene or dry rot. But never call them *her* limbs or leaves, for she indignantly denies the parentage, and asserts that they have fastened *on* her like leeches, but are not *of* her; and she protests that it would be as unfair to call the monarch oak by some parasitical vine that now and then coils over it, as to give herself epithets from the heresies and misdeeds that have so struck their roots into her bark as to be nourished by her juices.

Rather let it be our business to pull off the unnatural growth, or purge it with the physic of truth till it dies and drops away of itself, than to derive epithets to Christianity from slave-holders or Sabbath breakers, or any other class of sinners that contrive to shelter themselves under its lea. It is the duty especially of ministers in the ports where whalers are fitted out, to bring the law of God to bear upon this form of Sabbath breaking; to apply it pointedly and plainly to this sin, and to preach and pray against it till it shall cease to be allowed by owners in their congregations, or committed by persons going forth from their communities.

Let them, as the constituted expounders of the law of God, and the guardians of public morals and religion, boldly attack this sin, and show its contrariety to the Divine law and the Gospel of Christ. Let ministerial associations and societies, formed to promote the better observance of the Lord's day, pass resolutions expressing their sense of this sin. Let fathers, whose sons go down upon the sea in ships, protest against a practice by which those sons are rendered Sabbath breakers, and the high, homebred estimate in which they have been taught to hold that sacred day obliterated, and the way opened for any and all degrees of moral depravation to which that sin is the natural initiation.

Let ship-owners, as they fear God and have a regard to the judgment, separate themselves from this iniquity by positively instructing their agents not to whale on the Sabbath day. We call upon captains and officers to exercise the manly independence and regard for their rights to say that they will not sail except in Sabbath-keeping ships; and we call upon the men to stipulate beforehand that they shall be allowed the rest of the Sabbath. We call upon the editors of respectable journals, in whaling ports and elsewhere, to discuss the propriety of this practice. We ask religious men and good citizens there to express, in the intercourse of private life, their sense of the wrongfulness of so plain a desecration of the Christian Sabbath.

It is every where popular, at this day, to praise our Puritan ancestry, and, under God, to ascribe our liberty, and every thing that is dear to us, to their high principles and their conscientious practical regard to right. But with how many, it is to be feared, is it like the Jews building the sepulchres of the prophets, or like the base Athenians giving the hemlock to the virtuous living Socrates, and decreeing a statue and panegyric to upright Phocion, whom they had themselves put to death.

For it has come to pass that an institution which our fathers held in highest reverence and kept with strictest care, is now, both by precept and political statute and example, sadly desecrated, and that, too, with a boldness and publicity that prove how wide and general is our departure, both from their stern principles and severe Christian morals. A noble New England ancestry is justly a nation's boast; nor can the praise of our pious forefathers ever become too popular, or their memory be held in too high regard; but we would like better to witness a revival of their grave manners, and to see a holier regard paid to that sacred institution which they prized and guarded above all others, and therefore have we endeavored to draw attention to one form of its desecration, that is doing not a little to vitiate public morals, and impair that high sense of the Sabbath's sacredness which it is of vital importance to *have* maintained.

If the spirits of some of those upright old Puritans were now again to come among us, and see the whale ships of New England unscrupulously profaning God's holy day, steamboats and locomotives running, and stagecoaches carrying the Sabbath mail, would they not be likely to reproach us in accommodated language like this? In vain we made ourselves exiles, for conscience and the love of God, from the servile kingdoms of Europe. In vain we crossed the boisterous ocean, found a new world, and prepared it for the happy residence of civil and re-

the WHALE & *his captors*

ligious liberty. In vain we toiled; we bled in vain, if you, our offspring, thus need principle and purpose to maintain inviolate the sanctity of the Sabbath, and to defend the observance of that hallowed institution, which we kept so strictly, against the encroachments of hurrying worldliness and greedy gain. The blessed institutions we transmitted you can not long survive the desecration of that holy day, when, too, the penitentiaries and pauper-houses of Europe are disgorging upon your fair domain. Up, and rescue it from profanation, or your precious patrimony of liberty is gone!

The veteran Captain Scoresby, who, by age, and experience, and judgment, is entitled to speak on this subject with authority (having gone through twenty-eight of those perilous voyages successfully, and killed four hundred and ninety-eight whales), says that, in the Greenland whale fishery, much more perplexing, and more subject to sudden embarrassments and dangers than the voyages commonly pursued, "I have known public worship to be carried on so regularly that never a Sabbath passed over, for several years together, without one or more full services being performed. During these voyages severe gales have commenced on the Sunday; dangers from rocks, ice, and lee shores have threatened; frequent embarrassments from thick weather have occurred; yet time and opportunity were always found for the worship of God. The success of the voyage often seemed to be in the way, duty to the owners of the ship seemed to forbid, yet we persevered in waiting upon God, and certain I am that we found his blessing.

"At three bells (half past nine A.M.) every Sabbath morning, the hands were 'turned up' to prepare themselves for the forenoon service; then, according to the state of the weather, or the accommodations we had in the ship, the church was either 'rigged' upon deck, or arrangements made for divine worship below. At eleven the service commenced, and generally concluded a few minutes after twelve. From the calling of all hands until this time, every man was on Sabbath-day duty; and, although no man was *made* to join in the prayers against his will, yet he had only this option, either *to watch* or *to pray*.

"Before each of our services, whenever the weather was at all unsettled, the ship was put under a somewhat snug sail, and, the deck being left to the charge of the proper officer of the watch, with the

View of a Sabbath-keeping Whale Ship.

assistance of the helmsman, all the rest of the crew, or nearly all, could generally be spared to join the public prayers. When, indeed, there was any probability of squalls, or of any change being requisite in the sails, some few of the proper watch were placed within obser- vation of the officer on deck, so as to be easily called up without dis- turbing their comrades. But, if circumstances required, though for several years no such case occurred, the officer had orders to call up all hands to assist him.

"To the end of furthering the important object of sanctifying the Sabbath, it is good to remember it before it arrives. Prepare for the day of rest, as far as you can, on the Saturday. Let your men have time on Saturday evening for those needful acts of personal clean- liness which are better performed then than in the morning, so that the Lord's day be not unnecessarily broken in upon by these prepa- rations. In every nautical duty which requires attention on Sunday morning, bear in mind the hours fixed for divine worship, that every work which can possibly be anticipated may be completed. If your flying sails be taken in, your retirement will be more comfortable and secure, and you will seldom or never find the loss in your voyage. The

The WHALE *&* HIS *captors*

Lord's blessing will abundantly recompense this and every sacrifice made for his sake.

"Then call your men together, as far as possible, at the appointed hour, either in the cabin or on the deck, as may be most comfortable. Again, in the afternoon, let your crew and passengers, if any, have the opportunity of worshiping the Most High God, who made the heavens, the earth, and the wide sea; and, whether it be convenient to have any other service for the benefit of your apprentices or not, you will find it a good thing thus to wait upon the Lord. You will experience a benefit temporally as well as spiritually; your people will be more orderly and respectful, and Almighty God will be your shield and your exceeding great reward. *Yea, if thou acquaint thyself with him and return unto him, the Almighty shall be thy defense; for then shalt thou delight thyself in the Almighty, and shalt lift up thy face unto God; and thou shalt make thy prayer unto him, and he shall hear thee.*"

Now what rational subject of Almighty God can doubt this, having for it HIS own WORD! And what ship-master or common mariner will turn a leaden ear to this testimony and expostulation of one of their own craft, to whom a long and varied experience gives a right to be heard and regarded. Considerations like these, we fully believe, will yet have their weight upon owners, officers, and men. The sea shall yet have its Sabbath; the holy Lord's day shall be rescued from profanation by the great whaling and merchant fleets; the abundance of the seas shall be converted to God, and to the observance especially of this great ordinance of creation's Lord, THOU SHALT REMEMBER THE SABBATH DAY TO KEEP IT HOLY.

There's a good time coming for seamen, and that, we trust, not far. We thankfully recognize the law of progress and reform as true of them, and already remarkably developed in this day. We gladly share in the cheering faith of Dr. Bushnell, that the time is at hand when all that pertains to commerce is to be sanctified by virtue and religion, as of right it should be; "when commerce itself shall become religious, and religion commercial; when the mariners will be blended with all the other worshipers on shore, in the exercise of common privileges, and as members of a common brotherhood; when the ships will have their Sabbath, and become temples of praise on the deep; when habits of temperance and banks for saving will secure them in thrift, and assist to give them character; when they will no more live an unconnected, isolated, and therefore reckless life, but will have their wives and children vested here and there, in some neat cottage among the hills, to be to them, when abroad, the anchor of their affections, and the security of their virtue; when they will go forth also to distant climes and barbarous shores, with all their noble and generous traits sanctified by religion, to represent the beauty of Christ to men, and become examples of all that is good and beneficent in his Gospel. Be it ours to aid a purpose so desirable, theirs to realize it in their conduct and character."

Realized, we believe, it will be in the world's cheering progress, and that ere long, when MARINERS shall be missionaries from shore to shore, *from the river to the ends of the earth*; when the isles shall wait God's law at their hands, and continents, long wrapped in the darkness of paganism, shall be thrown wide open to messengers of salvation, borne and backed by those that *go down to the sea in ships, and do business in the great waters*!

> Lord! for those days we wait; those days
>   Are in thy word foretold.
> Fly swifter, sun and stars, and bring
>   This promised age of gold.
>
> Peace, with her olive crown, shall stretch
>   Her wings from shore to shore;
> The nations of the earth shall hear
>   The sound of war no more.
>
> Beneath the influence of HIS grace,
>   The barren waste shall rise,
> With sudden green and fruits array'd—
>   A blooming Paradise.
>
> Then shall bless'd seamen sing and tell
>   Of all Emanuel's love!
> AND SEA AND LAND, IN SABBATH LIGHT,
> SHALL SHINE LIKE HEAVEN ABOVE!

XVII

Nearing Home and
Analogies from the Sea

When one returneth from a distant land,
    Where he hath been in pilgrimage afar,
And seeks once more, his wanderings done, to stand
    Beneath the brightness of his country's star,
It is with beating heart and joyful eyes
    He views the long-remember'd scenes again,
The mountains far, ascending to the skies,
    The verdant hills more near, the flowering plain,
    The willow-shaded stream, the fields of golden grain.
—T.C.U.

Inside Nantucket Shoals.

If a man be coming off a long voyage, or from a lengthened absence in any foreign land, without having been so fixed as to allow of a frequent interchange of letters with those that are dear to him, he must be singularly stupid not to have throng thick into his mind many thoughts, hopes, and fears, imaginations and apprehensions, as he nears his native shores. There are few so alone in the world as not to have some dear friends to love and be anxious about; and two or three years will often make sad ravages in even the smallest circles. All this every one that has had much experience of life's realities thinks about, and hopes, and fears; and the flutter of blended anxiety and joy increases the nearer one gets to his fatherland.

Moreover, it is true, as matter of fact, that dangers actually multiply as you make the land; and you think how many events may step yet between you and home; and you remember how many that have braved the dangers of foreign travel, and remote, inhospitable seas, have been lost in returning, on the rocks and breakers of their own rude coast. You call to mind those lines of Dante:

For I have seen the bark, that all day long
Sail'd straight and steady, perish at last,
Even in the haven's mouth!

There is not a captain out of Massachusetts Bay, coming in from the southward and eastward, from a long voyage, a little in doubt, perhaps, about his chronometer, that does not dread to cross that fog-covered George's Bank, between Scylla on one side and Charybdis on the other, the George's Shoal on the right, and that fatal Nantucket South Shoal on the left.

We suddenly emerged from the warm water of the Gulf Stream right into the mist and cold of George's Bank, and a heavy northeast gale, in which we had to lay to during a most tempestuous night, and were drifted a long ways to leeward, so as to be in no little danger, uncertain as we needs must be of our whereabouts, and our sails being so old and rotten that it would have been impossible to beat off a lee shore. (Another ship and two schooners were wrecked upon the shoal in this same gale.) Day before yesterday there were occasional glimpses of the sun, just enough to give us doubtful observations, as his disk could be caught behind the dense flying scud,

Dim through the horizontal misty air,
Shorn of his beams.

But there has been blue sky visible only once since getting out of the Gulf. It was a dense Scotch mist, or else a downright rain all the time, and quite as cold here in May as off Cape Horn in January.

Sabbath night, however, after a day of almost entire calm,

Sounding on our dim and perilous way,

through fog and cold, a favorable breeze sprang up at eight in the evening, by favor of which we passed safely those dangerous shoals when we could not see them, trusting only to lead and line. From our position at that time we steered first northeast, then north-northeast, then north, then north-northwest, then northwest, so rounding those obscure and formidable dangers, sounding every hour.

This morning the light broke clear and cold, and it has been a glorious day. We made the dear land of New England about three in the

The WHALE *&* HIS *captors*

afternoon. Not long after we discovered Chatham light-house all as we desired, and have been gladly running up Pilgrim land ever since, until now, at nine o'clock, the noble, large, and steady light of Cape Cod bears about west.

The weary, weather-worn company in the May Flower, we have just been saying, had no such friendly beacons as this to shed light on their way when they came as pilgrims to a rock-bound and rude land. It is spring, too, with us, but we remember,

> That through *her* chafed and moaning shrouds *December's*
>   breezes wailed.
> Yet on that icy deck, behold! a meek but dauntless band,
> Who, for the right to worship God, have left their native land,
> And to a dreary wilderness this glorious boon they bring,
> A CHURCH WITHOUT A BISHOP, AND A STATE WITHOUT A
>   KING.

I preached for the last time, it is likely, at sea, yesterday afternoon. This evening we have had a very happy prayer-meeting, and probably our final one on shipboard. The captain, a boat-steerer, one of the fore-mast hands, and myself, led each successively in fervent supplication and thanks to the throne of grace. The two first have been converted during this absence from home, and they return evidently regenerated by the grace of God. Would that every *professing* ship-master gave as good evidence of *possessing* the reality of religion as ours.

When, lately, we were in the midst of a herd of sperm whales, it was my inward earnest prayer that God would give him good success in their capture, in order that he might yet realize a profitable voyage for his owners at its close, and enter port with a full ship, after all its first losses and misfortunes. Through no fault of his, however, this was not so to be. But the voyage has been productive to him, personally, of a better portion than many ship-loads all of spermaceti, for he has found during the course of it, and partly through the very discipline of disappointment, the pearl of great price, which he would not now part with for the wealth of the Indies or all California's gold. May he only keep it always, and find it to yield him a constant revenue of peace and joy!

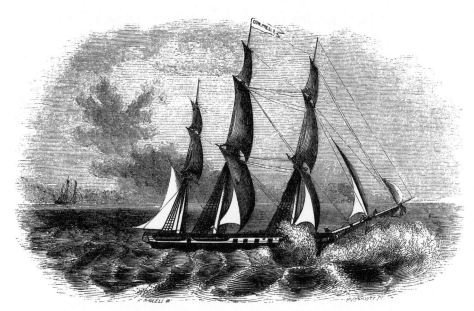

Picture of the Com. Preble Homeward Bound.

We have prayed and labored long in hope of a work of grace in the forecastle; but the power and mercy of God have not been shown that way, and there the men remain, and officers too, *dead in trespasses and sins*; hardened, I fear, by the very means of grace they have slighted, and the invitations and pleadings they have scorned. Alas! it is they only that will be the sufferers, as it is they only who are to blame for neglecting so great salvation!

We are trusting now, in God's good providence, to hail Boston Light by to-morrow evening, rejoicing and thankful to say once more,

This is my own, my native land!

To God be our grateful acknowledgments for all the mercies of this pleasant voyage, two hundred and thirty-six days to-morrow from the Sandwich Islands, eighty from Rio de Janeiro, where we put in for supplies.

The engrossing earnestness with which our captain, for a few days past, has studied the chart and watched the soundings, in order to make his way safely to port, may teach a lesson, I have thought, of the way in which we should all study and watch the answers of God's

the WHALE *&* HIS *captors*

word and prayer as we prosecute the voyage of life, having to steer by a thousand rocks, and shoals, and quicksands before we can make the port of peace. He would himself carefully put the tallow or soap into the hollowed end of the *lead*, then heave it himself, or hold the line, and carefully ascertain when it reached the bottom; then he would scrutinize it closely when hauled up, to see what report it brought from the bottom, whether it were sand, or gravel, or mud, or ooze adhering to the end, or whether it were dented, as if it had fallen on rocks.

Then he would go and sit down to his chart, with compass, and slate, and slide, to compare what he had found with what he was told there, in order to fix, if possible, upon his position on the great shoal, and shape his course accordingly for the next hour. Then he would lay down on the transom, in his great watch-coat, to catch half an hour's sleep, with the chart unrolled before him on the cabin table, and a lantern swinging over it with a sperm candle, a thing we had not had before for the voyage.

Now with the same carefulness, it has seemed to me, should we all ponder the Word of God, that we may be shaping our course aright over the tempestuous sea of life, where

Dangers of every shape and name
Attend the followers of the Lamb.

Yea, not only when we are exceedingly tossed with a tempest, and neither sun nor stars for many days do appear, but in the clearest weather and the best of times, how seldom is it, in our navigation for eternity, that we are not in peril from some out-jutting reef, or shoal, or sunken rock, or moving quicksand; to avoid which we must heave the lead and watch our soundings, and study well the *Chart*, and trim our sails, and keep a good look-out. I thank God that our captain, Lafayette Ludlow, has done both on the present voyage.

With the same steadiness and absorption that he now studied his chart, and worked and reworked his observations, and compared and reviewed his results, he used to study and pray over the divine Word till God showed him the way of salvation by faith in Christ, and he got his anchor on the promises, that proved good holding ground. I trust he will keep *fast* to them for life, be buoyed up by them in death, and afterward be received up unto glory, where faith is met with fruition, and the ransomed of the Lord return and come to Zion with songs of everlasting joy. May he and I, and those who are dear to me, and many that have followed us, it may be with interest, through this gallery of Daguerreotypes, be found in that blessed company when the voyage of life is up!

> When, soon or late, we reach that coast,
>   O'er life's rough ocean driven,
> May we rejoice, no wanderer lost,
>   BLESS'D WORSHIPERS IN HEAVEN!

XVIII

Knitting Up the Lessons of the Voyage at Its Close

I saw a wreck upon the ocean flood.
　　　How sad and desolate! No man was there;
No living thing was on it. There it stood;
　　　Its sails all gone; its masts were standing bare:
Toss'd on the wide, the boundless, howling sea!
　　　The very sea-birds scream'd, and pass'd it by.
And as I look'd, the ocean seem'd to be
　　　A sign and figure of Eternity.
THE WRECK AN EMBLEM SEEM'D of those that sail
　　　Without the pilot, Jesus, on its tide.
Thus, thought I, when the final storms prevail,
　　　Shall rope, and sail, and mast be scatter'd wide!
And they, with helm and anchor lost, be driven,
In endless exile sad, far from the port of Heaven!
—T. C. Upham.

Rounding Cape Cod, Massachusetts Bay.
In all probability, this beautiful sonnet must have been written some-where at sea, just after passing such a wreck as we met with a few days ago in the Gulf Stream. Such sad things (and they are melancholy ob-jects, indeed, to behold at sea) are often fallen in with there. Perhaps more wrecks are made within, and at the edges of the Gulf Stream, than in any other part of the ocean; squalls are so violent there, the lightning so terrific, and the wind and current so often opposed, as to raise an ugly, chopping, "head-beat" sea, that, if long continued, will beat to pieces, or start dangerous leaks in the very best of ships.

Wrecks, too, once made there, and ships abandoned without foun-dering, will stay for a long time in the course of the stream, being carried along and kept within it by the force of the current. Some captains think that the same wreck may sometimes go the whole round of the stream, being kept along in it to where it is lost, or turns southward by the Western Islands, then taken by the current from the north, and borne to the south and west by the northeast trades, until it falls into the identical Gulf Stream again, or a current sitting into it off the Windward Islands of the West Indies.

Just so in the political, religious, and philosophical world, you will see the wrecks of certain errors and fallacies exploded, dismasted, waterlogged, or quite foundered in one age, reappear in another on the revolving current of opinion. After having floated off into obscurity, and been quite lost sight of for a time, they will come round again, and perhaps be taken up and towed into port by some political novice or demagogue, or transcendental speculator, pretending to great originality of genius, or by some novelty-hunter in religion; by them re-ribbed, calked, and coppered, perhaps *razeed*, and set afloat anew upon the tide of speculation, with a great boast of newness and a mighty press of canvass.

As I happen to be in the mood for illustrations, I can not help writing out one that occurred to me lately while observing the behavior and management of our ship in the last severe gale. The conclusion we all came to was, that a ship in a storm or heavy sea must have sail enough on to run away from the waves and surmount them, or she will be buried *by them*, broaching to and being boarded by a disastrous wave.

So with the religious mind in the great waves of affliction, when the waters roar and are troubled—men's hearts failing them for fear and for looking after those things which are coming, it is often not so well and safe to *lie to* and wait for a lull, brooding meanwhile upon one's trouble, and anxiously casting eyes over what seems to be a great, heaving waste of impending adversity, as to keep busy, if possible, with carrying sail, and trying to scud before the gale.

I have learned, too, in the course of this voyage, that a ship's sails or rigging wear out more in a calm than in a gale. So the mind wears out faster in indolence or inglorious rest, than in well-braced nervous activity and productiveness.

Here also is an illustration of the workings of faith gathered from the experience of a young shipmaster. In first navigating a ship by

the WHALE & HIS *captors*

chronometer and lunars, until he has learned to live by faith in his observations, and the few figures he makes daily on his slate, with the tables of the Nautical Almanac, he is uneasy, doubtful, anxious, and will work his longitude over and over again, though sure there is no mistake, so hard is it practically to live on faith—that which is unseen, and for which we have no evidence of the senses, until a habit is formed: so strange is it to be steering one's way straight over the trackless ocean, without any way-marks, or sign-posts, or mile-stones, or any thing by which we can see that we are right or wrong. It is not until a captain has made three or four good land-falls, at wide intervals, and just according to his calculations, that living by faith in his chronometer and observations, and the results upon his slate be-gins to come easy.

Even so, I have thought, in the very nature of things, it is the *expe-rienced* Christian only that can live *perfectly* the life of faith. Use must have practically convinced him of the reliability of things unseen and eternal, before it can become the habit of his mind to navigate confi-dently the ocean of life, independent of sense.

While thinking much, lately, of life as a voyage, and every Christian the voyager that will soon be as close to the port of heaven as, I trust, we now are to our desired haven in Massachusetts Bay, it has seemed to my mind that the promises are to the Christian voyager what "life-lines" are to the sailor, for him to hold by to the yard when reefing or taking in sail, and to keep him from falling off. Yet, strange to say, many ships' yards are left without this protection for the exposed sailor, by reason of which many a poor fellow in a storm is shaken off that might have clung to the "life-line" had it been in its place at hand.

So Christians sometimes attempt the course of a Christian, and go to sailing over the troubled sea of life without being provided with the promises, without having learned how, or having them at hand, hidden in their hearts, to use and cling to in a storm. In good weather and ordinary times they get along without them, and do not feel the want; but let a storm arise, the wind blow fiercely, the sails be flap-ping, then it is they want the "life-lines," and are distressed and lost without them. Yea, it is not possible for the oldest and most expe-rienced Christian to live without a constant clinging to the prom-ises, still less is it for younger and more recent pilgrims: like a young sailor-boy, they must hold fast to the life-line of God's word, or they are sure to fall.

Sometimes there happens, even to praying, faithful Christians, what is true of large seabirds. When in the Pacific, we used sometimes, by hook and line thrown astern, to catch that most majestic and beautiful of all birds on the wing, the superb white-winged albatross, I observed that of itself it could never rise from the even surface of the deck and soar aloft, though unconfined and at liberty; but we must toss the noble bird overboard, and lift him quite clear of the ship's rail, before he could use his glorious pinions and mount aloft into the air. Then he would stretch those ample wings, and sail away through the ocean of space as easily as one breathes, and as if the elastic element of air and the bird were one, making the gazer wonder, and fairly long to be taking the same aerial flight.

Even so is it, in the economy of grace, now and then, with the real Christian. He is brought by Providence into straits and perplexities whence he can not rise and extricate himself alone; where the wings of faith and love seem to be of no avail to him, until a friendly hand lifts him up, and throws him out upon the deep, where he must say, with Peter, *Lord, save; I perish.* Then he loses despair; he surmounts the difficulty; he breaks his prison; he mounts up as on eagle's wings; the pinions of faith and love sustain him, and bear him away aloft; and he wonders now at the nightmare of doubt and fear that kept him from using them before.

He is ashamed of the wrong thoughts of God that had begun to gather and darken in his mind like gloomy clouds. He sees that God was infinitely wise and good in appointing the discipline to which he has been subjected; and those unuttered, perhaps, but felt murmurs against the dispensations of Providence, now fill him with sorrow and shame. Peculiar and trying as his case may have been, he now discovers many blessings and beneficial consequences to flow from it, which he could not see before. How happy the man whose sight is thus cleared, and his heart enlarged to trace the manifold wisdom and mercy of God in dispensations that once seemed dark and unaccountable!

We noticed in the late gale, and it is often observed by mariners in the beginning of bad weather, before the storm is fairly set in and fixed in its course, that the needle in the compass-box was consider-

The WHALE & *His captors*

ably affected, and there was unusual oscillation, probably through the changing or disturbance of the atmosphere's electric forces; but after the gale was fairly formed or at its height, the needle became true again to its polarity.

There is an analogy to this in the mind of a Christian under a storm of trial—a mind that has been once thoroughly magnetized by the grace of God, and stamped with the law of DIVINE POLARITY, making it to turn always to that POLE-STAR OF BETHLEHEM, the great magnet of the regenerated soul. Though ordinarily true to his pole, yet in sudden emergencies, on the first storm-burst of trouble, it is seldom or never that the Christian can at once repress the flutter and agitation of nature, control or understand its deviations, collect his energies, and repose calmly on God.

It is rare that Faith, taken by surprise, does at once steady the soul, and lift a man in a moment clear above hostile infirmities and fears. Be it true that, when once magnetized by the love of Christ, the soul does always point upward by kindred strong attraction, as the compass-needle to the north, yet, like that same needle, suddenly acted upon by a disturbing force, you must give it time to recover its balance, and, its oscillations done, to fasten upon the central point of rest.

I have sometimes known God's own dear children, when calamities came suddenly in prospect, when huge billows seemed ready to go over them, and a black cloud of sorrows was about to burst upon their heads, at first trembling and anxious, swinging a little with trepidation to this side and that of the central point of rest; but as the trial became more distinctly defined, the cloud's lightning began to flash, and its big drops to fall, the palpitating heart would be still, the vibrations of the will would cease, faith gather strength, and the eye of the soul be upturned and fastened on a faithful God, and its hand grasp firmly the promises, which neither death nor life, nor angels, nor principalities, nor powers, nor things present, nor things to come, nor height, nor depth, nor any other creature, can ever loosen.

With an extract, now, from the old poet George Chapman, lately met with in my sea-reading, somewhat accommodated and made pertinent to our present estate on shipboard, on the look-out for a pilot, these chapters of experience and observation in a whale ship must come to an end. The composition of them in the leaves of my

Knitting Up the Lessons of the Voyage at Its Close

journal has been a fitting employment for some of the hours of a long but every way profitable voyage. May they prove to have ministered a portion of entertaining knowledge and pleasure to some on the land, whom neither duty nor decaying health shall ever reduce to a like necessity with the writer, of being an exile so long from country and home. But if such a necessity do exist in the general prostration of health, without organic disease, I know of no means so feasible and hopeful for its restoration as a cruise in a whale ship, under as favorable circumstances as those with which I have tried it.

> Man is a torch borne in the wind; a dream
> But of a shadow, summ'd with all his substance;
> And as great seamen, using all their wealth
> And skills in Neptune's deep invisible paths,
> In tall ships richly built and ribb'd with brass,
> To put a girdle round about the world,
> When they have done it (coming near their haven),
> *Are fain to give a warning-piece, and call*
> *A poor stayed fisherman, that never pass'd*
> *His country's sight, to waft and guide them in:*
> So, when we wander farthest through the waves
> Of glassy glory, and the gulfs of state,
> Topp'd with all titles, spreading all our reaches,
> As if each private arm would sphere the earth,
> WE MUST TO JESUS FOR HIS GUIDE RESORT,
> OR WE SHALL SHIPWRECK IN OUR SAFEST PORT.
>
>   *   *   *   *   *
>   *   *   *   *   *

I did not think to have added more, but the news that awaited me in Boston of Death's visit to one inexpressibly dear, and that, too, on the very ocean which I had passed over in peace, and with greatly renovated health,

Through the dear might of HIM that walk'd the waves,

induces me to venture a word upon the natural and Christian graces of that beloved brother, whose mortal remains now lie treasured in the deep, till the *sea give up its dead.*

His was a lovely soul, formed to be blessed and bless.

He struggled long, even from early boyhood, with sickness and pain, but all the while patiently, even cheerfully, such was the buoyant energy of his natural temper, and so early was his trial sanctified by the grace of Christ.

> O, precious grace! that made him wise,
> And proved affliction, rightly used,
> Was mercy in disguise!

His disposition was so innately cheerful and lively, so irrepressibly buoyant and genial, that no weight of either maladies or misfortunes could keep him under. But still would he carry his head above the waves, and keep his eye cheerfully aloft in the saddest times, when the spirits of others were fainting. If, now and then, his cheerfulness seemed to suffer a temporary eclipse, it was only like the sun drifting through vapors that scattered as fast as they gathered, and it was but a moment before we would see again, through some open cloud-rift, the clear beams of his sunny face.

> If a sweet social temper, gushing love
> For kindred and for kind, spirits forever
> Sparkling and buoyant as a spring's light bubbles:
> Mirth, candor, frankness, and a love to give
> Pleasure to friends, and good to every one;
> And, more than all, true love for Christ and souls—
> If these be traits that make a blessing man,
> Beloved and form'd to bless, through God's rich grace,
> OUR CHERISH'D BROTHER WAS THAT HAPPY MAN.

> No more the tender offices of love
> We pay him here on earth, but all his virtues
> Still will we cherish; and that radiant face,
> From its calm sphere within the spirit world,
> Like a bright star shall still look down and cheer
> Our life's sojournings, till at length we come
> Where he the promises, through patient faith,
> Inherits, and enjoys the rest of heaven!

Knitting Up the Lessons of the Voyage at Its Close

It is all well with him now; and though I had fondly hoped to have seen him yet once more in the flesh, and to have knelt again in prayer with that blessed brother, and it would have been so comforting, if God's will, to have ministered to him in his last hours, I would not have it otherwise now. Through the mercy of Christ, may we soon bow in praise around the throne of God! Some of the birth-day lines addressed to him years ago by his elder brother, are, with a slight accommodation, equally appropriate now that he has passed the solemn threshold and BIRTH-DAY of a BLESSED ETERNITY!

How recollection paints anew
    The times when, in our own dear home,
We talk of mercies past, and view
    The heavenly life to come!

'Tis just in heaven, thy happy dawn—
    But ah! how full the mingled scene
On memory's pictured tablets drawn—
    Calm now, and all serene:

Serene because a blessed faith
    Throws o'er each melancholy line
That marks affliction's rugged path,
    The gleam of love divine.

Through all it sees thy Father's form,
    His gracious, guiding hand beholds;
And in the gloomiest of the storm
    Some bright design unfolds.

Amid the sufferings of years,
    Thou seest thou didst not walk alone;
Where all was agony and tears,
    There most His mercy shone.

'Twas thus he drew thy buoyant heart
    Up to a holier world above,
And bade thee choose that better part,
    A Savior's wondrous love.

      the WHALE *&* HIS *captors*

For this our fervent thanks we raise,
      That HE, whose love is wisdom too,
Made thee partaker of his grace,
      By trials here below.

CHRIST held thee* in his powerful hand;
      Now, every foe and fear subdued,
THY FEET DO PRESS THE SHINING LAND
      BEYOND DEATH'S NARROW FLOOD!

*To the American consul of Trinidad de Cuba, where he had been settled as a physician, he spake the precious words, a day or two before his death on shipboard, "*I wish you to understand, my faith is strong in Christ, my Redeemer.*"

NOTES

A, *p. 19*

When the islands of the Pacific Ocean were first discovered by Europeans, some of the natives were found very timid and friendly, while others were fierce, treacherous, and warlike. For many years after their discovery, these islands were visited only by those who were on voyages of discovery, or who were in the pursuit of gain. The natives were treated with great inhumanity; and drunken seamen, rioting through their villages and trampling upon all laws of right doing, soon introduced all the vices of civilized life to be added to those of the savage state. The natives generally became exasperated, and were ever watching for opportunities to cut off the ships and massacre the seamen. A Nantucket whale ship was at one time wrecked upon one of the Feejee Islands. The crew escaped, in their boats, to the shore, and before they were discovered by the natives, succeeded in constructing a fort for their defense. The natives, however, soon found them; and after a long and bloody battle, all of the sailors were slain except two little boys, whose lives were spared. One, after the lapse of many years, escaped on board a whale ship which stopped at the island. The other has never been heard from.

Such was the condition of these islands when the English missionaries, taking their lives in their hands, went among them to Christianize the inhabitants. The missionaries were ridiculed, opposed, and traduced by thousands at home, and they endured every species of privation and hardship from the habitations of cruelty, in the midst of which they took up their abode. God smiled, however, upon their exertions, and soon these wild men and women turned from their idols and their sins, and cultivated the arts of peace.

A few years after the missionaries had commenced their labors, an American whale ship came in sight of an unknown island in the Pacific Ocean. They had been for six months cruising in search of their gigantic game without having seen any land. Scurvy, that terrible scourge of seamen, had seized one after another of the crew, till there were not enough left in health to navigate the vessel in safety. Scurvy is a disease caused by living a long time upon salted provisions, without any vegetables; and the sufferers are almost immediately restored to health when they can breathe the fresh air of the land and eat freely of fruits and herbs. Here was this ship, several thousand miles from the South American coast. The crew were emaciated and dying.

Before them rose, in all the beauty of tropical luxuriance, one of those islands of the ocean, which appeared to the mariner, weary with gazing for months upon the wide waste of waters, like the Garden of Eden. But they dared not approach those shores. A foe, more treacherous and dreadful than disease, they apprehended there. The club of the savage, and the demoniacal revels of the cannibals dancing and shouting around their roasting victims, were more to be dreaded than death by slow and lingering approaches in the ship. They dared not draw near the shore, for they were too feeble to prevent the natives, should they come out in large numbers in their canoes, from climbing up the sides and taking possession of the ship. But with the glass they could distinctly see the clear streams of water foaming down their channels in the mountains. Meadows faded away in the distance, enchanting the eye with their shady groves and their rich verdure. The cocoa-nut tree reared its graceful head upon the beach, laden with its precious and its life-giving treasures; and forests rich with tropical fruits, juicy and luscious, were every where spread around.

These emaciated and dying men crawled from their berths and gazed with wistful eyes upon this tantalizing scene. Slowly they were borne along by a gentle breeze, and forest-crowned head-lands, and luxuriant valleys and groves, bending beneath the burden of fruit, glided by, like the changes of a kaleidoscope, and still no canoe pushed out from the shore, and no huts of the natives were to be seen. They began to cherish the hope that the island might be uninhabited, and cautiously approached it. But ere long they saw canoes upon the beach, and smoke here and there ascending from the cocoa-nut groves; and still, to their astonishment, no natives made their appearance, and no sound of human voices reached them from the shore.

As they rounded a promontory, which opened before them a quiet and lovely bay, a thickly clustered village of the natives burst upon their view, and in the center of it was reared a Christian church. A si-

the WHALE *&* HIS *captors*

multaneous shout of joy rang through the ship as the cry passed from stem to stern, *The missionaries are here!* It was the Sabbath, and the natives had learned the Divine command, "Remember the Sabbath day, and keep it holy." And the temptation of a ship entering the bay did not lure a single canoe to leave the shore. The crew were almost crazed with joy at this sudden change in their prospects. They speedily cast anchor, furled their sails, and, entering the ship's boats, went on shore. As soon as the natives were informed of their sick and suffering condition, they received them with the utmost hospitality, and supplied them with all the fresh fruit and vegetables they could need.

The next day the natives aided the emaciated crew in taking a sail from the ship, and spreading a large tent upon the green grass on the banks of a mountain stream. And here the crew reposed in inexpressible luxury. They bathed their limbs in the pure water, and quaffed it, in its coolness and its freshness, like Elysian nectar. They rolled with childish glee upon the green grass. Cocoa-nuts and bananas, and lemons and oranges, and other luscious fruits of the tropics, were brought to them in great abundance by the friendly natives. In a few days, the disease which had brought so many of them to the verge of the grave began to disappear. The missionaries, from their little stock of medicines, administered to their wants, and treated them with fraternal kindness.

In the course of two or three weeks, all were restored to health and vigor. They filled their casks with fresh water; laid in stores of vegetables; supplied themselves with pigs and poultry, and then, with invigorated bodies and rejoicing spirits, they raised their anchors and unfurled their sails, and departed on their adventurous way.

Thus is fulfilled the declaration of Scripture, that "godliness is profitable unto all things, having promise of the life that now is and of that which is to come." The labors of these missionaries were not only instrumental in promoting the moral elevation, and, we hope, the final salvation of these uncivilized men, but they also saved the lives of these seamen, and secured the success of the voyage upon which they had embarked.

What a different world would this be, could the spirit of Christian brotherhood pervade the hearts of all the inhabitants! Could woe, oppression, and injustice cease, and every man look upon his fellow-man as a friend, the larger portion of the sorrows of humanity would disappear forever. And none are doing more to hasten the advent of this happy day than those who are aiding by their personal influence and their purse to extend throughout the world the religion of Jesus Christ.

Ye disciples of Voltaire and of Paine, can you show us such a triumph as this? You profess to be humane men, to love your brethren, to desire to promote their happiness here and hereafter. Can you show us an instance in which the adoption of the principles of infidelity has been promotive of the moral or the physical welfare of an individual, or of a village, or of a nation? Have you ever known a young man to become more dissolute by becoming a Christian? Have you ever known a village to become less thrifty and prosperous in consequence of the observance by its inhabitants of the precepts of the Bible? Is there, on the surface of this globe, a more intelligent, virtuous, prosperous, and happy community than is to be found in the dwellings of New England, and is there any other portion of earth's inhabitants over whom the religion of Jesus Christ has greater supremacy? Give, then, your influence to aid this cause, and your fellowmen shall bless you, and conscience shall reward you, and your heavenly Father shall welcome you as his co-workers and his sons.

—*N. Y. Evangelist.*

B, *p. 71*

A boat-steerer in an American whaler, a man of more than ordinary thoughtfulness and intelligence, addressed an interesting communication to the Honolulu Seaman's Friend, while the author of these sketches was at the Sandwich Islands. It is feared that he has since been lost, it being a very long time since his ship was heard from. The communication referred to, being a slice of a sailor's autobiography, will be a good comment on the text that *there's many a heart under the rough pea jacket.*

When I look back (he says) upon my past life, with all its various scenes and occurrences, both by sea and land, it is on my lips to say, what hair-breadth escapes from death, what deliverance from threatening dangers have I experienced, even from my childhood. *Surely goodness and mercy have followed me all the days of my life.*

The WHALE & *His captors*

When a man is placed in a situation where no danger is apparent, where all is cheerful and happy, how apt he is to think and talk lightly of death; but let him be placed in the midst of the ocean, in a solitary bark, at the mercy of the winds and waves; let the tempest arise, and the wild waters be tossed by the howling winds, and we will suppose that the ship is trimmed for the storm, her sails furled, her top-gallant-masts are sent down, and when he casts his eye aloft, the naked spars and rigging strike a sort of chill—an unusual sensation to his heart. He looks to windward and to leeward, ahead and astern; there is nothing to be seen save the foam-clad billows in wild commotion.

Night comes, and no moon—not even a solitary star visible to cheer his sight; the land is hundreds of miles distant; he casts his eye upward to the heavens, the sky looks black; he leans over the bulwarks and peers away into the awful gloom around, nothing is to be seen, nothing is to be heard save the howling blast, the surging waters, and the creaking of the vessel. Wave succeeds wave, dashing with violence against the ship's side, the darkness is almost palpable, he can not distinguish a shipmate at the distance of a few feet, the ship labors heavily, and seems to struggle with the angry element as if conscious of the dread hour.

Then a man will *think*, ay, and his conscience will sometimes *speak*; strange thoughts, like unbidden guests, will at such times intrude themselves into his mind, whether welcome or not. He goes to his hammock and tries to sleep, but from the pitching and rolling of the ship it is almost impossible to rest; the night passes slowly and uneasily away in broken dreams and fearful fancies, and at length, when daylight comes, he discovers that the storm has increased in violence. Few words pass among his shipmates; perhaps a loud oath from some would-be reckless companion salutes his ear, which, if uttered at other times, would pass unheeded, but now, for some reason that he is at a loss to explain, sounds strangely out of place. The cheeks of some of the hardiest turn pale, and the restless glances of others betray the uneasy feelings within.

He will at such times reflect on the past, the present, and the future; what would have been the consequence if, on the previous night, some other vessel, imperceptible in the darkness, had come in collision with his; he shudders at the thought, and perhaps, at that moment, the idea will suggest itself that there is an overruling Providence who watches over and protects the poor mariner.

Well do I recollect my own feelings on several occasions of this nature, one of which happened on the coast of California. We were sailing in company with another whale ship, when a gale of wind came on which was favorable for the course we were steering toward Cape St. Lucas: both ships were kept before the wind during the day, but after sunset our captain thought it advisable to heave to, after which, from the position of our ship, it appeared probable that the other vessel, which was still kept on her course, would pass quite close to us, and a good look-out was therefore ordered to be kept to windward. In a short time it was very dark, the sea running "mountains high," and the gale blowing very hard, so that it was impossible to see any distance to windward.

When the other ship was last visible, she appeared to be heading right for us; and well do I remember with what anxiety I waited until I thought sufficient time had elapsed for her to pass. I know not why, but the thought seemed at that time to press very heavily on me, what the consequence would be should the other ship run into ours; very probably we should have all gone to the bottom; and my feelings were the more acute by the circumstance that the ship in question belonged to the same owners as ours, and had on board several young men who had often been my companions in pleasant parties.

At another time, while employed in *trying out*, on the coast of Kamtschatka, one very dark night the watch was busily employed on deck; we were boiling our last whale, and carrying more sail than is usual while boiling, for the purpose of making a port, when another vessel approached to leeward unseen by us; at this time, as it was blowing fresh, and the ship had a considerable heel, the officer of the deck ordered the helm to be put up to keep the ship before the wind, and consequently on an even keel, while the watch rolled a very large cask of oil away from the cooler. While running off for this purpose, we were suddenly hailed by a strange voice from the surrounding gloom, apparently close aboard of us; at first we thought the sound came from under the ship's bows, but fortunately it was not exactly there, and it turned out afterward, that while running off in the man-

The WHALE *&* His *captors*

ner described, we had unconsciously (but for being hailed) passed quite close to another ship.

At such times as these, most men will think, and that seriously; but, alas! it soon passes away; with the recollection of such dangerous occurrences vanishes, I may say, the recollection of the superintending care of an Almighty God. Who can tell how many unseen dangers are passed through by a ship during a three years' voyage?

If there be any class of men who ought, more than others, to feel grateful to God, I think that class is sailors, of whom many may well exclaim, "Surely goodness and mercy have followed me all the days of my life."

c, p. 110

An instance has come to the knowledge of the writer of a ship in the North Pacific, from which there was lost a boat and crew of six men, under the following circumstances. They had been lowered to take a whale, and had succeeded in plunging the harpoon into the monster's side, but he had rushed with them, at rail-road speed, out of the sight of the ship, which was making after them at what rate they could. Suddenly a fog began to rise, and enveloped both the ship and her lone boat, and to spread over the whole expanse of the ocean, involving a danger of very frequent occurrence to whalemen in high latitudes.

It was impossible to see any object at the distance of a ship's length; and there was an open whale boat, with six men in it, perhaps fifteen miles from the ship, with food and water for but a few hour's consumption, and utterly bewildered in the dense fog. The darkness of night soon came on; the wind began to rise, and the billows to swell. Every effort was made, by firing guns and showing lights, to attract the lost boat. The long hours of the night rolled away, a stormy morning dawned, and still no boat appeared.

For several days they sailed in circles around the spot, but all in vain. The boat was either dashed by the whale, or swamped by the billows of the stormy night, or, as it floated day after day upon the desert waste of the Pacific, one after another of the crew, emaciated with thirst and famine, dropped down and died.

Another, a sperm whaler, the bark Harriet, of Freetown, Captain Durfee, when cruising on the line, lowered her boats one day for sperm whales. The first and third mates had each secured a whale and made them fast alongside, when they returned to assist the second mate, who was fast to another. They came up with him about nine o'clock at night, and succeeded in killing the whale. They could then see the ship; but it soon began to blow, and they were obliged to lay by the whale all night. In the morning the ship was not in sight, it still blowing a gale and raining hard. They lay by the whale three days, when they ventured to stand off to the westward, in hopes of falling in with some ship. On the seventh day they caught a shark, which they ate with a good relish. They were then standing for the King's Mill Group of islands; but a new gale coming on, they were obliged to reef down and stand to the eastward, and finally to heave to, where they lay for thirty-six hours, in a gale unusual for those latitudes. On the morning of the tenth day they again stood to the west. On the eleventh they discovered a sail, and stood for her, which proved to be the bark Hanseat, of Hamburg. They were taken on board and treated with great kindness, having had nothing to eat during the eleven days excepting the shark they had caught and one or two flying fish, and no water except what they had caught in the linetubs. Some of them had lain down to die two days before they saw the ship, and all of them were so weak that they could scarcely support their weight. Captain Durfee, after cruising for several days in the vicinity, was making the best of his way to Oahu with the remnant of his crew, having given up all hopes of ever seeing any of his officers or crew again, when the bark Hanseat spoke him, January 20th. He was not more surprised than delighted to find his men all safe, and receiving all attention possible, as the third mate was a brother.

D, *p. 112*

Of the twenty thousand men who go in jeopardy of their lives under every accessible line of latitude and longitude, upon the great highway of nations; who, on an average, are exiles from home and country, from the social delights and most of the comforts of life for three or four years at a time, on purpose to bring back the means of enriching the owners of the whale ships, and of adding to the comforts and embellishments of the millions who are spared these privations, what can be said? what shall be done for them?

The WHALE *&* His *captors*

Very encouraging it is that, of late, some attention is given to this class of men. The fact that they are human beings begins to be recognized; nor are they altogether forgotten, as some notices of their condition and wants clearly prove. It could not be expected that our stately and dignified quarterlies would notice, except in the most general and gingerly manner, the worst features of the whaleman's case. You, however, who are fully committed to the work of philanthropic and Christian reforms, who do not fear to speak out plainly and boldly, who care more for the groans and degradation of humanity than for the frowns of its oppressors, who love to plead for the dumb, and whose honest boast it is that you faithfully hold up the mirror to reflect the evils which require to be repented of and reformed, as well as the good in which we may exult, surely of you and in your columns may be expected the full unmasking of whatever abuses and perversions have been allowed to spring up, and for a long time have been tolerated in silence.

From one whose position gives him ample facilities for unmistaking knowledge of the facts in this case, who has not, by a long course of familiar observation of flagrant abuses, become indurated to a sense of their turpitude; who, on the one hand, has no interests prompting to concealment, or glossing over frightful evils, nor, on the other, any feelings of goading retaliation for personal injuries, real or supposed, to cause an exaggerated picture, surely, from such a one, you ought to be able to rely on the simple truth. The former position, the subsequent tendencies, and the present state of the whalemen, in their physical and intellectual, their moral and religious condition, shall pass in brief review; and certain it is, that in more capable hands, it could not fail, in a surpassing degree, to awaken the deepest concern of the wise and good.

Only two or three generations since—at the very time when Burke poured forth, in the British Parliament, his splendid eulogium on the exploits of this class of men—they were, for the most part, the sturdy, intelligent, and comparatively virtuous yeomanry of New England. Not only the officers, but the crews of whale ships were of this character. But such is not the case now. Whether the deterioration of character in the crews especially has resulted from the hardships of the service, inducing all but the mentally imbecile to prefer some other branch of marine adventure, or whether the falling off has been occasioned by the grinding conditions as to remuneration which the ship-owner imposes, who is chiefly anxious to enrich himself, or perhaps some favorite officer in his employ, while the poor seamen are left to endure privations, and expose themselves to hazards of life and limbs in bootless disinterestedness; or whether the rapid extension of this enterprise has called for men faster than the good and worthy could be furnished; or, perhaps, from the joint influence of all these causes combined, it must be conceded that a lamentable deterioration of character in the crews of whaleships has been witnessed.

They are now made up to a great degree, and, of course, with some honorable exceptions, of the very refuse of humanity, gathered from every quarter, escaped from poor-houses and prisons, or gleaned from the receptacle of vagrancy and lazar-house corruption, with a large admixture of foreigners of all languages, complexions, and character.

Such constitute the experienced portions of the crew. To them you may add one third or one quarter part more of land lubbers, or raw hands, made up of very heterogeneous materials. Here will be found the young, roving adventurer, who pants for opportunity to see the world; he has heard marvelous stories of the facilities of foreign observation furnished in this service, while, at the same time, visions of easily-acquired wealth, golden harvests to be here reaped, have filled his mind, and he hurried from the interior to ship himself on board a whaleman. The reckless and impatient, who spurn all salutary control, are also here, thinking this is just the place to indulge unbounded license.

Here, also, you will find the spoiled sons of over-indulgent parents, who, having made themselves intolerable by their vicious propensities, and constantly in danger of bringing disgrace on themselves and their connections also, by their intemperance, their fits of passion, or unbridled licentiousness, are sent on a whaling voyage as a school of reform! To each of these a small advance of cash is made, on signing the shipping papers, for the ostensible purpose of paying their traveling expenses to the port of embarkation, or their board a few weeks or days before they are ready to sail, or for their partial outfit; the real object is to tie the poor renegade as firmly as possible to his new engagement.

With two thirds of the required number of men of the above de-

The WHALE & *His captors*

scription, the ship sails, relying on making up her complement in Portuguese sailors at the Western Islands or in Kanakas from the Sandwich or other islands of the Pacific Ocean. Both these classes are usually as filthy and disgusting specimens of humanity as can well be conceived, having this difference, however, that the former are perfectly incorrigible, while the latter do sometimes improve.

This motley crew are at length mustered on board, drunk or sober, though far less intemperance now prevails than in former years, thanks to the praiseworthy endeavor of reformers in one much-needed department of their endeavors. Sullen and sad, or jovial and light-hearted as they may seem, they are now in their quarters for several years. What *a home!* Look around for its facilities for comfort and improvement.

In that repulsive hole called the *forecastle*, of scarce twelve feet square capacity, not high enough to allow a tall man to stand upright, with little or no light or ventilation but what comes down the narrow hatchway (and even this must be closed in rough weather), here some twenty or five-and-twenty men are to eat, and sleep, and *live*, if such a state can be called living; here, in sickness and in health, by day and by night, without fire in the rigors of the polar regions, or cooling appliances under the equator, these men, with their chests and hammocks, or bunks, are to find stowage. After again and again examining this feature of their arrangements, and comparing it with the cells prepared for and *enjoyed* by the felons in all our principal prisons in more than half the states of our Union which I have visited, the latter would be pronounced princely, enviable even in all the requisites of roominess, light, ventilation, and facility for seclusion.

Here, with no possibility of classification and separate quarters, with few or no books, or opportunity to use them if they were possessed, with the constant din of roystering disorder, superabundant profanity, and teeming lasciviousness of conversation and songs, with no Sabbath, no prayer, no words and efforts by superiors to win them to something better and worthier, three fourths of their forty months' absence are passed. When they are on shore, or lying in port to refit, corruptions, by libidinous intercourse with impure women, intemperance, and other abominations, vary, while they by no means improve, their condition.

—*Christian Reflector.*

The Sabbath-keeping experience of Rev. William Scoresby, who, as well as the father, was for many years employed in the Greenland whale fishery, is of great practical value. In a volume entitled "Memorials of the Sea," he gives the following results of a strict and conscientious observance of the Sabbath at sea:

It was in the last four voyages, wherein my personal interest in the fishing was the greatest, that the providential testimonies to Sabbath observance were the most striking. During this period, the pecuniary interest to myself alone, in the capture of a large whale, was not unfrequently near £300, while a single day's successful fishing might afford a personal advantage, as in one instance or more it did, of upward of £800. Consequently every motive of self-interest was in favor of unceasing exertions, during the whole seven days of the week, for promoting the success of our undertaking. The practice, moreover, almost universally is, to pursue the fishery equally on the Lord's day, as at any other time, whenever whales were astir.

Works connected with the fishery, indeed, but considered of less importance, were, for the most part, suspended in honor of the Sabbath; but the capture of whales, if opportunity offered, was considered as such a kind of necessity as to justify that departure from the ordinary rest of the day; for it was argued, and that with reason, that the whales which were seen on the Sabbath might not remain till another day; and, therefore, it was inferred, though by no means with the same strictness of truth, that it was a necessary duty to pursue the objects of the fishery whenever they were within reach.

Through the goodness of God, however, I felt the line of duty to be otherwise. The strict command concerning the Sabbath, rendered, in my apprehension, the duty imperative—to refrain from laboring in a worldly calling for worldly advantage on that holy day; and this, for several of the most recent voyages in which I was engaged, became our undeviating line of conduct.

On the 13th of July, blowing hard, with rain or sleet, we moored to a large and heavy floe (a sheet of ice about three or four miles in diameter), in order the more commodiously to enjoy the Sabbath day's repose. A ship from Peterhead, which had for some days been accompanying us, followed our example, and a considerable number of her

the WHALE *&* his *captors*

officers and crew joined us in our usual Sabbath devotions. An evening service, designed chiefly for the instruction and benefit of the apprentices, had been concluded, the sacred day of the Lord was drawing to a close, and our visitors were preparing to return to their ship, when a large whale was descried by one of our own seamen in a situation very inviting for attempting its capture.

No doubt it was contemplated by many with an ardent and longing gaze; but the orders for sanctifying the Sabbath being quite peremptory, no attempt, on the part of any of our people, was made to pursue the tempting object. Our fellow-worshipers, however, being less scrupulous, instantly manned the boat which had brought them on board of the Baffin, and set forth, along with some others from their own ship, in eager pursuit. Nor were their ardent hopes disappointed; for in a short time, the usual quietness of the day, with us, was broken in upon by the shout of success from the pursuing boats, followed by vehement respondings from the contiguous ship. The attack, being followed up with the wonted vigor, proved successful, and the prize was fully secured by the middle of the night.

That such a result should not be exceedingly trying to the feelings of our people, who saw that their competitors had won the prize which we had first declined, was more than could be expected. Nevertheless, both the trial of their obedience and the exercise of their patience were so sustained as to be at once satisfactory to me and creditable to themselves. Their minds, in general, seemed disposed to admit the principle on which we acted; for, in addition to the religious sanctions, their repeated experiences had testified that the principle was acknowledged by heaven.

It was my intention to have "cast off," the morning of Monday, to explore the navigable spaces of the ice to the westward with a view to the furtherance of our voyage; but the day being still stormy, with constant thick weather from snow, sleet, or rain, we found it expedient to remain in somewhat anxious idleness, while our successful comrades were joyously and usefully occupied in flensing the valuable fish obtained almost under our stern. This was doubtless an additional trial of the good feelings of our crew; but whatever might be the regrets of any in yielding up, for conscience' sake, our chance of so fine a prize, I heard of no other dissatisfaction than the mere expression of a natural anxiety to be under weigh, that we might find a fish for ourselves.

The state of the weather, however, induced us to continue at our moorings till forced off by the movements of the contiguous ices, which threatened the safety of the ship. Soon afterward we set forward on our object; and having made a stretch to the westward, all hands were speedily called into exhilarating action by the discovery of several whales. The eagerness of the men, indeed, was, in the first instance, against us; more than one of the objects of their anxiety being unnecessarily scared, for want of that wise and considerate prudence which, under the circumstances, was peculiarly needed to temper and direct their excited zeal. At length, however, after a variety of mortifying failures, a harpoon was ably struck; and though the boat received a desperate heave, and some of its oars were projected high into the air, happily no accident ensued.

The excess of ardor among the men was now in full demand, being appropriately drawn off by the vigor with which the wounded monster struggled for its liberty and life. Outstripping the utmost speed of its pursuers, in the beginning of the chase, it obtained shelter amid the compact accumulation of numerous masses of ice where it was most difficult to reach, and from whence it seemed next to impracticable to be dislodged. After encountering, however, a variety of little adventures, as well as some very threatening obstacles, we succeeded in subduing the powerful animal; and no sooner was it clear of the lines, and in a condition to be removed, than the compact aggregation of ices by which it was enveloped began to relax, so that with little further embarrassment a channel was cleared out, and the prize effectually secured. Thus, before the very first day available for the fishery after the Sabbath had come to a close, all our anxieties were relieved, our forbearance compensated, and our efforts crowned with the desired success.

After a careful examination of the journals of my four last voyages in the whale fishery, being the same to which the foregoing records chiefly refer, I can only discover three instances wherein, after resisting the pursuit of whales seen on the Sabbath, we were not successful in the fishery of the ensuing week.

As to those who may yet question the result of our argument—that the statements here presented afford decisive evidence of a providen-

The WHALE & *his captors*

tial blessing on the endeavor to keep the Lord's day holy—we would claim, at least, this fair and candid admission, that our refraining from Sabbath violation, when urged to it by the prospect of worldly gain, was not the occasion of either loss or disadvantage, in the ultimate result of our labors. Could, however, the conviction of those who accompanied me in the voyages referred to, consisting, probably, of one hundred and fifty different men, be conveyed to their minds, an impression of a much more decisive and satisfactory character, methinks, would naturally and generally follow; for, on occasions when we refrained from fishing on the Sunday, while others were successfully engaged in that object, our subsequent labors, as has been seen, often succeeded under circumstances so peculiarly striking, that there was scarcely a man in the amount of our crew who did not seem to consider it as the effect of the Divine blessing!

Independently, indeed, of the positive duty of sanctifying the Sabbath, and of the blessing of Providence connected therewith, we ofttimes realize the wisdom of the institution, in the mere physical benefits resulting from its observance; for when the preceding week happened to have been laboriously employed, the day of rest became sweetly welcome, obviously beneficial, in its restoring influence upon the energies of the people, fitting them for a renewal of their arduous duties, while the temporary restraint thus put upon the ardor of the seamen, operated, no doubt, with no small measure of advantage, by stimulating to additional energy in their subsequent labors; so that, in every point of view, and in every relation to the well-being of man, spiritual and temporal, this sacred appointment stands commended both for wisdom and goodness.

F, p. 131

The writer has had many thoughts and conversations with others on the question whether the captain of a whale ship ought himself to go in the boats or always keep by the ship, and the opinion I have formed is (let it pass for what it is worth), that the commander, on whom so much depends, and whose safety should ever, therefore, be a prime consideration, not for his own sake merely, but for that of the ship and crew under him, should never leave the ship himself to engage in whaling.

This opinion is confirmed by the reflections had on one occasion, when our captain of the Commodore Preble was dragged out of our sight by an enormous sperm whale, to which he was fast, and had at last to cut loose from, lest he should be lost. Numerous melancholy facts in the annals of whaling confirm our estimate, then formed, of the danger and inexpediency of the captain's going in the boats, and naturally suggest to owners the propriety of instructing their captains to stay by the ship. Witness the recent narrative, from the New Bedford Mercury, of the sufferings of Captain Hosmer and a boat's crew, of the whaling bark Janet, who were separated from their vessel while on the coast of Peru. The account, furnished by the captain, is substantially as follows:

On the coast of Peru, 23d June, 1849, in latitude 30° N., longitude 104° W., while cruising for whales, a shoal of sperm whales appeared in sight from the Janet, and three boats lowered in pursuit. Captain Hosmer's boat's crew consisted of himself, Francis Hawkins, third mate, Edward H. Charles, Joseph Cortez, Daniel Thompson, and James Fairman, seamen. It blowing fresh at the time, the boats soon separated, each having made fast to a whale. After Captain Hosmer had succeeded in "turning up" his whale, and was towing him to the ship, from some inadvertence on the part of the third mate in putting about, the boat capsized, with loss of boat-keg, lantern-keg, boat-bucket, compass, paddles, &c. The crew succeeded in righting the boat, and lashed the oars to the thwarts across the boat, to prevent her from overturning, she being filled with water, and the sea continually breaking over her.

Two waifs, or flags, were immediately set as a signal of distress, the other two boats being in sight, at a distance of about one and a half miles. Captain Hosmer saw the other two boats take their whales alongside of the bark, which was then kept off in the direction for his boat; but, to his surprise and horror, when within about one mile of him, they kept off on another course until sundown. The crew of the captain's boat then got upon the whale alongside, and tried to bail the boat, but could not succeed. They then cut the line attached to the whale, and succeeded in setting some pieces of the boat-sail, and steered toward the bark, then about three miles distant.

During the night they saw a light at intervals, but in the morning

　　　　　The WHALE & *His* captors

the bark was at about the same distance off. Every expedient was resorted to, by making signals, to attract the attention of those on board the bark, but in vain. They saw them cutting in the whales, and apparently indifferent to the fate of their comrades. In this perilous condition, the unfortunate boat's crew made another attempt to bail the water from the boat, but, owing to their consternation, they did not succeed. They then continued on their course as above, hoping to regain the bark, but soon found that she receded from them, and it was then determined to put about to the wind and remain, whatever the consequence might be.

On the second morning, the weather being more favorable, all the whale craft was thrown overboard, and another attempt was made to bail the boat, which resulted in the loss of one man, without accomplishing the purpose. The effort was again renewed in the afternoon, the weather being yet more favorable, and they finally succeeded in freeing the boat from water, but with the loss of another of her crew, all on board having been up to their arms in the water during the last forty-eight hours. Two of the survivors were seized with delirium, all of them having been without a morsel of food or drink, and suffering painfully from thirst.

Thus disabled, no one on board being able to ply at the oars, and with only a small fragment of the boat's sail remaining, it was determined to make for Cocus Island, on the Peruvian coast, a distance of about one thousand miles, as the nearest land. Accordingly, the piece of the sail was used to the best advantage, and the ceiling of the boat was torn up, and also employed as a wind-propeller, and steering in a northeasterly direction.

Captain Hosmer says nothing occurred worthy of remark until the seventh day, the crew having, in the mean time, been without a particle of food or drink, and not a drop of rain having fallen. In this dreadful state of suffering, it was mutually agreed to cast lots as to which of the number should be sacrificed to prolong the lives of his companions; and the unfortunate victim upon whom the lot fell met his fate with perfect resignation and willingness. At the close of the day, a shower of rain proved a very grateful additional relief.

Being without compass or instruments of any kind, Captain Hosmer was compelled to rely entirely upon his judgment respecting the course, aided only by an occasional glimpse of the north star and the rolling swell of the sea from the south. On the eighth day another of the number died from exhaustion. It was found necessary to pursue a more northerly course in hope of rain, none having fallen during the last four days.

On the next day they were favored with another shower, and this benefaction was followed up by the remarkable circumstance of a dolphin leaping from among its finny companions directly into the boat. Several birds, also, approached so near to the boat as to fall a prey to the necessities of the crew, administering greatly to their relief. On the 13th of July land was discovered in an easterly direction, which proved to be Cocus Island (uninhabited), lying in latitude 5° 27′ N. longitude 87° 15′.

Captain Hosmer and the other survivors succeeded in reaching it, but in an almost helpless condition. They, however, secured a pig, and drank its blood, which revived their exhausted strength, and also obtained a plentiful supply of birds and fresh water. After remaining two days upon the island, they were overjoyed by seeing the approach of a boat, which proved to belong to the ship Leonidas (whaler), Captain Swift, of this port, then lying in Chatham Bay, for the purpose of procuring wood and water, and were relieved from their dreadful sufferings by being taken on board the ship and treated with every possible attention and kindness.

The names of those who perished on board the boat are, Francis Hawkins, third mate, of Augusta, Maine; James Fairman, seaman, of Ohio; Henry Thompson, seaman, of Philadelphia, Pennsylvania; Edward Henry Charles, place of residence unknown.

The mate of the Janet explained his apparent neglect of the captain, in a letter to his owners, as follows. After mentioning the fact of three boats putting off for whales, as stated above, he adds:

At three P.M. I had my whale alongside, and soon the ship came to me; and when I got on board there was but one boat in sight, and that was five miles to the leeward of the ship. I went down to it with the ship, and found that it was the second mate's boat. He had seen Captain Hosmer two hours previously, fast to a whale, and went to the leeward of him when last seen from the boat.

We proceeded in the direction in which the captain's boat had been

The WHALE & *His* *captors*

last seen, and lay to all night, with all sails set, and with all our lights fixed. In the morning saw nothing of the boat. We cruised three days, but, unfortunately, without meeting any trace of her. In the mean time, four of our hands were sick from fatigue, and we were under the necessity of making the best of our way to this port (Payta).

We had taken 100 barrels of oil for the last ten days previously, and lost 200 barrels during the same time by losing lines. I expect the captain's boat was taken down by a foul line, as he had a new line in his boat, coiled two days previous to the accident; we saved one whale the day the accident happened, and lost another that night.

THE END.

1853 ADDITIONS

NOTE F, *continued*

A recent instance, which puts almost all former exploits of the whale and perils by the whale fishery into the shade, is furnished in the destruction of a New Bedford whale ship by the malice aforethought of a sperm whale, who may have been the prototype or twin-brother to the notable "Moby-Dick." The account is given by the captain of said ship, and it is authenticated by nine of the crew in a protest under the seal of the United States consul, Alexander Ruden, Jr., at Payta.

The ship Ann Alexander, Captain S. Deblois, sailed from New Bedford, Massachusetts, June 1st, 1850, for a cruise in the South Pacific, for sperm whales. Having taken about 500 barrels of oil in the Atlantic, the ship proceeded on her voyage to the Pacific. Nothing of unusual interest occurred until, when passing Cape Horn, one of the men, named Jackson Walker, of Newport, New Hampshire, was lost overboard in a storm. Reaching the Pacific, she came up the coast and stopped at Valdivia, coast of Chili, for fresh provisions, and on the 31st of May last she called at Payta, for the purpose of shipping a man. The vessel proceeded on her voyage to the South Pacific.

On the 20th of August last, she reached what is well known to all whalers as the Off-shore Ground, in latitude 5° 60′ S., longitude 102° W. In the morning of that day, at about 9 o'clock, whales were discovered in the neighborhood, and about noon, the same day, they succeeded in making fast to one. Two boats had gone after the whales —the larboard and the starboard—the former commanded by the first mate, and the latter by Captain Deblois. The whale which they had struck was harpooned by the larboard boat. After running some time, the whale turned upon the boat, and, rushing at it with tremendous violence, lifted open its enormous jaws, and, taking the boat in, actually crushed it into fragments as small as a common-sized chair! Captain Deblois immediately struck for the scene of the disaster with the starboard boat, and succeeded, against all expectation, in rescuing the whole of the crew of the boat—nine in number!

There were now eighteen men in the starboard boat, consisting of the captain, the first mate, and the crews of both boats. The frightful disaster had been witnessed from the ship, and the waste-boat was called into readiness and sent to their relief. The distance from the ship was about six miles. As soon as the waste-boat arrived, the crews were divided, and it was determined to pursue the same whale, and make another attack upon him. Accordingly they separated, and proceeded at some distance from each other, as is usual on such occasions, after the whale. In a short time they came up to him, and prepared to give him battle. The waste-boat, commanded by the first mate, was in advance. As soon as the whale perceived the demonstration being made upon him, he turned his course suddenly, and, making a tremendous dash at this boat, seized it with his widespread jaws and crushed it into atoms, allowing the men barely time to escape his vengeance by throwing themselves into the ocean.

Captain Deblois again seeing the perilous condition of his men, at the risk of meeting the same fate, directed his boat to hasten to their rescue, and in a short time succeeded in saving them all from a death little less horrible than that from which they had twice so narrowly escaped. He then ordered the boat to put for the ship as speedily as possible; and no sooner had the order been given, than they discovered the monster of the deep making toward them, with his jaws widely extended. Fortunately, the monster came up and passed them at a short distance. The boat then made her way to the ship, and they all got on board in safety.

After reaching the ship, a boat was dispatched for the oars of the demolished boats, and it was determined to pursue the whale with the ship. As soon as the boat returned with the oars, sail was set, and the ship proceeded after the whale. In a short time she overtook him, and a lance was thrown into his head. The ship passed on by him, and immediately after they discovered that the whale was making for the ship. As he came up near her, they hauled on one wing, and suffered the monster to pass her. After he had fairly passed, they kept off, to overtake and attack him again. When the ship had reached within about fifty rods of him, they discovered that the whale had settled down deep below the surface of the water, and, as it was near sundown, they concluded to give up the pursuit.

The WHALE & *His captors*

Captain Deblois was at this time standing in the knightheads, on the larboard bow, with craft in hand, ready to strike the monster a deadly blow should he appear, the ship moving about five knots, when, looking on the side of the ship, he discovered the whale rushing toward her at the rate of fifteen knots! *In an instant the monster struck the ship with tremendous violence, shaking her from stem to stern!* She quivered under the violence of the shock, as if she had struck upon a rock! Captain Deblois immediately descended into the forecastle, and there, to his horror, discovered that the monster had struck the ship about two feet from the keel, abreast the foremast, knocking a great hole entirely through her bottom, through which the water roared and rushed in impetuously! Springing to the deck, he ordered the mate to cut away the anchors and get the cables overboard to keep the ship from sinking, as she had a large quantity of pig iron on board. In doing this, the mate succeeded in relieving only one anchor and cable clear, the other having been fastened around the foremast. The ship was then sinking rapidly. The captain went to the cabin, where he found three feet of water; he, however, succeeded in procuring a chronometer, sextant, and chart. Reaching the deck, he ordered the boats to be cleared away, and to get water and provisions, as the ship was keeling over. He again descended to the cabin, but the water was rushing in so rapidly that he could procure nothing. He then came upon deck, ordered all hands into the boats, and was the last himself to leave the ship, which he did by throwing himself into the sea and swimming to the nearest boat!

The ship was on her beam-ends, her top-gallant yards under water. They then pushed off some distance from the ship, expecting her to sink in a very short time. Upon an examination of the stores they had been able to save, he discovered that they had only twelve quarts of water, and not a mouthful of provisions of any kind! The boats contained eleven men each, were leaky, and night coming on they were obliged to bail them all night to keep them from sinking!

Next day, at daylight, they returned to the ship—no one daring to venture on board but the captain—their intention being to cut away the masts, and fearful that the moment that the masts were cut away the ship would go down. With a single hatchet, the captain went on board, cut away the mast, when the ship righted. The boats then came up, and the men, by the sole aid of spades, cut away the chain cable from around the foremast, which got the ship nearly on her keel. The men then tied ropes round their bodies, got into the sea, and cut a hole through the decks to get out provisions. They could procure nothing but about five gallons of vinegar, and twenty pounds of wet bread. The ship threatened to sink, and they deemed it imprudent to remain by her longer, so they set sail on their boats and left her.

On the 22d of August, at about 5 o'clock P.M., they had the indescribable joy of discerning a ship in the distance. They made signal, and were soon answered, and in a short time they were reached by the good ship Nantucket, of Nantucket, Massachusetts, Captain Gibbs, who took them all on board, clothed and fed them, and extended to them in every way the greatest possible hospitality.

On the succeeding day, Captain Gibbs went to the wreck of the ill-fated Ann Alexander, for the purpose of trying to procure something from her; but, as the sea was rough, and the attempt considered dangerous, he abandoned the project. The Nantucket then set sail for Payta, where she arrived on the 15th of September, and where she landed Captain Deblois and his men. Captain Deblois was kindly and hospitably received and entertained at Payta by Captain Bathurst, an English gentleman residing there, and subsequently took passage on board the schooner Providence, Captain Starbuck, for Panama.

At Payta, Captain Deblois entered his protest at the United States Consulate, which was authenticated by the following officers and seamen, on board at the time of the disaster; the two officers and the rest of the crew having shipped on board other vessels: Joseph K. Green, first mate; James Smith, third mate; John Morgan, carpenter; James Riley, cooper; James McRoberts, John Smith, William Smith, Henry Reid, and Charles F. Booth, seamen.

This is the third instance on record of a whale-ship totally destroyed by the leviathan of the deep; the other two having been the Essex, and the Union, of Nantucket.

On the Brazil Banks, in the Atlantic Ocean, one year before this disaster to the Ann Alexander, a similar attack was made by an enormous bull whale upon the ship Pocahontas, of Tisbury. Two boats had gone in pursuit of the whale, and one of them had struck and been fast to the monster about twenty minutes, and had hauled on the line;

the WHALE *&* His *captors*

but, in their attempt to lance the whale, he turned upon the boat and literally crushed it to atoms. The crew were uninjured, having been picked up by the other boat. After the crews had got aboard the ship, the vessel ran for the whale, which still continued round the fragments of the boat, and when about two boat's length off, the whale turned and struck the vessel's bow with such force as to start one or two planks, and break one or two timbers on the starboard side of the bow, at the water's line, causing the vessel to leak at the rate of 250 strokes per hour. Happily, the Pocahontas was enabled to reach Rio Janeiro for repairs.

A like disaster happened to the whaling bark Parker Cook, in the vicinity of the Western Islands. In a conflict with a large sperm whale, he had stove and capsized the boat with his head, and the line caught the leg of the boat-steerer, John Hoxie, nearly severing the foot. While in the water, Hoxie took his knife from his pocket and cut the line. The waste-boat picked up the crew. Finding the whale was very warlike, Captain Cook prepared his bomb-lance and gun, and in the mean time the whale attacked the bark and struck her on the stem, which penetrated the head of the whale to the depth of the stem. The shock was so great that it threw every one on board upon the deck, and started the false stem. The whale then went off about half a mile, and ran upon the vessel a second time, but with less force. Captain Cook then attacked the whale in his boat, with his bomb-lance, and fired three times, within eighty yards, the whale coming at him each time with his mouth open, and "showing fight" in the most desperate manner. The third lance caused him to spit blood, and he died soon after, yielding 103 barrels of oil.

APPENDIX:

LEAVES FROM THE LOG OF A PRACTICED WHALEMAN

Since the publication of the first edition of "The Whale and his Captors," a townsman and school-mate of the author (Mr. Joseph B. Gow, now of Edgartown, Martha's Vineyard) has submitted to our perusal certain desultory leaves from the log of his whaling life. Believing they will add somewhat to the value of this volume, as a memoir of the whaleman's adventures and the whale's biography, we give portions of them here in due order, and with such divisions and connectives as were naturally suggested. We begin with our friend's report in doggerel respecting a whaleman's outfit, which he made for a raw hand who had shipped for the South Pacific.

A Fitting Out

A chest that is neither too large nor too small
Is the first thing to which your attention I'd call;
The things to put in it are next to be named.
And if some I omit, I am not to be blamed.
Stow first in the bottom a blanket and quilt,
To be used on the voyage whenever thou wilt;
Thick trowsers and shirts, woolen stockings and shoes,
Next your papers and books to tell you the news;
Good, substantial tarpaulins to cover your head;
Just to say, keep a journal, "N. C., nuff sed,"
Carry paper and ink, pens, wafers, and wax,
A shoemaker's last, awls, pegs, and small tacks;
Some cotton and thread, silk, needles, and palm,
And a paper of pins as long as your arm;
Two vests and a thimble, a large lot of matches,
A lot of good cloth that will answer for patches.
A Bible and hymn-book, of course, you must carry,
If you expect at the end of the first voyage to marry.
Don't forget to take essences, pipes, and cigars;
Of the sweetest of butter, a couple of jars.
A razor you'll want, a pencil and slate;
A comb and a hair-brush you'll need for your pate;
A brush and some shaving-soap, plenty of quills;

A box of those excellent Richardson's pills:
Opodeldoc and pain-killer surely you'll need,
And something to stop the red stream, should you bleed.
Some things I've omitted, but never mind that;
Eat salt-junk and hard bread, laugh and grow fat.

First Whaling Voyage

Experience only can give an adequate idea of the pleasures and pains of the blubber-hunter in his first pursuit of the leviathan of the deep. One who has sailed in merchant vessels is acquainted with part of the business, but to the landsman every thing connected with the employment is entirely new. His maneuvers for the first few days after the ship sails are not a little amusing. When ordered to haul the mainbrace, away he starts forward and seizes the fore-tack, fore-sheet, or the biggest rope he can find. If ordered aloft, he creeps up at a snail's pace, ever and anon casting fearful glances downward, clinging all the time to the shrouds with a tenacity that almost squeezes the tar out of them. When he reaches the top for the first time, there's the rub. Unused to support the weight of his body by his hands alone, he hesitates, and looks about him for a safer passage. He sees the lubber-hole, and endeavors to ascend through that, when he hears the voice of the officer of the deck hailing him, and in not the most pleasant voice, or in the most insinuating manner, order him up the futtock-shrouds. With the utmost exertion he accomplishes it, the perspiration starting from every pore. He ascends the top-mast rigging. His point of destination is the top-gallant cross-trees. He holds the two shrouds in his hands and looks aloft, where he sees nothing but the bare ropes—no places present themselves on which to fix his feet. He has often, perhaps, at home shown his dexterity by climbing trees, but here is climbing of a different nature to be done. When he reaches the cross-trees, instead of looking out for whales, he is gazing on deck, thinking "what a fall there would be" should he lose his hold. If he spies a sail, he sings out at the top of his voice, perhaps, "Ship, ahoy!" greatly to the amusement of the officer and those of the crew who are acquainted with the usual manner of reporting vessels.

His eating utensils consist of a pot, pan, spoon, and knife. The manner in which the victuals are cooked, and the ironbound wooden kids (as they are termed) in which the food is served up to the crew, deprive him of his appetite for several days. He must wash and mend his own clothes, things which never occurred to him when he embarked. His nightly slumbers are disturbed by the harsh cry of "Larboard" or "Starboard watch, ahoy!" when he must turn out and "patrol the deck" while some of his "weary mess-mates soundly sleep." If by chance, overcome with drowsiness, he is caught napping by the watch-header, he is saluted with a bucket of salt water, or, with a rope made fast to his feet, is triced aloft, before he can extricate himself from the difficulty.

All this, however, is but the beginning of his sorrows. When the ship reaches the cruising-ground, should whales be plenty, he will have reason to curse the day of his birth and the hour in which he was induced to sign the articles of a blubber-hunter; for now there is call for constant and unremitted exertion, which will continue so long as there is any blubber in the ship, until a full cargo of oil is obtained. So long as the ship can carry any sail, or the rain does not pour in torrents, the fire is kept up; while the cutting and mincing of the blubber, the removal of the scraps, the filling and rolling away the casks of oil, keep him busily employed eighteen hours out of twenty-four. Boats are frequently stove, men injured, and sometimes killed by whales. The boat-headers and harpoonersmen, after unsuccessful attempts to strike a whale, often vent their spleen on poor Pilgarlick in curses, or perhaps in kicks and cuffs.

The time at length arrives when the ship steers for port to recruit. She is thoroughly cleansed, and Jack looks forward with delightful anticipation to the few days' liberty he will be allowed on shore. They reach port, where, the ship having recruited, Jack (who looks upon himself as quite a sailor by this time) puts on his best apparel, and away he pulls for the shore, where he endeavors to drown recollections of the past and care for the future by frequent recourse to the bottle, till, overpowered by such unusual potations, he falls senseless in the street, or on the first bench that offers. When the effects of the liquor have subsided, he finds himself relieved, perhaps, of his money, shoes, and hat, and in no fit state to resume his duty on board the ship. He then either conceals himself till she has sailed, or goes on board, with an aching head and a heavy heart, to labor and toil till the time for recruiting the ship again returns, when he acts the same scene over again, with the variation, it may be, of a black eye or broken head, obtained in a row.

Whale-ology

Having assisted in capturing more than three hundred whales, and having often read articles upon them, I am sure there is no animal about which people in general entertain such erroneous ideas. Five different species have come under my own observation: the Sperm, Right or Black Whale, Finback, Humpback, and Sulphur-bottom. Many small ones of the genus whale I have met with, as the Black-fish, Cowfish, Grampus, Killer or Thrasher, and five different kinds of porpoises. The most valuable of all is the sperm whale. The greatest number of them are found in the torrid zone; but they are not unfrequently taken in colder regions. As far as my observation extends, they are often found in "schools" of twenty, thirty, forty, and sometimes three or four hundred in number. When alone they are usually of the largest size (that is, yielding from ninety to one hundred and twenty barrels of oil), and are invariably of the male species. The cows, which are much smaller (not affording more than twenty or thirty barrels), herd together, having one of the males (termed by blubber-hunters their king) to accompany them. This king is selected by whalemen as the first object of pursuit when a "school" of this description is discovered, well knowing, if they can capture him, the remainder of the school will "bring to;" giving them an opportunity to "strike" several others. He is often, however, wary and cunning, having been chased perhaps many times before. He either starts off on the first intimation, leaving his female companions to follow in the rear, or, if captured, drags the boat through the water at the rate of fifteen or twenty miles an hour, till their "lessening bark" reminds them of the folly of "holding on" longer; when with the knife or hatchet the line is severed, and the wearied and dejected crew return to the ship. Should he start before he is struck, in ninety-nine cases out of a hundred he will go to the windward, and then it would be as easy to overtake a rail-road car on foot as to come up with him.

From the time the sperm whale ship discharges her pilot, till he is welcomed on board again after the toils and perils of the voyage are over, one or more of the crew are stationed on the top-gallant cross-trees or royal yard, to look out for whales, which are rarely seen away from their usual haunts, unless they are passing from one "ground" to another. The men aloft, aware of the fact, while away the time in whistling, singing, and building castles in the *air*; and not unfrequently fall asleep, supported in a standing posture merely by the slender rigging that passes from the royal mast-head through the extremities of the narrow cross-trees on which they stand. In pleasant weather, when it is calm, in warm latitudes, the most wakeful feel drowsy. The gentle motion of the ship, like the rocking of a cradle, induces sleep; while the death-like stillness that prevails is undisturbed by aught but the officer of the deck, who, wholly intent on the main object of pursuit, occasionally is heard to shout,

"Keep a sharp look-out aloft!"

"Ay, ay, sir!" is returned; but any one present may easily perceive by the answer that the officer and man aloft possess entirely different feelings, at least at the time. I will relate an incident during the early part of my first voyage, which is indelibly impressed upon my memory. We had just captured our first whale, and, after cutting off and hoisting in the blubber, had commenced trying it out, a process which requires constant labor, day and night, until it is completed. During the forty-eight hours previous I had scarcely closed my eyes, and on being sent aloft, I sat down on the top-gallant yard (the sail being furled), and was soon overpowered by sleep. The motion of the ship threw me from the yard, and I narrowly escaped being precipitated to the deck by seizing the running rigging which passes up abaft the yard from which I fell. My back and side were slightly injured by coming in contact with the top-mast cross-trees, and I was sadly frightened. Ever after, when aloft, if I felt drowsy, by recalling this occurrence to mind, every symptom of sleep left me; and this incident is one among more than a hundred during my sea life, where the hand of an all-merciful God was visible in snatching me from the jaws of destruction.

Thousands of the whale called Humpback frequent those parts of the ocean where their more valuable relatives of the Spermaceti and Right whale species are found. Hitherto they have been seldom molested for several reasons. They are very irregular in their movements,

The WHALE *&* HIS *captors*

and when "struck" move with such velocity that it is almost impossible to pierce them with a lance in a vital part. If captured, their blubber is found to be thin and tough, yielding but little oil. When whalemen find nothing else to do, should humpbacks be plenty, they sometimes give chase, but rarely capture one. We tried the experiment once, and, though successful, were poorly paid for our day's toil.

One morning, while cruising near the Island of Mocha, on the coast of Chili, we were called before the watch below had expired, and found, when we came on deck, that two boats had been sent in pursuit of humpbacks at daylight, and that one of them was "fast." Hurrying into the remaining boat, away we went. It was calm, and the sea was smooth, so that we were enabled, after a pull of nearly three hours, to come up with the "fast" boat and give them our warp, which having secured, we rested for a season from our labors. When the other boat came up, we conferred on them the same favor we had received, by taking them in tow. Thus far the whale had kept near the surface, moving with a velocity that frequently brought the water over our bows. Our ride for an hour was very pleasant, and we had calculated to let him "take his time," when he turned toward the reef at the northern part of the island.

We knew that if he kept on in the direction he had taken the game would soon be up, as we should be obliged to cut the line. In a few minutes he changed his course, and shortly after went down, taking about thirty fathoms of line. The moment he rose to the surface Captain R. pierced him in the region of the heart, which caused him to spout blood. While making preparations to tow him to the ship, he turned on his back, bringing to view two fins twelve or fifteen feet in length, and, before we had time to clear the line, sunk, overturning the boat and giving us a cold bath gratis. We cut our line, and, having attached a buoy to it, went on board, resolved to secure the carcass as soon as it floated. Two days after it rose, extremely bloated, surrounded by a host of hungry sharks and hundreds of sea-fowl; forming altogether a noisy and voracious assemblage. It was dark before we reached the ship with our mountain of blubber. A storm, that had been gathering during the day, broke upon us, and before we could attach a chain to our prize the line parted. The boats were lowered once more, and it was nearly midnight before our job was completed. The next morning we "cut-in" our whale. The blubber resembled India rubber in its elasticity, and produced just seventeen barrels of oil, worth, at that time, about twenty-seven cents per gallon. A right or sperm whale of the same size would have yielded at least ninety barrels, besides a large quantity of bone, of which humpbacks are destitute.

Domestic Discipline of a Whale Ship:
The Whipping, and a Man Overboard

I have witnessed many distressing scenes, and looked upon those who have been bereft of life by their own hands, or have suffered violent deaths in different ways, but the unpleasant sensations produced were trifling when compared with those occasioned by gazing upon a fellow-being bound to a ship's shrouds, his back bared, and the flesh lacerated by a monster in human shape. I was once an unwilling spectator of such a revolting sight, but hope that I may never be compelled to "look upon the like again." When a ship falls in with whales, and accomplishes the object of her voyage in a short time, though wearied with constant toil and loss of sleep, "all hands" are usually good-natured and obliging—kind words are spoken, orders are obeyed with alacrity, and, should there be a leisure hour, merry songs are sung, the officers occasionally joining in the chorus; yarns are spun by those who are best acquainted with the art of story-telling; and Jack turns into his berth, drops asleep in a moment, dreams of swimming in a sea of spermaceti, and is awakened, perhaps, at the dawn of day by the pleasant sound of "There she blows!" when he springs from his resting-place, hurries on deck, jumps into the boat with a light heart and a ready will, realizing that every whale captured shortens the voyage.

How widely different is the state of affairs on board the ship that rarely sees a spout and seldom takes a whale. The demon of discord has full possession of the unlucky vessel. The officers disagree among themselves, when hard words are not unfrequently followed by hard knocks, while the crew look on, without siding with either party, hoping the combatants will use each other up, after the fashion of the famous Kilkenny cats. The men grumble at their meagre allowance, and proceeding in a body aft, demand a greater quantity of food. The skipper, if he is one not easily frightened, retreating to the cabin, returns with his pistols, and threatens to blow them into eternity if they

the WHALE & *his captors*

do not go forward. The menace, perhaps, quells the disturbance for a few days, but the peace and harmony of the voyage are at an end; and when the ship drops anchor in port, a large number of the crew desert.

The "spouter" in which I first embarked was "one of 'em." Our ill-conditioned craft was named Arab. Her officers and many of her crew seemed to be, in disposition at least, true descendants of Ishmael—their hands being against every man. Our captain, among his disagreeable traits, possessed two essential qualities. He was an excellent whaleman, and when in port laid in a good stock of provisions. As to the mate, he did not possess a redeeming feature. No one (himself included) ever knew who his father was; but, judging from his diabolical disposition, Old Scratch might have been his paternal ancestor. When we entered port for the first time, ten months after we sailed from the United States, hard usage, mean food dealt out with a grudging hand, and last, but not least, the small quantity of oil we had taken, caused seven of our crew to desert. For a trifling compensation, several Spaniards were induced to go in search of them. Two days after, about noon, Captain C., of the ship P———, belonging to Nantucket, a man, or rather monster, noted for his cruelty, brought two of the deserters on board, and stopped to enjoy the pleasure of seeing their punishment inflicted. To have witnessed the death of my two shipmates, had they been prepared, would have been far less painful than the sight which soon presented itself. The man first "seized up" was an Irishman, about twenty years of age. He was a good-natured, active, generous young fellow, who had always been ready to perform his duty; who had done nothing worthy of stripes or censure previous to his desertion. Having ordered the mate to prepare a bucket of pickle, to apply to the backs of the unfortunate beings after they had received their flogging, he pulled off his coat, and, rolling up his shirt-sleeves, took the instrument of punishment in his hand, and, with a fiend-like smile, he ordered the back of the poor son of Erin to be bared. Although he applied the lash with all his might, Peter Malone did not suffer a moan to escape his lips till the skin was broken, and the blood flowed in a stream from the mangled flesh. His silence enraged Captain R., who seemed determined to make the man plead for mercy. The agonized victim at length called on the Savior to have pity on him, but our blasphemous skipper told him, with an oath, that he called in vain. It would be impossible to describe my feelings. None but those who have had the misfortune to gaze on such a scene for the first time can realize them. The smothered wrath consequent on such a scene in a whale ship often breaks out into the fire of mutiny; and it is to be wondered at that desperate frays, and murder in hot blood, are not oftener experienced on the deck of an ill-managed whaler.

We had now been buffeting the gales and tempests of Cape Horn for six weeks, when the dense clouds broke away for a few moments, permitting the captain to get an observation. In a few minutes the disheartening intelligence was brought us by the steward that our latitude and longitude were the same it had been five weeks previous. Those of us who had never visited that region of storms and icebergs before despaired of seeing the pleasant coast of Peru, to which we were bound. About ten o'clock the next day the gale abated and the wind hauled to the eastward. We squared the yards, shook the reefs out of our sleet-bound top-sails, and our captain being determined to make the most of the fair wind while it lasted, ordered the main top-gallant sail to be set. The ship tore through the water at the rate of eleven knots an hour, as indicated by heaving the log. It was with difficulty that two men at the helm could keep her within three points of her course. In a few minutes eight bells were struck, and we went below to satisfy the cravings of hunger with a few ounces of black, coarse beef, and a cake of hard bread filled with insects. The wind was evidently increasing, and, before we had finished our scanty meal, we heard the mate's voice at the gangway calling us to "jump up and take in sail." We hurried on deck, let go the topsail and top-gallant's halyard, hauled out the reef-tackles, and hastened aloft, the larboard watch going up forward, and the starboard watch, to which I belonged, laying aloft aft to reef the main top-sail. Every thing was in confusion. The ship was nearly on her beam-ends, and the sails were slatting at such a rate that it was with the greatest difficulty that we could cling to the yards. "A man overboard!" shouted some one from the opposite yard-arm to that on which I had stationed myself; and, turning my head, I observed poor Thornton, who had at that moment risen to the surface of the water, and was vainly endeavoring to buffet the seas, which were literally running "mountains high." The second mate seized an

The WHALE & *His captors*

oar, and jumping on to the taffrail, threw it in the direction of the drowning man, but it floated by him unnoticed. We cleared away the quarter-boat, which had been lashed and griped to prevent the seas from carrying it away, and six men jumped into her while she hung by the tackles. "Lower away," shouted the mate, and the frightened steward, who held the fall of the forward tackle in his hand, let go, while the after fall remained fast. A huge sea struck the boat at the moment and broke her in twain. The men hung to the wreck, and, after being much bruised by the force with which they were dashed against the ship's side, were providentially rescued from a watery grave. In the mean time poor Thornton had sunk to rise no more.

He was a fine intelligent Englishman, about twenty years of age—had been my mess-mate and most intimate acquaintance on board the ship. He was an excellent singer, and I had whiled away the hours of many a cold, weary watch listening to the rich melody of his voice. I never was superstitious, as sailors usually are, neither do I believe in signs and dreams; but some things have occurred during my sea-life, which, to say the least, were very mysterious. Thornton had been the life of the crew, and a merrier, lighter-hearted fellow never existed, till two days before his death, when he suddenly became depressed. His cheerfulness forsook him, and he scarcely uttered a word during the cheerless watch on the night previous, as we stood together on the forecastle looking out for icebergs, which we know were not far distant. On going below he spoke of his mother, whom he had not seen for many years, and said he had a strange foreboding that something was about to happen. I tried to allay his apprehensions and cheer him up, but in vain. In less than fifteen minutes after Thornton was lost, our unfeeling captain came forward, ordered his chest to be brought on deck, and sold his effects at auction. Turning to the carpenter, who was shedding tears, he asked him what he was sniveling about, remarking, at the same time, that we must lose two or three more of our crew before we could make a voyage.

Dissatisfaction had prevailed on board our ship for some time. Ten months of our voyage had elapsed, and but a small part of our cargo had been obtained. Every thing went wrong. In the cabin and in the forecastle things wore a gloomy aspect. We had been cruising on the coast of Chili for nearly six months, and had succeeded in obtaining but one hundred and fifty barrels of oil. Our food was of the coarsest kind; and we were on short allowance. It consisted of corn, coffee, moldy bread, samp (unhulled corn, mashed and boiled in salt water), and two ounces of black beef for each man during twenty-four hours. Add to this, hard usage and hard labor, and you may have some faint idea of the state of things in our unlucky bark at the time I refer to. Our captain and chief mate were Nantucket men. Their hearts (if they had any) were harder than the nether mill-stone, and oaths and abuses were all that escaped their lips. One of our crew, George Bunker, a native of the Society Islands, had been confined to his berth with a cough for some time, and was rapidly sinking under that wasting disease, consumption. The captain paid him no attention, and it was evident that, unless something was done immediately, poor George must soon (as the sailors term it) be consigned to Davy Jones. The whales having left the cruising-ground for the season, we shaped our course to the northward, and glided under easy sail along the pleasant coast of Chili and Peru. We were in latitude seventeen degrees south, and the weather, which had been tempestuous, was now mild and pleasant. Saturday evening had arrived; the decks had been cleared up, and most of the crew (who were a rough, vicious set) were seated on their chests around the low, dark forecastle, smoking, singing songs, and spinning yarns. I sat by the berth of the sick man, holding his feverish hand in one of mine, and fanning him with the other, for he complained of the heat; when suddenly he started up, his eyes shone with unwonted brilliancy, he spoke of his wife and children in Otaheite, of the missionaries who had taught him to read, and then seemed to be engaged for a short time in prayer. In a few minutes his extremities became icy cold, and indications of speedy dissolution rapidly succeeded. I begged of the crew to suppress their noise and mirth, telling them that their shipmate was very near his end. They would not believe me, and heeded not the groans of the dying man. In about five minutes George grasped my hand convulsively, gave a long, deep sigh, and all was over. His spirit had winged its way to God, who gave it. I hastened aft, and informed the captain that George was no more. He would not credit it until the mate went forward and found it was as I reported. The scene in the forecastle was instantly changed. When the hardened crew found that death had entered their confined limits, they hastily retreated, and but two of us remained with the corpse during the night. On the following morning (Sunday) the sun rose in a cloudless sky, and we were going through the water with a fine top-gallant sail breeze at the rate of five or six knots an hour. We brought the body of our deceased shipmate on deck, and, having sewed him up in his blanket, attached a bag of sand to his feet, placed him on the gangway board, which had been taken out for that purpose, and awaited the order of the captain, who was walking the quarter-deck. The mate informed him that every thing was in readiness, when, without deigning to speak, he waived his hand as a signal to launch the body into the deep. We did so, and the weight attached to the corpse being insufficient to sink it, after remaining below the surface of the water a moment, it rose and was seen floating astern. Never shall I forget that scene. I have witnessed the death and burial-service of many persons, both at sea and on shore, before and since, but the sufferings, exit, and the inhuman manner in which the mortal remains of that poor neglected islander were committed to the deep, left on my mind an impression never to be erased.

Incidents of a Calm

Nothing is more disheartening to the tempest-tossed mariner than a dead calm. Scudding under bare poles is pleasant when compared with it. During a sea life of six years, I never experienced but one calm of long duration, and I did not know as that would ever end. At the close of the season, when whales were to be found on the coast of Chili, we squared our yards, crowded all the sail we could conveniently carry, and pointed our black, greasy-looking ship's head toward Talcahuana for the purpose of recruiting. When within a few hours' sail of the mouth of the harbor, the wind hauled to the northward and blowed a "screamer." We were obliged to change our course to the westward. After scudding four days under a close-reefed main-top-sail and fore-topmast staysail, the lofty island of Massefuero loomed up through the mist. Having been rather lavish of our fresh water during the last month, with the expectation of a fresh supply in a few weeks, we were now obliged to be put on allowance of half a pint a day; and such water! of the consistency of soft soap. Our skipper determined, if possible, to obtain a small supply at this island.

After rafting a few casks, we towed them ashore, anchoring our boat outside the surf, for we could not land with the boat, and getting our casks to and from the boat by means of a guess-warp. We found a stagnant pool of water, resembling a frog pond, covered with a green mantle, from which we slaked our burning thirst and filled our casks. Having towed them to the ship and hoisted them on board, we braced forward and stood to the westward still further, hoping to fall in with sperm whales, which are sometimes found in that region. On starting our water, we found, in addition to the other rare qualities it possessed, that it was strongly impregnated with tar, the casks having contained hemp tow-line previous to being filled with the contents of the frog pond. But there was no remedy. We must either drink it or choke. After traversing ten or twelve degrees of longitude, and seeing nothing that looked like a *spout*, we concluded to return, when, *horribile dictu!* our breeze died away, and there we lay three long weeks with our top-sail yards on the caps, and not a cloud to be seen above the horizon during the whole time, the sun beating down on our devoted heads with an intensity that fried the tar out of our decks. We rattled and tarred down the rigging, cleaned and painted the hull, and manufactured all of our old rigging into spun-yarn and oakum —and still it was calm. Despair was depicted on every countenance. We whistled and whistled for a breeze, but all in vain; not a fish, not a bird, not even an insect was to be seen. When the last spark of hope was nearly extinct, and but a few gallons of water remained in the scuttle, a faint ripple was seen on the edge of the horizon, which tantalized us for several days. Gradually it approached us. A puff of wind would now and then lift our royals; and finally, to our great joy, a steady breeze set in, which wafted us into port, not, however, until the last drop of water was consumed, and our mouths were parched with thirst.

Again, it was a beautiful afternoon in Autumn that our noble ship, the Hercules, lay becalmed within a few miles of the shores of that lovely island, Juan Fernandez. The useless sails hung flapping against the mast, as our bark gradually rose and fell with the long, undulating swell. It was Sunday, and our crew, dressed in clean duck frocks and trowsers, were scattered about the decks, lying on the windlass and hatches, or leaning listlessly over the rail, watching the motions of a

the WHALE *&* his *captors*

large shark that had followed us for several weeks, seeking for blubber quite as anxiously as ourselves. To the landsman the Sabbath is emphatically a day of rest; but the sailor can not, with any certainty, call it so. It may be, and it may not, according to circumstances. Sail is sometimes to be *made*, and *taken in*. Should whales be seen, they are to be pursued. If captured, they are to be *cut-in* and *tried out*; otherwise nothing is expected of Jack, but to take his trick at the wheel, stand two hours on the top-gallant yard or cross-trees, looking out for whales, and to wash and holystone the decks in the morning. Our eagle-eyed skipper (from whose keen observation naught on the wide expanse of waters escaped, so far as the eye could scan) stopped suddenly, as he was pacing the deck, and clapping his hands, exclaimed in a suppressed voice, "Just look at that fellow, Mr. Folger." "Where?" asked the mate. "Not a mile off, two points forward of the larboard beam," returned the delighted captain, skipping about the deck in ecstacies, for we had seen no whales for several months.

The captain watched the monster at his uncouth gambols for a few minutes, now and then uttering exclamations like the following: "He lays like a log!" "He's slow as night!" "There she blows!" "There she lop-tails!" "There goes flukes!" "There she breaches!" &c., when hailing the man aloft, and cursing him for not keeping a better look-out, he called him down. Orders were then given to clear away and lower the boats without noise. Captain Howland charged the officers to be careful and not go on to the whale's eye; to lay well off, and to use the paddles instead of our oars, as they would make less noise. We were scarcely fifty yards from the ship when the whale turned and came directly toward us, quickening his speed as he advanced. His color was a dingy white, and I have noticed that whales of that complexion, without exception, are vicious and extremely cunning.

"Lay aside your paddles, boys," said the mate, "and be ready to take your oars. Work quick, for we must take him *head and head*. Stand up, Huzzy," addressing the harpoonsman, "and look out for him."

It was a moment of deep, anxious suspense, for we all anticipated trouble. Not a word was spoken; we scarcely breathed. It was such a stillness as generally precedes some dire convulsion of nature. "Give it to him!" shouted the mate, and the burnished harpoon glistened a moment in the air, and then buried itself to the socket in the bowels of the monster. With one convulsive sweep of his flukes he filled the boat half full of water, and then, throwing them high in the air, sought to escape his relentless pursuers in the fathomless abyss beneath. The velocity with which he descended caused the mate to be enveloped in smoke, occasioned by the rapid friction of the line around the logger-head. Before we were aware, he arose and took the boat in his mouth. Four of the crew jumped overboard. I remained in the boat. Just imagine yourself, if you will, in my situation, seated between those mighty engines of destruction. Now I confess that I was not more courageous than my companions, but always considered myself safer in a boat than in the water at such times. The thwart on which I sat prevented him from crushing the boat and myself. It was originally pine, had been broken and replaced by an ash one an inch in thick-ness. Had he seized the boat a few inches further toward the head or stern, I should not at this time be comfortably seated at my table in an easy chair relating this most providential escape. Finding he could not effect his object, he relaxed his hold, and, settling down, soon rose near the second mate's boat, who, by a well-directed lance, dis-patched him.

I know of no more terrific sight than that of a whale during its dying agonies. With his head raised a few feet above the surface of the water, he describes a circle from an eighth to a quarter of a mile in circumference, lashing the sea into a foam with his jaw and flukes, throwing the clotted gore from his spout-hole several feet into the air, with a noise not unlike the roaring of a mad bull, until exhausted with his mighty exertions and the loss of blood, he turns on his back and (what is a remarkable fact) dies with his head toward the sun.

If I ever experienced a moment of real joy during my "spouting" excursions, it was after a dangerous conflict with the leviathan of the deep, when I felt assured that the spark of life was extinct. The proud-est moment of my life was when I struck the first whale, and, as good fortune would have it, killed him with the harpoon, which is a rare thing. As I gazed upon his huge form, I thought, was it possible, with my puny arm, that I could bereave such a monster of life! I felt then that I was entitled to make a selection from that society of fair dam-sels in Nantucket, who have pledged themselves to unite in the silken bonds of Hymen with no one unless he has killed a whale.

Adventure with a Blasted Whale

Two most laughable incidents occurred in one of my voyages, which I will here relate. One pleasant morning while we were cruising on the coast of Chili, the man aloft reported a dead whale on our starboard bow two miles distant, and two living ones on the weather beam further off. Thinking it easier to take care of a dead whale than to kill live ones, our skipper sent the third mate to ascertain the state of the animal, and, if worthy, to tow him alongside. In order to test the soundness of his whaleship, Mr. Chambers went to the leeward of the bloated monster, and, taking up a spade thrust it into his bread-basket. The pent-up gas finding an outlet, escaped in large quantities, followed by a stream of corruption a foot in diameter, which descended upon the heads of the crew, and, before they could withdraw from their unpleasant situation, nearly filled the boat. Captain R., who was eyeing them through his glass from the ship, exclaimed, as he saw the effects of Mr. C.'s folly, "Mr. Brook, that whale isn't dead; he just spouted thick blood." As to the third mate, he did not stop to make another incision, but hurried to the ship, swearing terribly, and emitting an exceedingly offensive scent. Notwithstanding the catastrophe, the skipper, believing the whale to be valuable, commissioned the chief mate to tow the carcass alongside. He did so, and we saved nearly all the bone, and obtained from the blubber about eighty barrels of oil; but we were not free from the dreadful effluvium for several weeks. I presume that Mr. Chambers considered himself one of the initiated, and never afterward tapped a *blasted* whale on the lea side.

During the month following we were cruising near the Island of Mocha, where we took two or three whales, and, having tried out the blubber, secured two tall pipes, containing part of it, to the railing near the gangway. A gale coming on, the motion of the ship caused the ropes with which the casks had been secured to slip down below their bilge. At midnight, while the officer of the deck and the cooper were leaning against the circle-rail of the main-mast, a surge of the ship caused the pipes to fall at their feet. The heads flew out, and the contents thoroughly drenched the poor fellows. A part of it found its way into the steerage and cabin, while not a small portion flowed, through an aperture in the deck, into the butt containing all the fresh water we had. During three subsequent weeks our tea, coffee, and switchel had a rich coating of right-whale gurry, which caused the small quantity we drank for the purpose of allaying our thirst to slip down "amazing easy."

While writing the last sentence an old saying came into my mind, that every person must eat a peck of dirt during life. For one, I verily believe that while at sea I devoured more than a bushel of the dirtiest kind of dirt. Not unfrequently have I found shingle nails and rope-yarns in my duff. If we found hairs only, we considered that a mere circumstance. I was never perplexed with a very delicate appetite, but I am persuaded, had I been cast away, during the latter part of my sea life, on the "Cannibal Islands," I could readily have feasted with King "Hoky-poky" on any outlandish mess he might have had served up. Were cockroaches poison I should not have lived till this date. Many a time, during a night-watch, have I gone below, and groping my way in the dark to the place where I had kept my tin cup of cold tea or coffee, have found my swallow impeded by one of those rampscallions, who find a passage into every thing containing food or drink. Whalemen, however, it must be admitted are often favored with two dainties that landsmen can not obtain. The first is right whale's lip, fried in oil; the second, barnacles taken from the head of the same animal, and prepared in the same manner.

We had been cruising on the Off-shore Ground, near the Equator, for several weeks without seeing the spout of a whale. The sky had been cloudless during the day, and the weather oppressively hot. It was a stage of the moon when whalemen expect to see the object of their pursuit. Large quantities of squid, the fish (if they may be so called) on which the sperm whale feeds, had been observed during the last week. The decks had been cleared up, when, having eaten supper, I went aloft to relieve the man on the fore-topgallant cross-trees. I had remained about two hours, thinking (I confess) but little about whales, and caring less about seeing them at that late hour. My eyes were turned toward the glorious King of day, shooting forth his golden beams, as he was about sinking below the expanse of waters, when my attention was aroused by a column of thin vapor ascending from the surface of the ocean about four miles distant, in the direction of the setting sun. The wind was light, and the ship moved sluggishly along, at the rate of scarcely two knots an hour.

the WHALE & *his captors*

In a few moments it was evident, from the number of spouts, that a large school of sperm whales were approaching us slowly from the windward. I was as eager to obtain a voyage as any one on board, and as anxious to receive the bounty which our skipper had offered as an additional incentive to "look sharp;" but I had no desire to battle the monsters of the deep by moonlight. The school had gone down, and the sun was about doing the same, when the man on the main top-gallant yard shouted,

"There she blows," &c.

If you had thrust a stick into a hive of bees the effect could not have been more apparent.

"Where away!" yelled the captain, while the officers and half the crew flew to the railing and mounted aloft with as much speed as if the hull was just sinking beneath them.

The whales were now about two miles distant, unconscious of the proximity of their foes. After viewing the monsters at their uncouth gambols, through his glass from the top-sail yard, Captain Howland gave orders to lower the boats and use the paddles, cautioning us against making a noise. We moved along much more rapidly than I wished, and in fifteen minutes found ourselves in the midst of humps and flukes. It was an anxious moment, and when the harpoonersman stood up, with his burnished weapon poised, ready, at the word of command, to bury it in the back of a huge fellow under our bows, we scarcely breathed.

"Give it to him!" shouted the mate, as the head of the boat came in contact with the hump of a seventy-barrel whale. The order was obeyed, and the black mass disappeared beneath the surface of the water, apparently uninjured.

Like Agag of old, we thought "the bitterness of death had passed;" but we reckoned without our host. On feeling ourselves gently drawn through the water, we commenced "hauling line;" and the mate, having exchanged places with the boat-steerer, took up the second iron, and, just as the whale rose to the surface of the water, darted it. A crash followed, and for a moment we could hardly tell whether we were in this world or the next. A sharp pain in my side convinced me that I was still living, but that the extremity of the whale's flukes had reached me; and, upon examination, we ascertained that three of the thin cedar boards of which our frail boat was built were broken, leaving a large aperture. The thwart on which I sat was split from end to end. The mate proposed to cut the line, but we objected. It was trouble we had not sought, but now we were "in for it," we were reckless of the consequences. Careening the boat, we contrived, by filling the hole with some articles of clothing, and constantly bailing, to keep ourselves afloat.

After many fruitless trials, the mate, by chance, pierced a vital part, causing the monster to throw a column of thin blood into the air. But the victory was incomplete. Just at that moment the starboard boat came up, and the third mate, in endeavoring "to fasten," was upset. Away darted the enraged whale, and we as rapidly followed, holding on to our prize with a tenacity that frequently brought the water over our bows. Once more the mate asked the question, "Boys, shall we cut?"

But our organs of firmness and combativeness having been thoroughly aroused and brought into action, a unanimous "No, sir," was the only reply.

The white water near the bows of the boat, as the whale occasionally slackened his speed and lashed the sea into a foam with his flukes and jaw, together with the crimson stream which was now and then visible, satisfied us that the enemy must soon surrender.

Our utmost exertions were now insufficient to bring the boat nearer to the object of our pursuit, and whenever we relinquished our hold on the line and took our oars for the purpose of pulling up, he was off with the rapidity of a railroad car.

It was now after ten o'clock, and the sky was obscured with clouds. The second mate's boat had been carried by a whale to the leeward before we were "fast." The ship had long since disappeared, and the cooling night-breeze, together with the spray that flew over us, began to damp our zeal, and lead us to think seriously on our situation.

We knew that the ship was at the leeward far distant, but how far, or her precise direction, we could not tell. As the breeze began to freshen and the whale's speed to increase, the mate took up the hatchet, and without opposition severed the line. After rowing an hour toward what proved to be a star instead of a ship's light, we changed our course, and shortly fell in with the starboard boat. The

the WHALE & *his* captors

crew had righted her, and, placing their oars across the gunwales to keep her upright, opened their lantern-keg and struck a light which attracted our attention. They had seen the ship's signal, and directed us what course to steer. We were soon alongside, and shortly after took up the other boat.

The second mate, who had not been seen since dark, was soon discovered ahead towing a good-sized whale, which we secured with a stout chain, hoisted up the boats, and shortened sail. The watch was set, and the remainder of us turned in at two o'clock, to sleep two thirds of the time till daylight, which occurred at half past three. About six o'clock next morning, as we were hoisting in the last "blanket-piece," the boy stationed aloft informed us that a dead whale was floating on the water about a mile distant on our weather-bow. We lowered our boats, and soon ascertained, by the iron and line attached to it, that we had a better claim to him than any one else. He yielded seventy-five barrels of oil.

Whalemen Ashore and Homeward-bound

During the six years I was engaged in the whaling service, having visited many ports in South America and elsewhere, I became acquainted with the manner in which seamen spend their time and money when "on liberty" ashore. After several months of toil and privation at sea, destitute of many of the necessaries as well as the comforts of life, the ship is moored in some harbor, where, after water and provisions have been conveyed on board, each "watch" is allowed to spend two or three days alternately on shore, where, instead of improving the opportunity in recruiting the body and partaking of that which is nourishing, the means adopted have a tendency to weaken and derange the physical, mental, and moral powers. There are persons in every port who obtain a livelihood by catering to the depraved appetites of their fellow-beings. I can think of no more apt comparison of a ship's company landed on the pier in a foreign port than that of the inmates of one of our prisons (after several months' confinement, having in their intercourse matured plans for gratifying their evil propensities) being let loose for a few days, to spend their time as they please, in such a place as the Five Points, in New York. So long as men perform their duty on board the ship, and the officers are unmolested, it matters not of what misdemeanors they may be guilty. If young men in this Christian land run into excesses, what will they do, or, rather, what will they not do, where they are under no moral restraint, but where the multitude pursue vice for their chief gratification, and where intemperance and debauchery stalk abroad by daylight, decked in all the gorgeous array that wicked imaginations can invent? Some of almost every ship's company desert, after spending as much of their earnings as they can obtain, having sold a part, or perhaps the whole, of their "fitting out." It is a common saying among whalemen that a man who has passed three years on shore in South American ports is a confirmed villain.

Most of the intoxicating beverages sold in South America are far more destructive to the human system than those vended in the United States, a comparatively small quantity being sufficient to produce *delirium tremens* or *mania à potu*. It contains so much deadly poison that the use of it causes the body to be covered with loathsome sores, not unfrequently throwing the unhappy victim into convulsions. The liquor to which I refer is a cheap article manufactured in the country. Sailors usually buy this, as imported spirits are sold at a dear rate. I will relate an incident that occurred in Talcahuana, in Chili, just previous to our departure for home. Our captain shipped a blacksmith, who, when brought on board (for he was quite helpless), presented the most wretched aspect imaginable. His face was bloated and covered with carbuncles, his eyes were fringed with a deep scarlet, and he appeared to be perfectly saturated with the poisonous liquid he had imbibed. His chest contained about two gallons of ardent spirits, which he consumed in a few days. His rum exhausted, being unable to obtain more, he endeavored, after much persuasion, to take some refreshment. I went on deck to get some tea for him, and before I returned he fell from his chest in a fit. Some time elapsed before it left him, and for several weeks he remained feeble. Gradually he recovered his appetite and strength, and before we doubled Cape Horn he was an altered man. I never witnessed so great a change in the outward appearance of any person in so short a time. He was an excellent mechanic, possessed a good education, and was very intelligent. He told me that he went out to South America for the purpose of working at his trade, and that after pursuing it attentively for six or

the WHALE *&* HIS *captors*

eight months, he received his wages, came to Talcahuana, and, during six weeks previous to our arrival, spent his money, and reduced himself to the disgusting situation in which we found him. He solemnly pledged himself to drink no more. On our arrival at Fairhaven he went to New Bedford, and for a few days remained true to his vow; but "company, villainous company," as Falstaff says, induced him to commence a course of dissipation once more, and the last time I saw the poor fellow, he was engaged in a low, dirty cellar setting up nine-pins to obtain liquor.

Among the causes that lead to habits of dissipation among sailors, the examples of officers is not among the least. Many of those entitled temperance ships do not deserve the name, for although rum is expelled from the forecastle and steerage, it is not banished from the cabin. I have sailed in vessels of this description. When officers from other ships came on board, the steward was ordered to place the decanter and glasses on the table, and during storms *they* fortified themselves with a glass, while "Jack" was left to wet his whistle with salt or fresh water if he pleased. The ship in which I made my first voyage carried out two barrels of New England rum. After encountering head-winds, and being two months in the region of Cape Horn, we found ourselves one evening on a lee-shore near the Straits of Magellan. Captain R. deemed it necessary to carry a heavy press of sail during the night, and all hands were required to be on duty till morning. Among others, I was called into the cabin for the purpose of "signing my death-warrant," as Captain R. termed it. Never was the act of quaffing a glass of liquor more fitly characterized. To how many young men has the drinking a glass of rum been the death-warrant which has forever sealed their temporal and eternal destiny? Once afterward, before sailing for home (on an occasion when it was necessary to "cut-in" two whales during a night when a gale was expected), our *death-warrant* was signed.

Our provisions had been coarse and scanty during the voyage, and our captain, a severe man, had flogged two of the crew. To efface the remembrance of his hard usage, and prevent prosecution on his return home, during three months he came on deck every morning, and dealt out with his own hands the remnant of the two barrels of New England rum. It had the desired effect with many, but there are a few from whose minds the dreadful scenes enacted on board that vessel will never be effaced.

Wants of Seamen

Seamen need a *good library* on board ship. They have *mental* as well as bodily wants. They have not only the bone and sinew of other men, they have also, in proportion to their cultivation, the same intellectual powers, and the same capacity of mental elevation and enjoyment. They must be taught as other men, and the same importance attaches to the proper culture of their minds as is plead so wisely and successfully for the merchants, farmers, mechanics, and day-laborers of their native land. The sphere of their influence is wider than that of the mass of laboring landsmen, and, for evil, that influence has hitherto been much greater and more lasting. It has entered every port, and penetrated far into the interior of every empire. The wings of commerce have encircled the earth, and every where carried their physical and moral contamination. They are to vast multitudes, in every clime, the representatives of the nation under whose flag they sail. Entitled to their country's protection wherever they may roam, they may, by ignorance, indiscretion, or perverseness, cost more treasure and blood than the life-services of all their numerous class could ever redeem. Hence they have a moral and national importance far beyond their individual worth. They are, in a sense, the speaking trumpets and traveling preachers of the world. Their own characters and deeds have often been the darkest message they have conveyed, and the best exemplification of the necessity of useful knowledge and sound religious instruction. New England *gospel* and New England *rum* have freighted the same ship. The inconsistency and contradiction caught quickly the eye and stung deeply the heart of good men. But how few have discovered and mourned over the same, as exhibited in the band of praying missionaries in the cabin, and the profane and licentious crew of the forecastle; intelligence and ignorance—prayer and cursing—the hymn and the ribald song—the Sabbath and the day of lewd merriment—a Heaven and Hell going together to the conversion of the world! The day will come when the union will be severed, and the shame blotted out. But it will not be till more is done for the sailor. Sermons on shore will not do it. Nor will seamen's chaplains, unaided,

the WHALE *&* HIS *captors*

bring about the desired change. No combination of good influences on land will reform or preserve the sailor at *sea*.

Those influences must *follow* him around the world. They must be within his reach, and by his side, on his own element. They must be brought to bear upon him in his cabin and on deck; at the helm or aloft; on the "look-out" or in pursuit of the whale. Nor will any amount of *physical* reform accomplish the object. If all we have advocated, and much more, should be done for seamen, and a fair understanding, good government, wholesome fare, and suitable accommodations should be secured to him, he would indeed feel the impulse and exhibit a change. But if not followed by other and higher reforms, the sailor would, in the most important respects, remain the same. These changes in his physical condition would be necessary to the successful introduction of higher and better, and indispensable concomitants to complete reform. But they would *civilize* only, they could not essentially enlighten the mind. Certainly they could not renew the heart. And so intimately are the needed reforms linked together, that an *advance* beyond and above is necessary to the permanence even of physical improvement. Civilization, unsustained by intelligence and religion, will exhaust its own energies, and relapse into an indolent and sordid repose, and, if not resuscitated, die. The reforms we have been urging at the hands of masters and owners, if not followed by the better deportment, corresponding elevation of character, increased intelligence, and rational enjoyment of their men, would only confirm them in their false reasoning, and remand the half-delivered captive to his prison. It is, therefore, as necessary to *advance* as it was to come up to our present position. We have entered the enemy's territory and have taken a few fortresses, but complete victory must be gained at the *gate of the Capitol*, and in the very heart of the country. Our weapons, like the objects of our warfare, are not "carnal." Our colors are white, and our terms of peace, like our badge of victory, KNOWLEDGE and GODLINESS.

As the best practical means of securing intelligence among seamen, we insist on A LIBRARY adapted to their wants. Further than instruction in navigation, to those who may wish it, by the master or mate, and perhaps in reading to those ignorant of the art, by those kindly disposed, of their own number, we can not urge the school system of instruction; nor this, only as ships' duties will permit. The impracticability of this mode of imparting and gaining knowledge makes the resort to books more necessary.

Nor should the fragments of time at the sailor's command be wasted on *trash*. He should not be able to put his hand upon an unworthy book. The space it would occupy on the shelf, or in the mind and heart, had better be empty. *Comical, tragical,* and *fictitious* writings should, as a general rule, be kept from his perusal. Exceptions should be rare, and made with unwonted prudence. The first tends, in the sailor's mind, to excessive and empty joviality. The second raises in his adventurous spirit a careless boldness, and has sometimes stirred him up to treachery and blood. The latter excites an uneasy curiosity or unhappy discontent, and often ends in desertion, and consequent exposure and disgrace. Better if exceptions to entire exclusion of such works from the ship's library be never allowed. The influence of such works on the little informed, and the immature in principle, is always questionable. Besides, "*truth is stranger than fiction,*" and sobriety better than mirth, and the foul and bloody deeds of reckless men had better remain in the dark book of the judge for future reference in the trials of like criminals, than to be transcribed, and thus the "firebrands, arrows, and death" of hellish passions let loose on their fiendish errands of arson, murder, mutiny, and treason.

Infidel and *licentious* works should, of course, never disgrace a respectable library. No wise owner would ever put such combustibles in contact with a sailor's magazine. Better far scourge him to excessive toil, and fetter him a slave, than thus liberate him on the broad road to ruin. Mercy might rescue him in ignorance and in slavery, but in infidelity and the house of death infinite love could save neither him, nor yet the *murderer of his soul.* Who would write, or print, or sell, or scatter the leaves of such a Upas, whose deadly influence would collect from the north, and south, and east, and west, and from the ocean's depth, and the ship's cabin, so many and such swift witnesses of woe?

But books of HISTORY are peculiarly appropriate to the library we propose. And the selection might be made with particular reference to the countries lying in the track of the voyage. This circumstance would give additional charms to the best written history of any nation, and often induce the otherwise indifferent sailor to peruse its pages. He will feel at home on a foreign shore if his memory has chronicled any of the events connected with the race who people it. It will be an introduction to the intelligent and the good, if he can properly discover to them his knowledge of their national peculiarities, their soil, their wealth, their religious and literary institutions. Or, if he had no liberty and no inclination or opportunity on shore, or its clouded hills alone told the land was there as they passed it, the knowledge he had acquired would create self-respect and a thirst for more.

In connection with history, books on NATURAL SCIENCE would, of course, furnish ample amusement and valuable instruction. And these may be obtained in every dress, and with every illustration and embellishment, to suit the progress, style, age, and language of the reader. Entertaining conversation, or simple narrative, or pictorial illustration, or the graver style of scientific research and discussion, take the reader on through the various fields of useful knowledge, so various are the styles by which are pleased the equally various tastes of the reader.

Books of *travel*, of *voyages*, of *exploration and discovery*, should be found within the sailor's reach. They contribute to an interesting branch of knowledge, giving not only life-sketches of the actual state of the world, but revealing the *progress* of mankind, and the resources and wonders on the surface and in the bowels of the earth. Such knowledge would be interesting to the sailor as he plows the deep, or touches here and there in his voyage round the globe.

But, above all, RELIGIOUS books should meet the sailor on every shelf of his library. And it is a matter of rejoicing, that while religious instruction is most needed by this class of men, it is, at the same time, conveyed to us in all the variety and attractiveness that invite the taste and secure the attention of mankind to other and less important branches of education. Doctrine, history, biography, devotion, and practical duty are taught, related, illustrated, and enforced in every style, from the utmost simplicity to the height of dignity and sublimity. A suitable number and variety of these should tempt the sailor's eye, and reach the sailor's heart. This is but an imperfect sketch of an appropriate library for seamen. Good judgment, with a desire to benefit intellectually and morally this neglected class of men, could hardly fail of making a proper inviting selection. *Common school* books should not be overlooked. A judicious selection of periodicals would not be out of place. And, first of all, the *Bible* should be there; it should be his own. It needs hardly to be added, that these books should be for all; nor yet that a reasonable measure of time should be allowed for reading. With these facilities the complaint would soon cease that seamen have *no taste* for reading, or a taste only for books of a vile or unprofitable character. There has been but little chance for the cultivation of a better. It would have been a miracle if, with all their physical wants and abuses, they should, even with the best opportunities, have found any other. Nor need the proper use of this means of improvement interfere with the ship's duties. It should not, and would not. And it would be a libel on human improvement to suppose that such a course would *make men above an honorable employment or respectful and proper subordination.* Owners, and masters, too, would ultimately find such expenditure of time and means for the *interest of all.* While, then, so much is done on land to increase knowledge, and every town and village association and school district has its library, let a generous portion of the leaves of this great Tree of Life be scattered over the broad and peopled ocean.

A sailor, too, wants *a fair understanding as to the voyage before entering upon it.* This he does not always get. It may sometimes be his own fault. The buoyancy of youth brightens the dark horizon, smooths the rough seas, amplifies the narrow accommodations, and softens the hard words and the hard fare incident to the life he covets; and little does he think, and less does he care, as to where, with whom, and how long his home is to be upon the ocean wave. Without a tear he turns his back upon the dull scenes of his childhood, and with the blue deep in his eye, merrily shakes off the habiliments of the landsman, and with tarpaulin and trowsers welcomes mast-head, windlass, and helm. He makes few inquiries, and gets or cares but for little knowledge of what is before him. This is both his fault and his misfortune. His fondness for sea life must amount to a passion if stern usage and hard work do not dash his hopes and sadden his heart. But he has no one to blame. His own imagination blinded his eyes and thrust him into his prison. Be his bed hard, his fare coarse, his labor perilous, his thoughtlessness incurred them, and he must

the WHALE & HIS *captors*

bear them; the fault is his own. He must abide his time, as patiently and cheerily as may be, meanwhile dreaming of his praying mother, and sighing for his home. Had he known where he was to make his bed, with whom and how he was to eat, what perils and escapes of wrecks and flukes he was to meet, he would have thought old ocean a deceiver, and the oil of her monsters easier *bought* than *obtained*. Perhaps his disappointment will wear upon him, and sicken him of his adopted element; if so, Jack will become landsman again, having learned one valuable lesson, to "*look* before you *leap*."

Some do "look." They have before hardened their hands to the same work, and their ears, and perhaps their tongues, if not their hearts, to sea profanity, and often to obscenity. Though in one sense it is often "in the *dark*," yet they know where they are to "leap." They know the "dark hole" under the bows of the ship; they have sat down to their "grub" on the deck, or on their chests, or under the lee of the bulwarks; they have dodged to escape the fragments of their shivered boat, and heard the "whiff" of the descending fluke that hurried their less fortunate shipmate into eternity. They have tugged long at the dying whale, which perhaps at length sunk from their reach, leaving them through sudden fogs, and with much weariness, and with no prize to repay them, to toil back all day, over a "chopped sea," to their lost vessel, and perhaps an ordinary supper. All this they know, and they will have it again. Perhaps they have no better home on land; or, having a better, still love the exposures and excitements of the worse. They enter the lists again, and, if not trampled on by their superiors, these sturdy fellows will fill the ship with little trouble to her officers, only anxious of promotion, or content at their voyage's end to draw their well-earned "shares." They have got what they expected, a sailor's berth and a whaleman's toil, rigid rule and a full ship. They have generally no ground of complaint.

But there is a class who *have*. It would be foolishly credulous to believe every tale of abuse that reaches our ears; yet, if the word of officers and men can be at all relied on, there is on the part of those who ship men a *gross amount of deception* practiced in the whaling fleet. Flattering and often false representations are made of the ship, its accommodations, character of the master and officers, shortness and profitableness of the voyage, &c., thus creating expectations which the first day at sea dooms to disappointment and chagrin. Perhaps it is his first voyage to sea. No matter what cause led him to the enlisting office. There he receives such replies to his inquiries as induce him cheerfully to give in his name. He takes the boat or car to the place of departure. He is provided at the shipping establishment with a chest and clothes suitable to his new life. He looks at his bill, then looks again, but he tries to suppress the growing conviction that it is rather extravagant. But the master seems obliging, and the officers are familiar and pleasant, the ship is newly painted and in trim, and a merry song reaches his ear from her jovial "tars;" the sky is fair and the wind favorable, so he looks at the stars and stripes waving at the stern, and gladly hears the clanking of the cable that is to go down again in distant waters and bind him to a strange soil. All ready, he is taken aboard. A strange kind of sensation creeps over him as he stands upon the deck and recognizes himself a "raw hand." But he has hardly looked *down* where he saw his chest go, and wondered why it should be thrust into *such* a hole, when a stern voice from the starboard quarter orders his trembling limbs aloft. He thinks that *somebody's* voice has very *much changed* in tone, but "loose the jib," and "shake out the foretop-sail," startles him to do *something*, and go *somewhere*. He is naturally awkward in his first attempt aloft, and a louder voice hurls an *oath* after him that nearly brings him to the deck. "What," thinks he, "*it was a law of the ship that no profane language should be used on board!*" Perhaps *another oath* from the consistent master or under officer breaks for a while his reflections, while he exerts himself to his utmost at his work, to save them another curse and his own feelings further pain. Sails unfurled, and anchor hauled in and made fast, the ship fills away and sails quietly out to open seas. The halyards properly adjusted, and the decks clear, he begins to think of where he is to lodge, and with whom he is to associate. The lewd song and the profane words of those about him send the cold chills over his frame, and he shrinks inwardly from their companionship. He asks himself, "Are these the 'likely chaps' I was told would be my shipmates?" The most unpleasant anticipations begin now to cloud his brow. He ventures at length to ask for his berth, and he is pointed where he saw his chest go down. He approaches and looks down. "But I was told," he says to himself, "that the accommodations were every way comfortable." He

the WHALE *&* his *captors*

undertakes his descent, and the first step sickens him; but he "plucks up," and through bilge stench and tobacco fumes, his ears meanwhile pained with oaths and ribald songs, he makes his way to the place for which he has exchanged his own soft bed and cheerful lodgings. He throws himself in, but not to rest. He listens to the loose talk of older tars, and realizes that he must be like them or be alone—go along with their muddy current, or make head against it if he can. He learns that he is bound for *three* years instead of *two*; that the ship is *old and leaky* instead of *new*; that he is to have *no Sabbath*; that the *books are not for foremast hands*! He shrinks from the prospect before him, and he would give all the oil of all oceans could he be freed from his prison. In short, he finds himself *grossly deceived*. Naturally enough his heart resents the injury. What wonder that dissatisfaction exists among this class of seamen; and what else can be expected but that they should seek their discharge, or discharge themselves at the first port they enter? Though this is not the class to give the most trouble, yet who can blame them if they should make some? Sailors are often unreasonable as well as their officers, and it is generally a dissatisfied and worthless set that desert and give most offense to their superiors; yet who will not say but that the deceived class we have mentioned above are the injured party? Justice would respond "Amen," should they *demand* a discharge, and make the guilty party smart for their deception.

It is to be regretted that offices for enlisting whalemen are ever opened in cities distant from the places of departure. But the number of seamen required in this service created the necessity. But no plea of necessity can justify deception. Better leave the king of the deep undisturbed in his dominions, and their own purse to a lighter burden or to emptiness, than man their ships by means so detestable. Let young men know *where* they are bound, *who* they are going with, what *treatment and accommodations* they may expect, that *hard work and dangers* are their lot, nor *overrate* their *shares*, nor *underrate the duration of their voyage*. In a word, *be honest*; and honesty here, as every where else, would be found the best policy. One great source of discontent would thus be removed, and a great favor conferred both upon officers and crews.

—Honolulu Friend.

APPENDIX TO THE
SEAFARING AMERICA
EDITION

CONTEMPORARY REVIEWS
AND COMMENTARY

"THE VICIOUS APPETITE OF A SAILOR"
Review of *Typee* in the *New York Evangelist*, April 9, 1846.
Reprinted in Brian Higgins and Hershel Parker,
Herman Melville: The Contemporary Reviews
(New York: Cambridge University Press, 1995), 46.

This is apparently Cheever's first encounter with Melville in print; see
Randall Cluff (2001) exhaustively for attribution. If this review is indeed by Cheever—and there is very little evidence for believing otherwise, if indeed there is any—then Cheever must have mellowed in his
old age. His obituary in the Andover Theological Seminary *Necropolis*
(1897) states, "He was absolutely fearless, and so earnest in his views
on matters of reform, such as temperance, that he was apt to overlook
considerations of practical wisdom and sometimes to be unduly vehement in his expressions. . . . He never showed the least sign of personal resentment toward those who opposed him, even if they treated
him abusively. He was unsparing in his denunciation of wrong, but
always had a heart of kindness toward the wrongdoer" (240–241).

The "H. C." of this review, however, writes with a tiger heart.

If this be not sheer romance, (which there is reason to suspect,) it is the
extremely exaggerated, but racily-written, narrative of a forecastle-
runaway from an American whale ship, who met the fortune those
fish did in fable, that jumped out of the frying-pan, into the fire. He
had life among Marquesan cannibals to his liking; a plenty of what
pleases the vicious appetite of a sailor, or of sensual human generally.

He seems to have been pleased enough with his captors, but glad to get away uneaten. "Horrible and fearful (he says) as the custom of cannibalism is, still I assert that those who indulge in it are in other respects humane and virtuous!"

The book abounds in praise of the life on nature, *alias* savageism, and in slurs and flings against missionaries and civilization. When the author alludes to, or touches matters of fact at the Sandwich Islands, he shows the sheerest ignorance, and utter disregard of truth.

The work was made, not for America, but for a circle, and that not the highest, in London, where theatres, opera-dancers, and voluptuous prints have made such unblushing walks along the edge of modesty as are here delineated to be rather more admired than we hope they are yet among us. We are sorry that such a volume should have been allowed a place in the "Library of American Books." It can only have been without reading it beforehand, and from deference to the publisher on the other side.

We have long noted it as true in criticism, that what makes a large class of books bad, immoral, and consequently injurious, is not so much what is plainly expressed, as what is left to be imagined by the reader. Apply this rule to the work in hand, and while everybody will admit it is written in an attractive vivacity, and (except where it palpably lies) with great good humor, it cannot escape severe condemnation.

—*H.C.*

"THE CAPTAIN'S CRUEL LANCE"
Specimen passage from "Letters from a Whale-Ship," in
The Christian Parlor Book: Devoted to Literature, Morals, and Religion, vol. 5 (New York: George Pratt, 1849), 24–26.

Some chapters of *The Whale and His Captors* were initially published serially. The chapter from which this brief example comes is the prototype for chapter III of *The Whale and His Captors*, with minor but persistent tinkering for book publication. The article is signed "H.T.C. New Zealand Cruising Ground, Pacific Ocean, lat. 42°. S. long. 160°. W." Chapter IV is also printed in this volume as "A Chapter on Whales and Whaling" (106–108). That these are not just prepublications puffs is indicated by the passage "According to Wilkes's Narrative . . . easy prey" from the latter chapter. In the *Parlor Book* (as in the *Evangelist*), this passage appears as a footnote; in the Harper edition, the note has been incorporated into the text with the addition of "The same thing . . . called a 'drag.'" *The Christian Parlor Book* was edited by Joel Tyler Headley, whom Melville met at the famous literary picnic in Stockbridge on August 5, 1850—the same occasion at which he met Nathaniel Hawthorne.

There leviathan,
Hugest of living creatures, on the deep
Stretch'd like a promontory, sleeps or swims,
And seems a moving land; and at his gills
Draws in, and at his trunk spouts out, a sea.
—Milton.

For the first time on the passage from the Sandwich Islands, ten weeks to-day, we heard day before yesterday from the mast-head, "There she blows." The usual question and orders from the deck quickly followed: "How far off?" "Keep your eye on her"—"Sing out when we head right." Three whales were descried from aloft in different parts, and in a short time the Captain gave orders to "stand by and lower" for one a little more than half a mile to windward. Three boats' crews pulled merrily away, glad of something to stir their blood, and with eager hope to obtain the oily material wherewith to fill their ship. The whale was going leisurely to windward, blowing every now and then two or three times, then "turning tail," "up flukes," and sinking. The boats "headed" after him, keeping a distance of nearly one quarter of a mile from each other, to scatter (as it is called) their chances.

Fortunately, as the seamen were "hove up," that is, had their oars a-peak about the place where they expected the whale would next appear, the huge creature rose just by the Captain's boat, and all the boat-steerer, in the bow, had to do, was to plunge his two cold irons, which are always secured to one tow-line, into the blubber sides. He did it so well as to hit the "fish's life," and make him spout blood. It was the first notice the poor fellow had of the proximity of his powerful captors, and the sudden entrance of the barbed harpoons made him caper and run most furiously. The boat spun after him with almost the swiftness of a top, diving through the seas, and tossing the spray, and then lying still while the whale sounded, for the space of an hour; in which time another boat "got fast" to him, and the Captain's cruel lance had several times pierced his vitals. He was killed, as whalemen call it, that is mortally wounded, an hour before he went into "his flurry," and was really dead or "turned up" on his back.

"CONTEMPLATIVE EYE AND CHRISTIAN HEART"
Review of *The Whale and His Captors* in the
New York Evangelist 20 (51) (December 20, 1849): 204.

All of Melville's works had been published since the issue of Dana's book. The imprecise diction of "swung" could be a dig at Melville, but if so it would rest on literary gossip. Melville had not yet presented himself in print as a boat-steerer (harpooner), although he was to represent himself as one shortly to his English publisher Richard Bentley. See Horth, *Correspondence*, 163.

Since the issue of Dana's justly celebrated "Two Years Before the Mast," we have read nothing of sea life and adventure so fresh, lively, and instructive as this beautiful little book. Mr. Cheever does not boast of having swung a harpoon, but he admires the daring, the enterprise, and the many sterling qualities that constitute the whaleman, and yields his imagination in all its fervor, to the sublimity and terror of the scenes which make up the whaleman's history. The book is full of life, anecdote, facts, incidents and character, and succeeds in keeping the reader intensely occupied with the glories and wonders of the deep to the end. The contemplative eye and Christian heart with which the writer looks abroad upon the deep, and the fertile fancy with which he links the incidents and even phraseology of sea life, with the most important and beautiful matters of religion and truth, are among the peculiar charms of the book. It is printed uniform with the Abbott's beautiful series of histories, and is well adapted for the reading of the young. It is also embellished with several very fine engravings, which themselves are full of instruction, and is neatly printed. It possesses so many attractive qualities, and appears at so opportune a moment, when parents and friends are seeking gift-books, that its popularity cannot be doubted.

"THE MYSTERY OF THE WHALE SHIP"
Review of *The Whale and His Captors* in
the *Literary World* 6 (January to June 1850): 11.

Melville was at sea on his way home from England when this slight review appeared in *the Literary World; a Journal of Science, Literature, and Art*, edited by his friend and mentor Evert Duyckinck.

The Whale and His Captors; or the Whaleman's Adventures and the Whale's Biography, as gathered on the homeward cruise of the "Commodore Preble," by Rev. Henry T. Cheever (Harper & Brothers.) Mr. Cheever, after an opening chapter, of interesting statistics of the American whale fishery, takes us with him on his cruise, relating its various incidents with animation, and telling many a good fish story. He seems to share his brother's admiration for John Bunyan, introducing several bits of poetry into his narrative, which have the earnestness with something of the homeliness of the great allegorist. Mr. Cheever never loses a chance to "point a moral," and always does it well. The book has a better chance than many a one more bulky in size and pretending in subject, to be known all over the world, for it cannot but find its way into the chest of many a sea-smitten youth or weather-beaten tar, and be read in all latitudes. The woodcuts solve many of the perplexities of the young reader taking his first lesson in the mystery of the whale ship.

Appendix to the Seafaring America Edition

Advertisement in the *Literary World* 6
(January to June 1850): 96.

In the issue for January 26, 1850, Harpers ran a full-page advertisement for recent books, reprinting notices from several of the early reviews of *The Whale and His Captors*, which Harper offered in "16mo.
muslin. Price 60 cents." Cheever's book is the third listed, and its notices take up about a column in the advertisement's three-column
format. On February 23 (192), Harper advertised *The Whale and His
Captors* (retaining only the *Albany Argus* quotation) only an inch or
two beneath a notice for Melville's *Redburn*—right where the latter
author, looking attentively for news of his most recent books, would
have noticed it had he been interested in whaling books at the time. In
their advertisement for April 27 (436), Harper listed Melville's *White
Jacket* in the first column and *The Whale and His Captors* in the third,
both along with three dozen other "recently published" books. On
June 29 (648), Cheever's book was featured (last, but rather boldly)
in the Harper advertisement, this time with the *Christian Examiner*
quotation.

"From the graphic pages of this little volume, and from its startling
engravings, we have actually learned more about the excitement and
perils of the whale fishery, than from more ambitious and extended
volumes."
— *Christian Examiner.*

"Replete with incidents and valuable information."
— *Yankee Notion.*

"The author found adventures enough, and saw enough of veritable
monsters to make a pleasant book and one well stored with readable
information."
— *Anti Slavery Standard.*

"Written in the lively and picturesque style of the author—its perusal
cannot fail to both please and profit."
— *Southern Christian Advocate.*

"There is very much valuable information contained in a small compass. Interspersed are glowing and graphic pictures of the ocean—its dangers—its storms—its calms—and the peculiar habits of those that roam its depths. It is a very readable and pleasant as well as profitable volume."

—*Albany Atlas.*

"A very interesting book, abounding in well executed illustrations. It contains valuable information as well as striking incidents."

—*N. Y. Recorder.*

"Since the issue of Dana's justly celebrated 'Two Years before the Mast' we have read nothing of sea life and adventure so fresh, lively, and instructive as this beautiful little book. It is full of life, anecdote, facts, incidents, and character, and succeeds in keeping the reader intensely occupied with the glories and wonders of the deep to the end. It is embellished with several very fine engravings, which themselves are full of instruction."

—*Evangelist.*

"A most attractive work both as a composition and for its pictorial interest."

—*Albany Evening Journal.*

"Mr. Cheever takes us with him on his cruize, relating its various incidents with animation, and telling many a good fish story."

—*Literary World.*

"ALMOST MARVELLOUS"
William Scoresby's preface to *The Whaleman's Adventures in
the Southern Ocean; as gathered, by the Rev. Henry T. Cheever,
on the Homeward Cruise of the "Commodore Preble"*
(London: Sampson Low and David Bogue, 1850).

Ironically, Scoresby reveals some of the same skepticism about events
in Cheever's book that Cheever himself had evinced in his review of
Typee three and a half years earlier. Scoresby, however—perhaps recog-
nizing the pious use to which his own writings had been put in Cheever's book—refrained from challenging too directly a work that he had
already endorsed by the plain fact of editing it for his British audience.

The following pages comprise, in substance, the private notes of a
pious and observant American clergyman, whilst embarked, on account of his health, on a whaling voyage to the South Seas and Pacific
Ocean. Whilst the original work was in progress, a copy came into the
hands of the present publishers, who, considering the matter of it to be
novel and interesting, as well as calculated for conveying useful moral
impressions, applied to the Editor in respect to his approval of it, with
a view to his superintendence of an edition of it for the British public.

Finding, on undertaking this task—which the sound and excellent character and lively spirit of the work inclined him to do—that
revision and alteration would be necessary to adapt it for the class
of readers designed; application was made to the Author (the Rev.
Henry T. Cheever) for the requisite permission, which was so fully
and frankly conceded, as to leave the discretion and taste of the Editor quite unfettered.

Of this kind confidence he has freely availed himself wherever he
has deemed alteration or correction needful. And thus, so far as pertains to the natural history of the "right whale," or mysticetus, or to
the usual practices of the northern whale fishery, or to the general
character of the Arctic regions, he has made himself, in a considerable degree, responsible. But in respect to the natural history of the
sperm whale, with the modes, adventures, dangers, and conflicts of
the southern whale fishery, he has not ventured on any essential alter-
ations; for what the Author states respecting what he himself saw, or

Appendix to the Seafaring America Edition   { 209 what, from credible information, he received as facts, the statements given will, no doubt, carry that favourable impression to the minds of the readers which a credible, conscientious, and intelligent witness has a right to expect.

In respect to certain surprising incidents herein recorded, the Editor has not felt himself authorized to offer either opinion or comment; first, because incidents are not unfrequent in the whaler's hazardous pursuits so special as to be deemed almost marvellous in comparison of the occurrences of ordinary seafaring adventures; and, secondly, because he himself, being in possession of no more information than the reader, could merely offer, at the best, an uncertain judgment. The terrible combats, for example, described in Chapter VII., betwixt the whale and its various enemies, are thus inserted without observation, the Editor having no knowledge personally of these conflicts, not, indeed, that his own negative experience can guide in forming a judgment thereon, further than in indicating the probable fact, that such combats are vastly less frequent in the Arctic regions, if they occur there at all, than in the regions traversed by the southern and north-western whalers.

Whilst the Editor has taken much liberty with the construction of the work, and occasionally with its phraseology, he has been careful not to interfere with the free, frank style, and lively spirit, of the Author, either in the descriptions of what he personally witnessed, or in his interesting reflections on the circumstances with which he was surrounded.

These explanations having been given—both in justice to the confiding author, and for the guidance of the public as to the real integrity of this London edition of his work—it only remains to the Editor to commend this publication as embodying, he believes, a considerable quantity of novel incident and curious information, which can hardly fail to interest the youthful, and, he hopes, the general reader; and as having interwoven, (to adopt a hope expressed by the Author, when addressing his own countrymen in America,) "moral hints and lessons, which may catch the eye and touch the heart of the casual reader, like sober threads of green in tapestry of gold."

—*The Editor.*

Torquay, Nov. 18th, *1850.*

Appendix to the Seafaring America Edition

"PURELY ACCIDENTAL"

Scoresby's note on the *Essex* from *The Whaleman's Adventures,*
202–203 (to follow "their strange, eventful story" in chapter XIV).

The "narrative" of this extraordinary shipwreck was published at New
York in 1821; a copy of it is now in my hand. It is deeply and painfully
interesting, and bears every indication of accuracy, as well as general
authenticity. In one particular, however, I have come to a different
conclusion from that arrived at by the author of the present work,
and that of the original "narrative," this is, as to the first collision of
the whale with the Essex being a *designed* attack. I do not myself believe that a whale, not being itself attacked, would willfully drive its
head against so huge an object as a ship. All that I have myself ever
seen or heard of the habits of whales, indicates his disposition to flee
from any unusual object, whether ship or boat, which might approach
them, or lie in their path. I have frequently seen the Mysticetus pass
under the bottom of my own ship, or of boats in which I have been
embarked; and some of the whale tribe I have seen, when deep under
water, (as they sometimes be so discovered by an observer placed almost perpendicularly above them at the mast-head), to turn their side
in passing below the keel, evidently with the purpose of viewing the
strange object floating on the surface. In such case, where the ship
was lying to, or tolerably quiescent, the whale would go on its track
but little, if at all disturbed, and might be seen quietly to rise for respiration at no very great distance from the object which had engaged
its attention.

The collision of the whale with the Essex, therefore, I believe, in
the first instance, to have been purely accidental. The vessel was going
moderately ahead, when the whale, advancing obliquely across her
track, came into contact with her on the weather bow. The succeeding stroke, not inconsistently with the habits of the sperm whale, to
give battle when attacked or hurt, might be designed. The fatal result
of the double collision is very intelligible, when the class and build of
the vessel are considered. From the small number of her boats, and
comparative fewness of her crew, the ship appears not to have been
of large tonnage, and, probably, was but slightly built. The southern
fishery, indeed, does not require the strength and solidity of ships

Appendix to the Seafaring America Edition   { 211

which the formidable ices of the north call for. A stroke from a whale, such as that described in the narrative referred to, would, I am well persuaded, have produced no serious effects upon an Arctic whaler, strengthened and fortified as these ships always are, which are perpetually subject to heavy blows, and hard nips whilst navigating the icy seas of the north.

—*Ed.*

Appendix to the Seafaring America Edition

Excerpts from chapter II of *The Island World of the Pacific*
(New York: Harper and Brothers, 1851), 37, 54–57, 60.

Cheever's preface is dated June 11, 1850. Although Melville is widely known for cribbing factual material, one might argue that he was rarely metaphysically inspired by his whaling sources—the greatest exception probably being "Benito Cereno" (1855). When *The Whale and His Captors* led Melville to Cheever's *The Island World of the Pacific*, however, Melville transformed a chapter on natural history into the most significant footnote in *Moby-Dick*: the encounter with the albatross in the chapter "The Whiteness of the Whale." As in other cases in the novel, the appearance of this material in a footnote is not an indication of its insignificance but reflects Melville's habit, late in composition, of inserting a footnote so he would not have to recopy a long passage.

Melville drew almost the entire substance of his note from Cheever's chapter: the Cape Horn setting, the rough winds, the method of capturing the albatross, the nobility of the bird, the emphasis on the bill and eye, the reminder of Coleridge's *Ancient Mariner*, the prosaic name of *gony*—even the tally-boards attached to the necks of the birds. With his typical flourish, however, Melville's oceanic messengers ascend to heaven itself.

South Pacific Albatross from Cheever's The Island World of the Pacific.

Penguin Roosts and Albatrosses
of Cape Horn and the Pacific

At length did cross an albatross:
   Through the fog it came;
As if it had been a Christian soul,
   We hail'd it in God's name.
It ate the food it ne'er had eat,
   And round and round it flew,
The ice did split with a thunder-fit,
   The helmsman steer'd us through!
And a good south wind sprung up behind,
   The albatross did follow,
And every day, for food or play,
   Came to the mariner's hollo.
—*Rime of the Ancient Mariner.*

The first introduction of my readers to the good ship Wales, whereby we pass to the Pacific, is as she is lying off and on in Berkley's Sound, at the islands called Foul Weather Group, otherwise named Falkland, after an English lord. Cape Horn weather here begins, and the ship and her company put on their Cape Horn suit; which, so far as some of our men are concerned, is quite as unique and nondescript as the notable "White Jacket." . . .

While off the coast of Patagonia, what time the weather would permit, some of the passengers, and the watch on duty, occupied themselves in fishing for albatrosses. They are caught by baiting a hook with pork or blubber, fastening a piece of wood near the bait, so that it may be kept floating, and letting it tow astern. The noble birds would wheel and hover over it, and at length alight on the water like a swan, and often succeed in getting all the bait without being hooked. But six or seven times they were taken and hauled aboard, the unsuspected hook catching within their long bills. They measure nine and ten feet across the wings. The first one was killed and stuffed, to be carried home for some museum. The rest were sacrificed for their long bills, wings, and large web feet. This bird is uncommonly beautiful and majestic, whether soaring sublimely upon the wing, or seen as a prisoner upon a ship's deck, from which we found they are unable to rise. Their motion through space is the easiest and most graceful conceivable. In storm or calm, once raised upon their strong pinions, you never see them flutter, but away they sail, self-propelled as naturally as we breathe; a motion of the head, or a slight curl of a wing serving to turn them, as the course of a rapid skater will be ruled at pleasure by an almost imperceptible inclination to right or left. It is the reality of that motion through space, which we sometimes conceive of in dreams, when we are borne along without conscious effort on our part, or any means of propulsion but our own free will.

If the eagle be the king of birds, the albatross ought to be called the queen, so queen-like and stately is her course on the wing, and so dignified, mild, and unfearing is her expression when captured. Her eye is full, bright, and expressive, like that of a gazelle; the head and neck large, but admirably proportioned; the feathers either a pure white or delicately penciled and speckled, except on the upper side of the wings, which are mostly black. There was an expression of pathos and intelligence about the eye of the first one captured that made it seem to me like a sin to take its life. Could I have had my way, that look should have given it liberty. . . .

This glorious bird, the albatross, is the most beautiful and lovable object of the animate world which the adventurer meets with in all the South Pacific. Philosophers might take a lesson of it in æsthetics, for when on the wing it is the very beau ideal of beauty and grace. Seamen ought to love and prize it dearly, for the drear monotony of life at sea is often relieved by its always welcome appearance, and by watching with admiration, almost envy, its glorious gyrations and curves, and swoops in the elastic ocean of air, a free race-ground, where it has no competitor. . . .

Sailors generally, but especially right-whalemen, have many yarns to tell of this noble bird, which they call by the unclassical name of *gony*. They have a partiality, which is not to be wondered at, for this superb specimen of oceanic ornithology, although coarser ones among them are too apt to show it in a way not so pleasing to humanity, and which I have often tried to dissuade them from, that is, capturing them so cruelly by hook and line. When so taken, knowing ones often carve little billets of wood with inscriptions, which they tie to their necks, and then set them loose again. These birds in repeated instances have afterward been captured in different and distant latitudes by other ships, and curious information has been so communicated.

"THE BOLD POLYNESIAN ROMANCE"

A note from *Life in the Sandwich Islands: or, the Heart of the Pacific, as It Was and Is* (New York: A. S. Barnes & Co., 1851), 257.

Cheever's preface is dated August 20, 1851. Randall Cluff discusses in detail the publication of this note in serial form in the same number of the *New York Evangelist* in which his review of *Typee* had appeared. By 1851 the quotation marks setting off "the enormities . . . such examples" had disappeared, but Cheever is partially quoting from chapter IV of *Typee*. Cheever omits all of one paragraph and most of a second between "bottom of the sea" and "It may be asserted." See *Typee*, 26–27, and Cluff, 69–71.

The author of the bold Polynesian romance entitled "Typee," very properly remarks that the enormities perpetrated in the South Seas upon some of the inoffensive islanders well-nigh pass belief. These things are seldom proclaimed at home; they happen at the very ends of the earth; they are done in a corner, and there are none to reveal them. But there is, nevertheless, many a petty trader that has navigated the Pacific, whose course from island to island might be traced by a series of cold-blooded robberies, kidnappings, and murders, the iniquity of which might be considered almost sufficient to sink her guilty timbers to the bottom of the sea. It may be asserted without fear of contradiction, that in all the cases of outrages committed by Polynesians, Europeans have been at some time or other the aggressors, and that the cruel and blood-thirsty disposition of some of the islanders is mainly to be ascribed to the influence of such examples.

"THE JUDGMENT DAY WILL HOLD HIM LIABLE"
Review of *Moby-Dick* in the *New York Independent* (1851).
Reprinted in Brian Higgins and Hershel Parker,
Herman Melville: The Contemporary Reviews
(New York: Cambridge University Press, 1995), 379.

The following review appeared in the *New York Independent* for November 20, 1851. It is generally considered to have been penned by Henry T. Cheever, signing himself "H." See Hershel Parker, *Herman Melville: A Biography, vol. 2: 1851–1891* (Baltimore: Johns Hopkins University Press, 2002), 25.

The name given to this burly volume reminds us of an observation of Burton in his Anatomy of Melancholy, where he says that it is a kind of policy in these days to prefix a fantastical title to a book which is to be sold, because as larks come down to a day-net, many readers will tarry and stand gazing like silly passengers at an antic picture in a painter's shop, that will not look at a judicious piece. There are harlequin writers at this day as ready as in Burton's time to make themselves Merry-andrews and Zanies, in order to raise the wind of curiosity about their literary wares.

In the volume before us there are some of the queerest specimens of ground and lofty tumblings in the literary line, to which the world has been lately treated. Up to the middle of the book the writer is half the time on his head, and the other half dancing a pirouette on one toe. By the time these *outré* gayeties are a little spent, the reader gets an inkling that Moby-Dick is a very famous and most deadly Monster, a Sperm Whale of an uncommon magnitude and malignity, having as many lives as a cat, and all of them immortal. After this the realities and fabrications of whaling life are dashed into with a bold hand; and mixed with a great deal of myth and mystery, there are exciting descriptions, curious information, and strange adventures, which would have not a shade of probability, were not truth in whaling life often stranger than fiction.

The writer evinces the possession of powers that make us ashamed of him that he does not write something better, and freer from blemishes. And yet we doubt if he could, for there is a primitive formation

Appendix to the Seafaring America Edition

of profanity and indecency that is ever and anon shooting up through all the strata of his writings; and it is this which makes it impossible for a religious journal heartily to commend any of the works of this author which we have ever perused. Let his mind only turn on the poles of truth, and be fixed with the desire to do good rather than to tickle and amuse by the exposure of his foolish vagaries, and few could do more than the author of Moby-Dick to furnish instructive literary aliment for the Sons of the Sea.

The Judgment day will hold him liable for not turning his talents to better account, when, too, both authors and publishers of injurious books will be conjointly answerable for the influence of those books upon the wide circle of those immortal minds on which they have written their mark. The book-maker and the book-publisher had better do their work with a view to the trial it must undergo at the bar of God.

—H.

AFTERWORD

"The Cruel Harpoon" and the "Honorable Lamp": The Awakening of an Environmental Consciousness in Henry Theodore Cheever's
The Whale and His Captors

MARK BOUSQUET

In 1999, environmentally invested scholars Leo Marx and Lawrence Buell had a well-known exchange of competing ideas in the *New York Review of Books* over, among other things, the presence of humans in environmental texts and their effect on raising the environmental consciousness of the reader. Marx takes Buell to task for his belief that a "book devoted to whales 'for their own sake' . . . wholly independent of *Homo sapiens* is more likely to heighten environmental awareness than a book depicting the actual existence of whales in oceans dominated by humanity and its ingenious whale-killing technologies."[1] Marx favors the pastoral approach (where man occupies the space between art and nature), as its anthropocentrism (the idea that man is at the center of all things) leads to depictions that reveal the "ecological consequences that follow from humanity's socioeconomic, political, and cultural arrangements" with the natural world. Ultimately, I believe Marx and Buell create a false dilemma, as books that raise environmental awareness are more attributable to the quality of the writer and not the mere presence or absence of humans, but what's of greatest interest to me is that Marx and Buell focus their debate on the completed narrative and not the actual experience that inspired an author to recreate the moment in print. In *The Whale and His Captors* (1850), Henry Theodore Cheever bridges the gap between Marx and Buell, standing in the pastoral position between nature and art and crafting a whaling narrative that depicts how the "ingenious whale killing" awakens an environmental consciousness inside of the Christian man; as a result, Cheever becomes the first writer to produce a whaling narrative that demonstrates sustained sympathy for the plight of the whales. In the process, Cheever's narrative serves to question the masculine identity of both the whaling industry and the nation, as his sympathy for the hunted whales aligns with the demonstration of maternal love as mother whales refuse to leave the side of their calves during their slaughter.[2]

Cheever's stated goal in *The Whale and His Captors* is to "finish the complement of whaling literature, and supply what was wanting, in order to put the reading public in possession of a full-length portraiture of the whaleman as seen in the actual pursuit and garb of his perilous occupation" (9). Cheever is true to his word, filling his narrative with numerous such adventures, but his text also reveals a confrontation with the unexpected emotions brought forth by witnessing the slaughter of whales. Cheever finds himself caught between sympathy for the whale at being hunted (what he calls the "cruel harpoon," 51) and a practical appreciation for the whale as nation-driven commodity (the "honorable lamp," 60). The result is that Cheever becomes caught between the competing desires of sympathy and economy after witnessing the brutality of the whale hunt.

My interest in Cheever's narrative comes from my larger examination of nineteenth-century whaling narratives and my larger interest in creating a water-specific branch of ecocriticism. Lawrence Buell articulates a call-to-arms for water ecocriticism when he writes, "Few episodes in the history of modern environmentalist consciousness have been more dramatic than this late twentieth-century awakening to the awareness that three-quarters of the globe, hitherto thought virtually immune from human tampering, might be gravely endangered" (201). He posits that this "attitudinal shift" can be thought of both as a "great *de*mythologization" and "great *re*mythologization," noting that in the wake of the reevaluation of the "ocean as sanctuary" myth, the whale was recast as an environmental icon (201). The whale has undergone a stark transformation in American culture, starting out as a commodified mammal that was eventually hunted in all corners of the World Ocean and transforming into a sacred symbol of the environmental movement in the latter half of the twentieth century. My search for the moment when the whale stopped being the former and started becoming the latter led me to the genre of whaling nar-

Afterword

ratives, which led me to Cheever, whose narrative, I argue, serves as the literate moment when the national attitude regarding whales begins to change toward conservation instead of exploitation. It is one thing to have the product of the whale hunt in one's home, and another, Cheever's narrative makes clear, to watch how that product is acquired.

At the time of Cheever's voyage aboard the *Commodore Preble* in 1844–1845, both the industry of whaling and the genre of the whaling narrative are about to reach their apexes. Whaling in the United States occurs in three distinct hunting phases: pre-1650s drift whaling (in which the American Indians and colonists would simply wait for dead pilot whales to wash up on shore); 1650s to early eighteenth-century shore whaling (in which rowboats were launched from shore); and finally, post-1700 deep-sea whaling (in which large vessels were built and launched for oceanic hunting). The "Golden Age" of the American whaling industry ran from the end of the War of 1812 through the 1850s; this is the era of *Moby-Dick*, of whaleships launched from Nantucket and New Bedford for multiple-year voyages to the South Pacific, the time when whaling narratives were at their most popular, and the era during which Henry Cheever voyaged on the *Commodore Preble*. While exact sales figures are unavailable, the genre was popular enough for Cheever's intended desire to "finish the complement." Building off the work of J. Ross Browne, Francis A. Olmsted, and William Scoresby, Cheever's narrative is the last significant nonfiction whaling narrative of this time period.

While it is impossible to determine the exact number of whales killed by the American fleet during the Golden Age, the best estimates place the annual kill at nearly eight thousand whales.[3] Scientists argue the specificity of the numbers but not the lasting damage. Farley Mowat insists that industrialization turned the "Sea of Whales" into the "Sea of Slaughter" across the World Ocean: "Had it not been for the appearance of our kind, there is little doubt but that the whales would have remained the great presences dominating the seas that they still were when the Europeans crossed the North Atlantic to possess the New World."[4] Whalemen were less interested in the number of whales caught than in how many barrels of oil they would produce, and Charles Scammon estimates that between 1835 and 1872 the American fleet averaged 96,625 barrels of sperm oil and 172,448 barrels of all other whale oil combined (244). Whatever the exact numbers, we can see the end result of the hunting as whale cruises that once lasted weeks in the relatively nearby waters of the Atlantic Ocean now lasted years and took whalemen from Atlantic seaports around Cape Horn and into the far reaches of the Pacific, Indian, and Arctic Oceans.

Cheever's environmental awakening occurs because the reverend places himself at Buell's nexus of environmental reflection and technological power (and at Marx's nexus of nature and art), and the result is a narrative that starts to give voice to the consequences of the whale hunt for the whales and not just for the industry supported by the existence of whales. In *The Environmental Imagination*, Lawrence Buell provides a clear, simple rationale for the importance of an ecocritical lens on American literature, arguing that we should look for the "most searching works of environmental reflection that the world's biggest technological power has produced; for in these we may expect to find . . . the pathologies that bedevil society at large and some of the alternative paths it might consider."[5] Carolyn Merchant argues that the importance of environmental historians lies in their ability to "explain the consequences of various past interactions with the natural world and warn us of potential problems as we form policies and make decisions that affect our lives and those of our children."[6] Cheever's unexpected emotional reaction to seeing whales hunted, killed, and processed is the most striking part of his narrative, and heralds the potential for change in the nation's environmental consciousness.

The view of whales in the nineteenth-century public's eye is largely a result of their positive attitude toward the whaling industry; since the industry is noble and heroic, its behavior is justified by the public —especially since that same public reaps the benefits of the post-kill processing. There is a marked difference in how those outside and inside viewed the profession of whaling in the mid-nineteenth century, with the former offering a romantic view of the noble pursuit of whaling combined with a frontieresque opportunity for man to prove himself, and the latter offering a subdued, cautionary view of a hard life of dangerous, time-consuming labor. An 1856 *Harper's New Monthly*

Afterword

Magazine article offers a version of the romantic approach to whaling, framing the whale hunt as a modern quest to slay the dragon, as the article waxes poetically of the opportunity to "gather wealth in the face of danger, and snatch subsistence from the impending jaws of death."[7] In his *Five Years on the Pacific Ocean* (1858), whaleman J. C. Mullet is very conscious of the attitudinal difference between the inexperienced public and experienced whalemen, as he himself fell victim to industrial romanticism. Walking off the boat that brought him to Staten Island from London, Mullett is approached by a man selling him on the economic riches that will come his way if he joins a whaling cruise; this "soft-tongued, black hearted schemer," he writes, "plead with me until I consented to go with him. Without delay we went to the shipping office; my name was signed to the ship's articles and I was entrapped before I was sensible of the act."[8] Cognizant of how his feelings toward whaling have changed through his own personal experience, Mullett combats a potentially disbelieving public in his Preface, informing them directly that "the Narrative is not written for the purpose of deceiving the community, or to impose upon the minds of the Public, any untruths, but rather a true relation of the incidents and hardships experienced by the Author in his travels over the trackless main" (3). His awareness of the disconnect in attitudes about whaling between the general public and the industry's labor force is evidenced even in the alternate title of his memoir, *Blind Man's Narrative*. Mullett refers not to a blindness of physical sight but of his own culturally imposed lack of awareness, a form of blindness that was just starting to alert the nation toward the plight of animals.

The concept of animal rights, or more accurately in this essay's context of whales, animal advocacy, had no widely held appeal to the American public through the mid-nineteenth century, and thus there was little reason for either Henry Cheever or the whalemen to have a sympathetic attitude toward the hunted whales. Historian Diane L. Beers notes that the concept of animal rights in the colonized United States is evidenced as far back as the original Puritan communities, when the Massachusetts Bay Colony "enacted the earliest known law in this part of the world to afford some sort of legal protection to animals."[9] It wasn't for another two hundred years, however, when "dynamic social and cultural shifts facilitated the emergence of a more broadly based animal advocacy movement" (20). Beers points to three major influences on the burgeoning animal advocacy movement in the mid-nineteenth century: the model set forth by the English Royal Society for the Prevention of Cruelty to Animals (RSPCA), the evolutionary theories of Charles Darwin, and the growing questions raised by industrialization. While Henry Cheever demonstrates no engagement with either of the first two ideas, he becomes increasingly interested in the industrialization of the whale hunt and the impact it has on both the labor force and the environment as he observes through his devout Christian lens.

In making its transition from England to America, Beers argues that animal advocacy was built on the increasingly successful arguments for human rights, along with the growing awareness of environmental issues (especially the destructive effects of industrialization on the natural world) and romanticism's appreciation for nature. The movement began in earnest in England in the eighteenth century, highlighted by Jeremy Bentham's *An Introduction to the Principles of Morals and Legislation* (1789), which extended the rights of humans to include animals, famously arguing, "The question is not, Can they reason? Nor, Can they talk? but, Can they suffer?"[10] The sentiment behind Bentham's words would hold sway with the dedicated abolitionist Henry Cheever but not with the whalemen who were being paid to kill whales throughout the World Ocean.

There is very little environmental reflection in whaling narratives regarding the ethics of hunting the whales themselves.[11] Prior to *The Whale and His Captors*, whaling narratives offer economic rather than sympathetic attitudes toward whales, who are viewed primarily as what I call "economic monsters," a combination of the two attitudes most displayed by whalemen. The "economic" half of the phrase comes from the status of the whale as purely commercial objects—the job whalemen are employed to do is hunt, kill, and process whales into oil, and they cannot return home until they have filled the waiting barrels down in the holds of their whaleships. In *A Whaling Voyage in the Pacific Ocean and its Incidents* (1882), George Dodge repeatedly represents whales to the reader by the size of their processed state: "Not a ripple was on the water," Dodge writes of the Chinese Sea, "except the spouting of a large eighty-barrel whale."[12] The "monster" half of my configuration is borne in the mythohistorical configuration of whales as monsters, a trope that many whalemen and nonwhalemen (including Charles Darwin) continue through the nineteenth century. J. C. Mullett is terrified during his first whale hunt, and he's relieved when their first hunt is a failure: "I found myself courageous when going towards the ship," he recounts, "but I will leave you to imagine how I felt when going towards the monster" (8). Given that whalemen are going to sea to hunt whales, they are conditioned to think in economic terms, but Cheever has no such lens placed before him; the result is that he gains a sympathetic attitude for the whales that the other whalemen never express.

At the heart of Cheever's inner struggle are the competing desires of sympathy and economy. Cheever presents a proeconomic rationale, desiring to glorify the whalemen at work in their "perilous occupation" for the audience at home. Key to Cheever's conversion is witnessing the disconnect between the mythic whale of the books he'd read prevoyage and the actual, living creature that the whalemen slaughter before his eyes. Cheever's initial narrative formulation of the whale is not his own, nor a scientist's, nor a whaleman's, but the poet Milton's conception, which emphasizes the immense size of some generic whale.[13] "Here leviathan," Milton writes, "Hugest of living creatures, on the deep / Stretch'd like a promontory, sleeps or swims, / And seems a moving land; and at his gills / Draws in, and at his trunk spouts out, a sea" (21).[14] Witnessing the raw brutality of the whale hunt, however, turns that disinterested giant into a slaughtered and processed creature of God, and this change tugs at Cheever's sympathetic heart. Cheever slowly finds himself having to reconcile his sympathy for the hunted with his desire to glorify the hunter.

The Whale and His Captors provides a unique opportunity to look at the direct effect of experience on writing as Cheever constructs his narrative while still aboard the *Commodore Preble*, providing us with a near-immediate cause and effect dynamic. He does not wait until he has returned home to write a cohesively orchestrated narrative, nor does he edit out his conflicted, changing thoughts on whalemen, whaling, and whales—all of which helps to give an honest immediacy to his narrative. Writing the narrative apparently as the voyage unfolds, the pious Christian is unknowingly setting up his own environmental awakening; by focusing on the significant consequences of the whale hunt, the death of whales will have a much greater impact— both on the narrative and on Cheever himself. It is his religion that creates the foundation for this transformation. He is a devoutly religious man and his narrative is infused with pious reflections on the state of whalemen. He is concerned about whalemen breaking the Sabbath, yet understanding about how the nature of whaling, with its long droughts between sightings, encourages its breaking. Throughout a narrative tinged with the sense of inevitable decline, Cheever's narrative captures whaling, the whaling narrative, and the spermaceti whale closer to the end of their reign than the beginning.

The thematic structure, the movement in overall tone of *The Whale and His Captors*, continuously reinforces the inevitable end of all three whaling areas. Cheever mimics the quick rise of the whaling industry's Golden Age post–War of 1812 and also its slow decline as his narrative shifts between glorifying and lamenting the occupation of the whalemen and between the competing desires of sympathy and economy with regard to the whale. Like almost all industrial whaling narratives, Cheever's offers a brief history of the whaling industry, dating back to the twelfth-century Biscayans, who are "believed to have been the first people who prosecuted the whale fishery as a commercial pursuit" (5).[15] Even here, at the very start of his narrative and his historical overview, Cheever prepares his readers (and perhaps himself) to expect the inevitable end of the whaling industry.[16] He writes that the Biscayan industry ultimately failed "by reason of whales ceasing to visit the Bay of Biscay" (5).

As he works through his European history, Cheever reveals his own lack of understanding of whales and the natural world, arguing that animals and nature operate completely separately and not as part of the same system. He labels the seventeenth-century Dutch port of Smeerenburg, built on the shore of Spitzbergen "within only eleven degrees of the North Pole" as "perhaps the most remarkable instance on record of what commerce can do against unyielding laws of Nature and over obstructions which it would seem impossible to surmount" (6). Now, just under two hundred years later, however, evidence of

Afterword

the "great rendezvous of Dutch whale ships" is negligible, a fact that Cheever attributes to the power of Nature: "But how soon does Nature, if ever temporarily displaced, resume her sway. Now that the whales have long since deserted these parts, even the site of the old Arctic colony is hardly discernible" (6). Cheever disconnects the natural world from one of its component parts (fauna), attributing the recapturing of Smeerenburg to the awesome power of Nature, but does not see its limitations in the absence of whales. Instead, Cheever simply believes that the whales have gone elsewhere; he attributes the end of whaling in Biscay and Smeerenburg to the whales "ceasing to visit" and deserting the waters near these two industrial centers and not to a dwindling population caused by the industry's massive operational hunting practices.[17]

Beginning with the classic "THERE SHE BLOWS!" identifier of the impending hunt in whaling narratives, Cheever delivers an account of what transpires for the whalemen when a whale has been sighted.[18] Though he relates the story from the perspective of the whalemen, Cheever is already giving hints of his impending feelings of sympathy for the whales when he writes of the kill. The whalemen are in their boats, rowing after a whale, keeping a quarter mile between each boat, and Cheever states that "fortunately" the oarsmen had placed the boat in excellent position when the "huge creature rose hard by the captain's boat, and all the harpooner in the bow had to do was plunge his two keen cold irons . . . into the monster's blubber sides" (21). At the moment of the harpooner's attack, the whale is a "monster," yet in the second sentence following this monstrous designation, Cheever switches his narrative to the whale's perspective and immediately offers a sympathetic response to the animal; after noting how the harpooner hits the "fish's life," causing the whale to "spout blood forthwith," Cheever notes the plunging in of the harpoons is "the first notice the poor fellow had of the proximity" of his captors (22). With the whale now wounded, a second boat attaches itself to the whale with its harpoons, and "the captain's cruel lance had several times struck his vitals" (22). Thus Cheever's first narrative representation of the hunt moves from a description of the whale as a "monster" to a representation of the animal as a "poor fellow." He also shifts the terms of his description of the hunting tools: first they are "keen steel irons," but later they become "cruel harpoons." This dual, sympathetic interpretation of the whale is completely antithetical to the cold, mythical whale in Milton's opening quote, but Cheever isn't yet willing to completely endorse or foster this emerging attitude.

After witnessing the hunt and indicating his first signs of sympathy, Cheever watches the processing of the whale and sidesteps the sympathy vs. economy question by focusing on the whale (particularly its size) and aligning himself with the hunters. Despite his stated intention at the beginning of the text to offer his readers "a full-length portraiture of the whalemen," Cheever focuses very little attention on the whalemen during the processing of the whale; instead, his focus is locked on the whale being processed and not on those who are doing the processing. After describing the scene of the "mammoth carcass" being secured to the ship and the captain and two mates falling "lustily to work chopping off the blubber," Cheever's fascination is continually drawn to the dismembering of the whale itself. "First came one of the huge lips," Cheever writes, offering a description of the lip being hoisted to the ship, and then informing that "next came one of the fore-fins; after that its other lip, and then the upper jaw along with all that peculiar substance called whalebone, through which the animal strains his food" (22). Cheever offers a long description of the whalebone, or baleen, but nothing of the whalemen who process it, or even how the whalemen remove it from the carcass. The enormity of the whale is the key subject of his narrative, and he reveals his own ignorance of the whale's condition or status in its native element when he informs his audience that the best way to properly understand the whale is to see it on land; in other words, the best way to comprehend the whale is to see it dead. After the baleen, the lower jaw, throat, and tongue are removed with the latter item catching Cheever's eye. "The tongue," he writes, "alone must have weighed 1,500 or 2,000 pounds; an enormous mass of fat" (23). Tongues were tricky parts, as "whalers often have to lose it . . . it being impossible to get it up on deck detached and alone, because it would not hold, and it is generally too large and heavy to raise along with the throat" (23). Once the head is removed to the deck, attention was turned to removing the blubber from the whale's body. The blubber is "cut and peeled off, in huge unbroken strips, as the carcass rolled over and over" and then hoisted

Afterword

onto deck by the windlass, the massive individual strips of blubber "nearly reaching to the top of the main mast" as they hung in the air, waiting to be cut down and lowered into the blubber room, where they'd be cut again into six- to eight-pound pieces to be stowed away before boiling (23).

At this moment, Cheever's attention is drawn again to the dissected whale carcass secured to the side of the ship, and we see his first acknowledgment and appraisal of his own changing attitudes toward animal life as his preconceived notions come into conflict with actual experience. Blood and guts from the dismantled whale carcass escape into the ocean, attracting the attention of "albatrosses . . . gonies, stinkards, horsebirds, haglets, gulls, pigeons, and petrels," all of which had "many a good morsel of blubber. . . . Sharks, too, appeared to claim their share" (24). It is the "magnificent, swan-like albatross," however, that upsets Cheever's expectations; as the whalemen remove piece after piece of the whale, hundreds of albatrosses surround the ship "eagerly seizing and fighting for every bit and fragment that fell off into the water, swallowing it with the most carnivorous avidity, and a low, avaricious greed of delight, that detracted considerably from one's admiration of this most superb of birds" (24). Cheever's romantic view of the albatross is now exposed as fantasy in the light of the violence of actual experience, and he frames his realization in human terms for his audience, comparing his reaction to that of an adult confronting the fantasies of childhood; "just as your veneration for one whom the coloring of a youthful imagination has made a little more than human," he writes, "is not a little abated by finding him subject to the necessities and passions of poor human nature" (24).

Cheever's romantic notions seem to sink right along with the whale carcass itself: "I hoped the peeled carcass would float for the benefit of the gonies and other birds," Cheever admits, "but no sooner was the last fold of blubber off, the flukes hoisted in, and the great chain detached, than it sank plumb down" (24). Cheever is confronted, for the first time, with the difference between how he believes the natural world should operate and how it actually functions; the "magnificent, swan-like" albatross is revealed to him as just another bird gorging itself on an abundant meal. Cheever ultimately admits to his readers that the experience of witnessing a whale far outstrips the expectation of it formed through stories and literature. "As is usually the case," he admits, "the observed reality of the mammoth animal, prodigious as it is, hardly comes up to the preconceived vague idea of it, still less to the poetic notion" (26).

In the aftermath of his first processing, Cheever begins to recognize the tension between economics and animal advocacy that is brought into sharper relief by the decrease in the whale population. His transformation into a whale sympathizer starts with what he refers to as the "useless devastation" of whaling, and he laments that on "some voyages they say more whales have been sunk than have been saved" (32). Cheever frames the issue of the decreasing global whale population by putting it in the economic terms of the whalemen; until recently, he notes, "this gigantic game has been everywhere so abundant that whalemen have used no means to keep their rich prizes from sinking" (32). No matter the value of the individual whale (Cheever puts the value at upwards of $3,000), during abundant times whalemen considered the loss of one sunk whale as little more than a "whaleman's fortune, and have gone to capturing others instead" (32). Times have changed, however, with voyages going deeper into the Pacific in order to fill their holds, and Cheever suggests adapting American Indian techniques for saving a killed whale from sinking: "would whalemen go provided with India-rubber or bladder buoys," he writes, drawing on historical evidence discussed in Commander Wilkes's *Narrative of the United States Exploring Expedition*, "ready to be bent on to harpoons and darted into a whale's carcass as soon as 'turned up,' or when he is perceived to be going into 'his flurry', we are persuaded that many thousands of barrels of oil might be saved, and not a few poor voyages would be made good ones" (33). Cheever cites the use of sealskin floats by Northwest Indians and wooden blocks by Cape Cod Indians as historical precedents that can be adapted for modern usage. The scarcity of whales, he believes, is a challenge that can be met by "Yankee sense and forehandedness" which will "soon see to this, and go prepared against such disheartening catastrophes as losing their game by its sinking" (33). Through this economic lens, Cheever offers a subtle critique of the whaling industry, arguing that American whaleships are not hunting as efficiently as they could or should, and assuring his readers that if

Afterword

"owners knew how much might be saved by it, they would never let a ship go from port to port without buoys to hold up dead whales" (33). Here the focus is primarily on the economy, but the sympathetic seed has been planted through his introduction of the declining whale population, and in short order the emphasis on labor economy will become mingled with advocacy for the whales.

The turning point for Cheever is when he begins to make the sustainability argument (even though he does not voice it in those terms), arguing that we need to save young whales in order to ensure that there are enough mature whales to continue the survival of the species. Cheever's emphasis is still on the economy of the situation, however; he does not argue that we need to save whales for ecological reasons, but so that the whaling industry can continue to have whales to kill. In discussing the Russian policy of banning bay whaling at Kamchatka (spelled Kamtschatka), Cheever notes the reason for the ban is to prevent American whalers from killing the cows at the time of calving, which keeps the population of whales high, allowing for greater hunting between May and October in what Cheever terms the "great harvest-field" (44). The abundance of whales in Kamchatka mirrors the former abundance of whales off the coasts of New England (where many of the whalers are from) and New Zealand (where the *Preble* has just been), and though Cheever does not make that historical connection, he recognizes the lesson learned—an abundance of whales leads to industrial wastefulness. At Kamchatka, at New Zealand, at New England, wherever in the World Ocean whales exist in large numbers, the whalemen do not have to mourn sunk whales. Cheever gives several examples of the wastefulness of sunk whales— one ship that had killed six whales in one day, all sunk; another that killed nine before she secured one; and a third that sunk twenty-six in one voyage—but the overall abundance, supported by the ban on bay whaling, still allows for "almost all ships [to] fill up there," and results in some ships throwing overboard provisions to make way for more oil. The sustainability argument clearly holds some appeal for Cheever, however, and soon after the Kamchatka sequence, he finally begins to shift his narrative to a more sympathetic, whale-centric point of view.

The end of the whaling industry is clearly coming and Henry

Cheever's sustainability argument is made with the intention of keeping the industry healthy for as long as possible. In arguing for ways that Northwest whaling (meaning the northern Pacific region of Alaska and Russia) can exist for another quarter decade, Cheever notes how the lack of year-round bay whaling will mean that "nearly all the calves born will arrive at an age where they can take care of themselves before the old whales are encountered in the summer season by their sworn enemy, man" (48). Man is now transformed as the enemy and the whale has been transformed in Cheever's narrative from object to sympathetic being: "The poor whale," he recounts a captain telling him, will be "chased from sea to sea . . . doomed to utter extinction, or so near it, that too few will remain to tempt the cupidity of man" (48). Cheever is approaching his "almost epiphany," but he cannot escape his desire to see the industry continue. Though he clearly recognizes the inevitable end of the industrialized global whaling industry, Cheever's focus remains on what is best for human interests and not whale interests; for the whale, he offers only a lament, rhetorically asking his readers back in the industrialized American Northeast if "before the end of the present century . . . is it likely that the hunting of whales on the sea will be any more prosecuted as a business than the hunting of deer on the land?" (49) The unnamed captain offers specific numbers for Cheever to impart to his readers, estimating that with three hundred whaleships in the northwest oceans, the seasonal devastation amounts to twelve thousand whales killed, and "as many of these, perhaps full half, are cows with calf, the number of whales to be born and arrive at maturity, in order to make up for this sweeping destruction among them, must not be less than 18,000" (48). The captain's lament over the killing of pregnant or nursing mothers feeds directly into Cheever's decision to retell a story of the killing of a mother and calf that he was told by a member of the *Preble* crew. His experiences begin to offer Cheever a foundation for sympathy.

Cheever's sympathetic breakthrough finally occurs when he retells this story of the killing of a right whale cow and her calf, and he is both touched by the loyalty the mother shows for her calf and disturbed by the killing technique of the whalers—one that exploits that mother-child bond.[19] Importantly, it is Cheever's deeply held religious beliefs that lay the foundation for his shift in attitude, and it is his recognition of the whale as one of God's creatures that spurs him to advocacy. In his most emotional sequence, Cheever describes how the right whale is an animal of peace: "Its disposition," he writes, "is mild and inoffensive. It never shows fight except when wounded, and then in an awkward and blind way, that proves it is not used to war either offensive or defensive" (50). The right is also an extremely loyal animal, whose "immediate recourse is to flight, except when it has a young to look out for, and then it is as bold as a lion, and manifests an affection which is itself truly affecting" (50). The experience of the whaling cruise has revealed to Cheever that the mythohistoric representation of the whale as a violent monster is incorrect; instead of presenting his readers with a destructive leviathan, Cheever gives them a right whale that "grazes quietly through the great deep, never using its prodigious strength to seize it or lord it over other inhabitants of the sea" (50). Cheever recasts the mysterious monster of the deep as a gentle giant, even taking the animal's feeding habit as a sign of God's magnificent design; the right whale doesn't destroy with its powerful jaw but instead "strains its insect-like food through its admirably contrived apparatus of bone and hair, that strikingly evinces His beneficence and wise design" (50).[20] Cheever's earlier focus on the processing of the killed whale, combined with his new conception of the whale as beneficent ruler of the deep, lays the groundwork for his recognition of the right whale's mouth as evidence of God's handiwork in the animal's design. Cheever subtly conflates God and His creation, insofar as the former like the latter is imbued with "prodigious strength" that is never used to seize or lord power over the earth.

With the right whale now reframed as the gentle master of the ocean, Cheever moves even closer to a stance of sympathetic advocacy by discussing the maternal affections of a mother cow towards her calf. The affection that Cheever is drawn to, and the act that momentarily turns him against the whaling industry, is the hunting practice of first killing the calf rather than the mother. Cheever describes a whale cow "when driven into shoal water, being seen to swim around its young, and sometimes to embrace it with her fins, and roll over with it in the waves, evincing the tenderest maternal solicitude." Cheever could insert this scene at any point in the narrative, but his usage here, after recasting the whale as gentle giant, suggests he is now reinterpreting the story in light of his personal experiences aboard the *Preble*. He does not tell us who relayed this story to him, or when he heard it, but given the nature of the narrative's construction—with Cheever largely writing his observations while still aboard the *Preble*—it is not unreasonable to conclude that he was reinterpreting the meaning of the mother-calf story in light of his recent exposure to the decidedly unromantic elements of the whale hunt. Cheever continues by emphasizing the actions of the mother: "As if aware of the impending peril of her inexperienced offspring, as the boat drew near," Cheever writes, "she would run round her calf in decreasing circles, and then try to decoy it seaward, showing the utmost uneasiness and anxiety" (51). Cheever is attributing human emotions to the whale's behavior; perhaps most important is his decision to tell this story as if it is his own instead of giving credit—as is often the case in the narrative—to the story's original teller.

The hunting of the mother and calf turns Cheever against the whalemen for the first time in the narrative. The whalemen know the mother will not abandon the calf and so they attack the smaller whale first, burying a harpoon in the mammal and letting the weapon slowly kill it from the inside, while the mother stays close instead of making her own escape. "Reckoning well that, the calf once struck," Cheever writes of the practice, "the dam would never desert it, the only care of the harpooner was to get near enough to bury his tremendous weapon deep in its ribs" (51). The whalemen plunge the harpoon into the calf, sending it fleeing in panic and pain and pulling out one hundred fathoms of line, but the whalemen simply needed to wait death out, and shortly, with "the barb lacerating its vitals, it turned on its back, and, displaying its white belly on the surface of the water, it floated a motionless corpse" (51). What touches Cheever isn't the death of the calf as much as it is the actions of the mother cow: "The huge dam, with an affecting maternal instinct more powerful than reason, never quitted the body till a cruel harpoon entered her own sides; then, with a single tap of her tail, she cut in two one of the boats, and took to flight, but returned soon, exhausted with loss of blood, to die by her calf, evidently, in her last moments, more occupied with the preservation of her young than of herself" (51).

Experience has given this story a new meaning for Cheever due, I believe, to his role as an outsider on the ship; because his livelihood calls for him to observe and preach instead of participate in the hunt, he is more open to sympathetic feelings than a member of the labor force whose economic prosperity depends on killing and processing as many whales as possible in the shortest amount of time.

Though he ultimately turns his back on these new feelings, Cheever cannot completely escape them. Even after pushing such feelings aside to provide a clinical discussion of sperm whales, Cheever quickly returns to the emotional dimensions of the whale hunt. When a killing stroke has been delivered to a sperm whale, "the whalemen will soon know the items of its last bill of fare; for, while the waters around him are purpled with its gore, and a crimson tide is flowing from its spiracles, portions of its lance-lacerated lungs and the contents of its capacious stomach also are being vomited at the mouth" (52). What Cheever offers here is a normal death scene, but it affects him more than he would have expected: "It is painful to witness the death agony of any creature," Cheever laments, especially "of one in which life is so lively and tenacious, and animating so vast a bulk" (52). Cheever now offers his narrative's greatest lament—articulated in the form of an epiphany and founded on the principle of the whale body's organization that first caused him to conflate the animal with its Heavenly creator: "I am not one that can coolly observe the last agony of so mighty an organized creature as the whale with as little emotion as some persons feel at the crushing of a reptile or the writhing of a worm" (52). Cheever feels "painful enough" at the thought of any of God's creatures "forcibly bereft of the boon of life," and calls upon the words of Cowper to explain his changed attitude. Cowper argues that man's convenience, health, and safety take precedence over animal rights, but otherwise animals should be "as free to live, and to enjoy that life, / As God was free to form them at the first, / Who in his sovereign wisdom made them all" (53).

Cheever finds himself now caught between the unexpected sympathy for the hunted whale and the economic necessity of killing and processing it to satisfy the nation's desire for whale oil. Extinction now seems inevitable to Cheever, just as it does to the veteran whalemen he encounters on his travels; caught between "natural foes and its predatory human enemy, the great mammoth of [the] ocean seems doomed to extinction" (57). He admits to the reader that he has "no scruple at confessing that, since I have become closely acquainted with the habits of the great right whale, how it quietly grazes through the great pasture-ground which God has ordained for it," and because he has seen the "hazards . . . and perils to be surmounted in its capture by men" his thoughts on the whaling industry have been altered: "I begin to be somewhat doubtful," he gravely asserts, "about the lawfulness and expediency of the whale fishery." In the narrative's most ecologically sympathetic passage, Cheever recounts an older whaleman telling him, "Whales has feelings as well as any body. They don't like to be stuck in the gizzards, and hauled alongside, and cut in, and tried out in them 'ere boilers no more than I do" (58). Cheever goes on to frame the whaleman's remarks within a religious argument, but the result is the same: the man who went to sea to glorify the whaleman comes away disturbed by the process and sympathetic to the hunted. Cheever will never fully realize his conservationist impulses, but the fact that such feelings even arise in the first place helps to show that, by the mid-nineteenth century, the experience of witnessing the hunting and killing had the power to raise doubts and questions about the practice as a whole.

Ultimately, Cheever favors the needs of humanity over the lives of whales, despite his growing sense of the need to advocate for the animals. After the *Preble* rounded Cape Horn, crossing from the Pacific to the Atlantic, Cheever notes the presence of a school of sperm whales heading in the opposite direction. He mentions that boats were lowered and the hunt was unsuccessful, but his sympathy now rests firmly with the whales instead of the whalers: "Poor fellows!" he laments, noting the whales' victory is likely temporary, as they "will find keen human enemies enough where they were going" (60). Cheever, however, is still unwilling to condemn the practice of whaling or the desire of American consumers for whale oil: by the time he transforms the experience into published narrative, he knows it is likely that "the blubber sides of one or more of them are already headed up in the hold of some ship, and biding their time to fill honorable lamps with light ten thousand miles off" (60). The death of a whale may come at the pointed end of a "cruel harpoon" out on the World Ocean, but

Afterword

the result of this cruelty is to fill "honorable lamps" back home in the United States, and though Cheever has felt an unexpected sympathy for the whale, his epiphany does not sustain itself. Shortly after lamenting the fates of these Pacific-bound whales, Cheever "had the pleasure of climbing the mizzen rigging to witness the capture of our first Atlantic whale" (60). From high above the deck, the effect of the ocean in its "stillest, loveliest mood, its breast heaving only like a sleeping infant; the morning sun most glorious; the sky without a cloud" turns Cheever nostalgic for his youth. "That glimmer of reflection from the molten steel mirror beneath," he writes, thinking fondly of childhood, "which I remember being so much struck with the first time I ever saw the sublime sight when a boy" (60).

Nostalgia is the champion of human economy, and even though the hunt he witnesses from the mizzen rigging involves a mother whale and her calf, there is no longer any ecological advocacy in Cheever's narrative. He notes how the whales were "putting their heads together as in love," but then he immediately changes tone, offering the scientific interpretation that instead of being a sign of affection, the rubbing was practical, "to rub off the crab-lice and barnacles that adhere by millions to the top and sides of their heads" (60). This time, there is no great lament. Cheever clinically informs us that the "calf was soon struck, and made little ado of being killed, not going into a flurry, or sounding long, or making the water foam, fly, or splintering the cedar with strokes of his tail" (60). The actions of the calf read like an absolution for Cheever and the reader: if the whale doesn't struggle or mourn his own passing at the end of the cruel harpoon, then why should we? Even the mother absolves the "honorable lamps" back home as she "prudently made off a mile and a half to windward, while we got the cub alongside the ship" (60). The mother, in this instance, does not wait around to be killed alongside her young. In the struggle between human economy and ecological sympathy, Cheever ultimately accepts the latter as a cost of the former. Yet as the title of his narrative suggests, he comes away with some sense that whales are as much sympathetic captives of human desire as they are "prey" to be killed without remorse. Cheever's title foreshadows the unexpected emotional arc of the narrative; what begins as a celebration instead becomes, for whales and industry, a lament.

Though the narrative is barely at its midpoint, Cheever provides no further commentary on the possibilities for sympathy and advocacy. Rather, he moves on to offer several adventure-driven tales of the whale hunt that speak as much to romanticism as they do realism. In doing so, Cheever returns to his original purpose of celebrating whalemen and their industry. He chooses not to elaborate on his emotional response to the hunt and instead embraces the mythohistoric mode, including in his narrative tales that glorify the whalemen in the "garb of their perilous occupation." Perhaps as a reaction to his sympathies for the whale, Cheever now saves his emotions for the whalemen; after a particularly long and dangerous story about a hunt that sees whalemen die in the pursuit, Cheever assures his readers that "under many a rough, pea-jacket bosom there beats a heart, which you will be feeling long for, and be slow in finding under the purple, and silks, and satins of fashion and frivolity" (71). Fittingly, he ends with the *Preble*'s return home and the unexpected news of "Death's visit to one inexpressibly dear" who died "on the very ocean which I had passed over in peace, and with greatly renovated health" (140). Cheever suggests that whaling is a business of death that no one can escape, even one whose only purpose was to observe and report.

NOTES

1. Lawrence Buell and Leo Marx, "An Exchange on Thoreau," *New York Review of Books*, December 2, 1999.

2. In 1839, Jeremiah N. Reynolds published "Mocha Dick: Or the White Whale of the Pacific: A Leaf from a Manuscript Journal," which includes a scene of a mother whale defending her calf from the whalemen's attack. Unlike Cheever's account, however, there is no sustained sympathy demonstrated for this act, merely a reporting of the events that transpired.

3. The most profitable year for the American whaling industry was 1853. According to Charles Scammon, the American whaling fleet killed over eight thousand whales, generating total sales of $11 million. See Charles Scammon, *Marine Mammals of the Northwestern Coast of North America, Together with an Account of the American Whale Fishery* (San Francisco: John H. Carmany and Company, 1874), 244.

4. Farley Mowat, *Sea of Slaughter: A Chronicle of the Destruction of Animal Life in the North Atlantic* (Shelburne, VT: Chapters Publishing, 1996), 206.

5. Lawrence Buell. *The Environmental Imagination: Thoreau, Nature Writing, and the Formation of American Culture* (Cambridge, MA: Belknap Press of Harvard University Press, 1995), 2.

Afterword

6. Carolyn Merchant, *American Environmental History: An Introduction* (New York: Columbia University Press, 2007), xvi–xvii.

7. "The Story of the Whale," *Harper's New Monthly Magazine* 12 (March 1856): 466–467.

8. J. C. Mullett, *Five Years on the Pacific Ocean, or the Blind Man's Narrative* (Cleveland: E. Cowles, 1858), 4.

9. Diane L. Beers, *For the Prevention of Cruelty: The History and Legacy of Animal Rights Activism in the United States* (Athens, OH: Swallow Press, 2006), 200.

10. Jeremy Bentham, *An Introduction to the Principles of Morals and Legislation* (1789; rpt. Oxford: Clarendon Press, 1907), 301.

11. Many narratives do contain passages of environmental reflection on the ports they visited in such diverse locations as Lima, Japan, Madagascar, and the Sandwich Islands. Interestingly, this nonemotional response to whales did not extend to all creatures the whalemen killed. There is ample evidence in whaling narratives centered in the Arctic that whalemen had a great deal of sympathy for the seals they were forced to hunt and kill to supplement their stores of whale oil.

12. George Dodge, *A Whaling Voyage in the Pacific Ocean and Its Incidents*, Kenneth R. Martin, ed. (Fairfield, WA: Ye Galleon Press, 1981), 12.

13. Throughout his narrative, Cheever seems perfectly content to simply use "whale" to stand in for any of the particular species of whales, often saving the specific designation until the end of a particular whale's time in his narrative.

14. John Milton, *Paradise Lost*, quoted in Cheever (21). (Original: John Milton, *Paradise Lost: A Poem, In Ten Books. The Author John Milton*, London, Samuel Simmons, 1667, lines 412–415). Note that Cheever quotes, "here Leviathan" instead of "there Leviathan."

15. Cheever acknowledges that the "Northwest Indians, Esquimaux, and Norwegians were in the habit of capturing whales in their rude way, in order to supply themselves with fat and food," but he is most interested in the industrial origins, as they provide a direct line to the American whaling industry that is the subject of Cheever's narrative.

16. Curiously, chapter I is the only chapter in the text that Cheever clearly writes in a postexperiential voice, which reinforces the sense of the inevitable ending. While there is a five-year gap between his experience on board the *Preble* and the publication date of *The Whale and His Captors*, the remainder of his text has been constructed to feel like it is occurring in the immediate aftermath of each individual experience. He tells his audience at the end of this chapter that the voyage lasted 236 days and that the "comforts of this long voyage far exceeded its discomforts" (10).

17. It is important to note, too, that when Cheever moves into his history of the American whale fishery, he focuses largely on statistical evidence to illustrate the overall economic impact.

18. Cheever (21). Emphasis is Cheever's. Cheever's description of the whale hunt begins very dramatically but quickly becomes clinical and instructive by the time the whale has been hauled to the ship for processing. The effect indicates that his burgeoning sympathy for the whale mutes his representation of the dramatic conflict, turning a

moment of hot heroic masculinity cold due to his increased sympathy for the creature at the center of the hunt.

19. While Cheever does not experience this mother-calf killing himself, hearing the story while in the midst of this experience aboard the *Preble* opens him up, I believe, to a greater sense of sympathy for the plight of the hunted whales.

20. Note that this is an instance where Cheever's continued treatment of whales as generic can lead to false assumptions, either on his part or on the audience's part. While Cheever does identify the whale here as a right whale, he doesn't put the right immediately into contrast with other whales. The right whale is a baleen whale, evidenced by the "contrived apparatus of bone and hair" instead of teeth. A sperm whale—the primary target of whale hunts—has teeth instead of baleen, and thus Cheever's reading of the right whale wouldn't work with a sperm. Perhaps aware of this potential for misunderstanding, Cheever quickly moves to a discussion of sperm whales immediately following the retelling of the hunt of the mother-calf duo.